KU-281-869

THE ESSENCE OF

MICROPROCESSOR ENGINEERING

Sid Katzen

Leabharlann James Hardiman
Ollscoil na hÉireann, Gaillimh
385

Prentice Hall Europe

LONDON   NEW YORK   TORONTO   SYDNEY   TOKYO
SINGAPORE   MADRID   MEXICO CITY   MUNICH   PARIS

First published 1998 by
Prentice Hall Europe
Campus 400, Maylands Avenue
Hemel Hempstead
Hertfordshire, HP2 7EZ
A division of
Simon & Schuster International Group

© Prentice Hall Europe 1998

All rights reserved. No part of this publication may be
reproduced, stored in a retrieval system, or transmitted,
in any form, or by any means, electronic, mechanical,
photocopying, recording or otherwise, without prior
permission, in writing, from the publisher.

Printed and bound in Great Britain by
MPG Books, Bodmin, Cornwall

Library of Congress Cataloging-in-Publication Data

Katzen, S. J.
        The essence of microprocessor engineering / S.J. Katzen.
        p.   cm. — (The essence of engineering series)
        Includes bibliographical references and index.
        ISBN 0–13–244708–8 (alk. paper)
        1. Microprocessors—Design and construction.   I. Title.
II. Series.
        TK7895.M5K38   1998
        621.39′16—dc21   97–43886
                                                                     CIP

British Library Cataloguing in Publication Data

A catalogue record for this book is available from
the British Library

ISBN 0–13–244708–8

---

    2   3   4   5   02   01   00   99   98

In memory of Val Jones

Contents

Preface

Microprocessors and their microcontroller derivatives are a ubiquitous if rather invisible part of the infrastructure of our electronic and communications society. These are the intelligence behind singing birthday cards and talking children's books, appliance controllers and smartcards, intelligent test equipment and aircraft control systems.

Of course microprocessors are better known as the engine behind the personal computer (PC). Names like the Intel Pentium are freely bandied about. But even the PC relies on a multitude of anonymous microprocessors to support its operation, for example for its disk controller and video card. Microprocessors in these dedicated control roles are often known as embedded, that is they are just another, albeit programmable, digital chip entrenched within the rest of the circuitry. For example the Nikon F5 35mm SLR camera has three 16-bit, one eight-bit and one four-bit processor.[1]

Almost all courses in electronic engineering, and many in the physical and computing sciences, have at least one module covering this hybrid hardware/software subject. The aim of this text is to present the subject in a self-contained manner suitable for first-exposure modules in this topic. Within the limitations of a modest-sized text this is not an easy task if the outcome is not to be simply a watered-down version of a standard textbook in this area. Rather I have chosen to take an engineer's approach, dealing with the microprocessor as the embedded intelligence of a digital circuit. This will hopefully give the reader the confidence that, even at such an introductory level, he/she can design, construct and program a complete working embedded system. The text is not a book on computer architecture in the traditional sense, but in mastering the material presented here, the reader will have the confidence to proceed to topics at other levels, such as software design methods, real-time operating systems and high-level embedded coding. Given the practical aim of the book, real-world hardware and software products are used throughout to illustrate the material. In particular, the 68000 microprocessor is the target device. It is one of the more popular industrial standard 16/32-bit products, and is certainly one of the simplest microprocessors without descending back to the eight-bit devices of the 1970s. The 68000 is the

---

[1]Warwick, L.; Electronics in Photography, *Electronics World*, **103**, no. 1735, July 1997, pp.542–546.

base member of the microprocessor family extending up to the 68060 and the new ColdFire RISC devices.

The book is split into three parts. Part I covers sufficient digital, logic and computer architecture to act as a foundation for the microprocessor engineering topics presented in the rest of the text. Inclusion of this material makes the text suitable for a stand-alone module, as it does not require a prerequisite digital systems module.

Part II looks mainly at the software aspects of the 68000 microprocessor, its instruction set, how to program it at assembly and high-level C coding levels, and how the microprocessor handles subroutines and exceptions. Modular concepts are used throughout this part.

Part III moves on to the hardware aspects of interfacing and interrupt handling, with the integration of the hardware and software being a constant theme throughout. A practical build and program case study integrates the previous material into a working system as well as illustrating simple testing strategies.

With the exception of the first two and last chapter, all chapters have both fully worked examples and self-assessment questions. As an extension to this, an associated Web site at

$$\text{http://www.nibec.ulst.ac.uk/~sidk/essence}$$

has the following facilities:

- Solutions to self-assessment questions.
- More self-assessment questions.
- Additional material.
- An evaluation kit giving a limited capacity 68000-based assembler/linker and cross C compiler/simulator.
- A 68HC001 data sheet.
- Useful pointers to 68000-based material.
- Errata.
- Suggestions.

The manuscript was typeset on a Siemens Scenic D Pentium 133 PC by the author using a Y&Y implementation of LaTeX 2_ε in the Lucida Bright font family. Camera ready copy was produced at 1200dpi on a Lexmark Optra R postscript laser printer. Line drawings were created or modified with Autocad R12 and incorporated as encapsulated PostScript files.

S.J. Katzen
Jordanstown
February 1998

PART I

The fundamentals

This book is about microprocessors (MPUs). These are digital engines modelled after the architecture of a stored-program computer and integrated on to a single very large-scale integrated circuit. Although the MPU is better known in the role of the driving force of the ubiquitous personal computer, the vast majority are embedded into an assemblage of other digital components. The first MPUs in the early 1970s were marketed as an alternative way of implementing digital circuitry. Here the task would be determined by a series of instructions encoded as binary code groups in read-only memory. This is more flexible than the alternative approach of wiring hardware integrated circuits in the appropriate manner.

We will look at embedded MPUs in a general digital processing context in Parts II and III. Here our objective is to lay the foundation for this material. We will be covering:

- *Digital code patterns.*
- *Binary arithmetic.*
- *Digital circuitry.*
- *Computer architecture and programming.*

This will by no means be a comprehensive review of the subject, but there are many other excellent texts in this area[2] which will launch you into greater depths.

---

[2]Such as S.J. Cahill's *Digital and Microprocessor Engineering*, 2nd edn., Prentice Hall, 1993.

CHAPTER 1

Digital representation

To a computer or MPU, the world is seen in terms of patterns of digits. The **decimal** (or denary) system represents quantities in terms of the ten digits 0...9. Together with the judicious use of the symbols +, − and . any quantity in the range ±∞ can be depicted. Indeed non-numeric concepts can be encoded using numeric digits. For example the American Standard Code for Information Interchange (ASCII) defines the alphabetic (alpha) characters A as 65, B = 66...Z = 90 and a = 97, b = 98...z = 122 etc. Thus the string "Microprocessor" could be encoded as "77, 105, 99, 114, 111, 112, 114, 111, 99, 101, 115, 115, 111, 114". Provided you know the context, i.e. what is a pure quantity and what is text, then just about any symbol can be coded as numeric digits.[1]

Electronic circuits are not very good at storing and processing a multitude of different symbols. It is true that the first American digital computer, the ENIAC (Electronic Numerical Integrator And Calculator) in 1946, did its arithmetic in decimal[2] but all computers since handle data in **binary** (base 2) form. The decimal (base 10) system is really only convenient for humans, in that we have ten fingers.[3] Thus in this chapter we will look at the properties of binary digits, their groupings and processing. After reading it you will:

- *Understand why a binary data representation is the preferred base for digital circuitry.*
- *Know how a quantity can be depicted in natural binary, hexadecimal and binary coded decimal.*
- *Be able to apply the rules of addition and subtraction for natural binary quantities.*
- *Know how to multiply by shifting left.*
- *Know how to divide by shifting right and propagating the sign bit.*
- *Understand the Boolean operations AND, OR, NOT and EOR.*

---

[1] Of course there are lots of encoding standards, for example the six-dot Braille code for the visually impaired.

[2] As did Babbage's mechanical computer of a century earlier.

[3] And ten toes, but base-20 systems are rare.

The information technology revolution is based on the manipulation, computation and transmission of digitized information. This information is virtually universally represented as aggregrates of *binary digits* (**bits**).[4] Most of this processing is effected using MPUs, and it is sobering to reflect that there is more computing power in a singing birthday card than existed on the entire planet in 1950!

Binary is the universal choice for data representation, as an electronic switch is just about the easiest device that can be implemented using a transistor. Such two-state switches are very small; they change state very quickly and consume little power. Furthermore, as there are only two states to distinguish between, a binary depiction is likely to be resistant to the effects of noise. The upshot of this is that both the packing density on a silicon chip and switching rate can be very high. Although a switch on its own does not represent much computing power; 5 million switches changing at 100 million times a second will manage to present at least a façade of intelligence!

The two states of a bit are conventionally designated **logic 0** and **logic 1** or just 0 and 1. A bit may be represented by two states of any number of physical quantities; for example electric current or voltage, light, pneumatic pressure. Most MPUs use 0 V (or ground) for state 0 and 3–5 V for state 1, but this is not universal. For instance, the RS232 serial port on your computer uses nominally +12 V for state 0 and −12 V for state 1.

A single bit on its own can only represent two states. By dealing with groups of bits, rather more complex entities can be coded. For example the standard alphanumeric characters can be coded using seven-bit groups of digits. Thus the ASCII code for "Microprocessor" becomes:

1001101 1101001 1100011 1110010 1101111 1110000 1110010 1101111
1100011 1100100 1110011 1110011 1101111 1110010

Unicode is an extension of ASCII and with its 16-bit code groups is able represent characters from many languages and mathematical symbols.

The ASCII code is **unweighted**, as the individual bits do not signify a particular quantity; only the overall pattern has any significance. Other examples are the die code of Fig. 5.2 on page 83 and the seven-segment code of Fig. 8.7 on page 139. Here we will deal with **natural binary** weighted codes, where the position of a bit within the number field determines its value or weight. In an integer number the rightmost digit is worth $2^0 = 1$, the next column to the left $2^1 = 2$ and so on to the nth column which is

---

[4]The binary base is not a new fangled idea invented for digital computers; many cultures have used base-2 numeration in the past. The Harappān civilization existed more than 4000 years ago in the Indus river basin. Found in the ruins of the Harappān city of Mohenjo-Daro, in the beadmakers' quarter, was a set of stone pebble weights. These were in ratios that doubled in the pattern, 1,1,2,4,8,16..., with the base weight of around 25 g ($\approx$ 1 oz). Thus bead weights were expressed by digits which represented powers of 2.

worth 2^{n-1}. For example the decimal number one thousand nine hundred and ninety eight is represented as $1 \times 10^3 + 9 \times 10^2 + 9 \times 10^1 + 8 \times 10^0$ or 1998. In **natural binary** the same quantity is $1 \times 2^{10} + 1 \times 2^9 + 1 \times 2^8 + 1 \times 2^7 + 1 \times 2^6 + 0 \times 2^5 + 0 \times 2^4 + 1 \times 2^3 + 1 \times 2^2 + 0 \times 2^1 + 1 \times 2^0$, or $11111001101b$. Fractional numbers may equally well be represented by columns to the right of the binary point using negative powers of 2. Thus $1101.11b$ is equivalent to 13.75. As can be seen from this example, binary numbers are rather longer than their decimal equivalent; on average a little over three times. Nevertheless, two-way switches are considerably simpler than ten-way devices, so the binary representation is preferable.

An n-digit binary number can represent up to 2^n patterns. Most computers store and process groups of bits. For example the first microprocessor, the Intel 4004, handled its data four bits (a **nybble**) at a time. Many current processors cope with blocks of eight bits (a **byte**), 16 bits (a **word**), or 32 bits (a **long-word**). 64-bit (a **quad-word**) devices are on the horizon. These groups are shown in Table 1.1. The names illustrated are somewhat de-facto, and variations are sometimes encountered.

As in the decimal number system, large binary numbers are often expressed using the prefixes k (kilo), M (mega) and G (giga). A binary kilo is $2^{10} = 1024$; for example 64 kbytes is 65,536 bytes. In an analogous way, a binary mega is $2^{20} = 1,048,576$; thus a 1.44 Mbyte floppy disk holds 1,509,950 bytes of information. Similarly a 2 Gbyte hard disk has a storage capacity of $2 \times 2^{30} = 2,147,483,648$ bytes.

Bit (1 bit) 0–1 (0–1)		
Nybble (4 bits) 0–15 (0000–1111)		
Byte (8 bits) 0–255 (0000 0000–11111 1111)		
Word (16 bits) 0–65,535 (0000 0000 0000 0000–1111 1111 1111 1111)		
Long-word (32 bits) 0–4,294,967,295 (0000 0000 0000 0000 0000 0000 0000 0000–1111 1111 1111 1111 1111 1111 1111 1111)		

Table 1.1 *Some common bit groupings.*

Long binary numbers are not very human-friendly. In Table 1.1, binary numbers were zoned into fields of four digits to improve readability. Thus the address of a data unit stored in memory might be $1000\ 1100\ 0001\ 0100\ 0000\ 1010b$. If each group of four can be given its own symbol, 0...9 and A...F, as shown in Table 1.2, then the address becomes $8C140Ah$; a rather more manageable characterization. This code is called **hexadecimal**, as there are 16 symbols. Hexadecimal (base-16) numbers are a viable number base in their own right, rather than just being a convenient binary representation. Each column is worth $16^0, 16^1, 16^2 \ldots 16^n$ in the normal way.[5]

Decimal	Natural binary	Hexadecimal	Binary
00	00000	00	0000 0000
01	00001	01	0000 0001
02	00010	02	0000 0010
03	00011	03	0000 0011
04	00100	04	0000 0100
05	00101	05	0000 0101
06	00110	06	0000 0110
07	00111	07	0000 0111
08	01000	08	0000 1000
09	01001	09	0000 1001
10	01010	0A	0001 0000
11	01011	0B	0001 0001
12	01100	0C	0001 0010
13	01101	0D	0001 0011
14	01110	0E	0001 0100
15	01111	0F	0001 0101
16	10000	10	0001 0110
17	10001	11	0001 0111
18	10010	12	0001 1000
19	10011	13	0001 1001
20	10100	14	0010 0000

Table 1.2 *Different ways of representing the quantities decimal 0...20.*

Binary Coded Decimal (BCD) is a hybrid binary/decimal code extensively used at the input/output ports of a digital system (see Chapter 15). Here each decimal digit is individually replaced by its four-bit binary equivalent. Thus 1998 is coded as $(0001\ 1001\ 1001\ 1000)_{BCD}$. This is very different from the equivalent natural binary code, even if it is represented by 0s and 1s. As might be expected, arithmetic in such a hybrid system is difficult, and BCD is normally converted to natural binary at the system input and processing is done in natural binary before being converted back (see Program 6.3 on page 107).

The rules of arithmetic are the same in natural binary[6] as they are in the more familiar base-10 system, indeed any base-n scheme. The simplest of these is **addition**, which is a shorthand way of totalling quantities,

---

[5]Many scientific calculators, including that in the Accessories group under Windows 95) can do hexadecimal arithmetic.

[6]Sometimes called 8-4-2-1 code after the weightings of the first four lowest columns.

as compared to the more primitive counting or incrementation process. Thus $2 + 4 = 6$ is rather more efficient than $2 + 1 = 3; 3 + 1 = 4; 4 + 1 = 5; 5 + 1 = 6$. However, it does involve memorizing the rules of addition.[7] In decimal this involves 45 rules, assuming that order is irrelevant: from $0 + 0 = 0$ to $9 + 9 = 18$. Binary addition is much simpler as it is covered by only three rules:

$$0 + 0 \quad = \quad 0$$
$$\left.\begin{matrix} 0 + 1 \\ 1 + 0 \end{matrix}\right\} = 1$$
$$1 + 1 \quad = 10 \quad (0 \text{ carry } 1)$$

Based on these rules, the least significant bit (LSB) is totalized first, passing a **carry** if necessary to the next left column. The process ends with the most significant bit (MSB) column, its carry being the new MSD of the sum. For example:

```
  1                              1
  0 1                            2 6 3  1
  0 0 1                          8 4 2 6 8 4 2 1
    96   Augend                   1100000   Augend
  + 37   Addend                 + 0100101   Addend
  ─1─1─  Carries                 ─1─1────── Carries
   133   Sum                     10000101   Sum
```

(a) Decimal   (b) Binary

Just as addition implements an up count, **subtraction** corresponds to a down count, where units are removed from the total. Thus $8 - 4 = 4$ is the equivalent of $8 - 1 = 7; 7 - 1 = 6; 6 - 1 = 5; 5 - 1 = 4$.

The technique of decimal subtraction you are familiar with applies the subtraction rules commencing from the LSB and working to the MSB. In any given column were a larger quantity is to be taken away from a smaller quantity, a unit digit is **borrowed** from the next higher column and given back after the subtraction is completed. Based on this borrow principle, the subtraction rules are given by:

$$0 - 0 = 0$$
$$^{1}0 - 1 = 1 \quad \text{Borrowing 1 from the higher column}$$
$$1 - 0 = 1$$
$$1 - 1 = 0$$

For example:

---

[7]Which you had to do way back in the mists of time in primary/elementary school!

	1 0 1			6 3 1 4 2 6 8 4 2 1	
	96	Subtrahend		1100000	Subtrahend
	− 37	Minuend		− 0100101	Minuend
	1	Borrows		1 1 1 1 1 1	Borrows
	59	Difference		0111011	Difference

(a) Decimal   (b) Binary

Although this familiar method works well, there are several problems implementing it in digital circuitry.

- How can we deal with situations where the minuend is larger than the subtrahend?
- How can we distinguish between positive and negative quantities?
- Can a digital system's adder circuits be coerced into subtracting?

To illustrate these points, consider the following example:

	37	Subtrahend		0100111	Subtrahend
	− 96	Minuend		− 1100000	Minuend
	1			1	
	41	Difference (−59)		1000111	Difference (-0111001)

(a) Decimal   (b) Binary

Normally, when we know that the minuend is greater than the subtrahend, the two operands are interchanged and a minus sign is appended to the outcome; that is −(subtrahend − minuend). If we do not swap, as in (a) above, then the outcome appears to be incorrect. In fact 41 is correct, in that this is the difference between 59 (the correct outcome) and 100. 41 is described as the **10's complement** of 59. Furthermore, the fact that a borrow digit was generated from the MSD indicates that the difference is negative, and therefore appears in this 10's complement form. Converting from 10's complement decimal numbers to the 'normal' magnitude form is simply a matter of inverting each digit and then adding 1 to the outcome. A decimal digit is inverted by computing its difference from 9. Thus the 10's complement of 3941 is −6059:

$$\overline{3941} \Rightarrow 6058; +1 = -6059$$

However, there is no reason why negative numbers should not remain in this complement form — just because we are not familiar with this type of notation.

The complement method of negative quantity representation of course applies to binary numbers. Here the ease of inversion ($0 \rightarrow 1; 1 \rightarrow 0$) makes this technique particularly attractive. Thus in our example above:

$$\overline{1000101} \Rightarrow 0111010; +1 = -0111011$$

Again, negative numbers should remain in a **2's complement** form. This complement process is reversible. Thus:

$$\text{complement} \iff \text{normal}$$

Signed decimal numeration has the luxury of using the symbols + and − to denote positive and negative quantities. A two-state system is stuck with 1s and 0s. However, looking at the last example gives us a clue as to how to proceed. A negative outcome gives a borrow back out to the highest column. Thus we can use this MSD as a **sign bit**, with 0 for + and 1 for −. This gives $1,1000101b$ for −59 and $0,01110011b$ for +59. Although for clarity the sign bit has been highlighted above using a comma delimiter, the advantage of this system is that it can be treated in all arithmetic processes in the same way as any other ordinary bit. Doing this, the outcome will give the correct sign:

0,1100000	(+96)	0,0100101	(+37)
1,1011011	(−37)	1,0100000	(−96)
0,0111011	(+59)	1,1000101	(−59)

(a) Minuend less than subtrahend   (b) Minuend greater than subtrahend

From this example we see that if negative numbers are in a signed 2's complement form, then we no longer have the requirement to implement hardware subtractors, as adding a negative number is equivalent to subtracting a positive number. Thus $A - B = A + (-B)$. Furthermore, once numbers are in this form, the outcome of any subsequent processing will always remain 2's complement signed throughout.

There are two difficulties associated with signed 2's complement arithmetic. The first of these is **overflow**. It is possible that adding two positive or two negative numbers will cause overflow into the sign bit; for instance:

0,1000	(+8)	1,1000	(−8)
0,1011	(+11)	1,0101	(−11)
1,0011	(−13!!!)	0,1101	(+3!!!)

(a) Sum of two +ve numbers gives −ve   (b) Sum of two −ve numbers gives +ve

In (a) the outcome of $(+8) + (+11)$ is −13! The 2^4 numerical digit has overflowed into the sign position (actually, $1011b = 19$ is the correct outcome). Example (b) shows a similar problem for the addition of two signed negative numbers. Overflow can only happen if both operands have the *same* sign bits. Detection is then a matter of determining this situation with an outcome that differs. See Fig. 1.5 for a logic circuit to implement this overflow condition.

The final problem concerns arithmetic on signed operands with different sized fields. For instance:

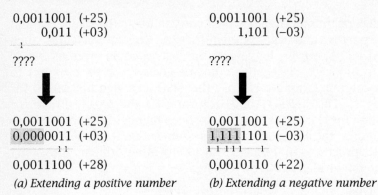

0,0011001 (+25)		0,0011001 (+25)
0,011 (+03)		1,101 (−03)

????   ????

0,0011001 (+25)	0,0011001 (+25)
0,0000011 (+03)	1,1111101 (−03)
0,0011100 (+28)	0,0010110 (+22)

(a) Extending a positive number   *(b) Extending a negative number*

Both the examples involve adding an eight-bit to a 16-bit operand. Where the former is positive, the data may be increased to 16 bits by padding with 0s. The situation is slightly less intuitive where negative data requires extension. Here the prescription is to extend the data by padding out with 1s. In the general case the rule is simply to pad out data by propagating the sign bit left. This technique is known as **sign extension**.

Multiplication by the nth power of 2 is simply implemented by shifting the data left n places. Thus $00101(5) << 01010(10) << 10100(20)$ multiplies 5 by 2^2, where the $<<$ operator is used to denote shifting left. The process works for signed numbers as well:

0,00000011 (3)	1,11111101 (−3)	0,00000110 (3 x 2)
<<	<<	+ 0,00011000 (3 x 8)
0,00000110 (6)	1,11111010 (−6)	0,00011110 (3 x 10 = 30)
<<	<<	
0,00001100 (12)	1,11110100 (−12)	
<<	<<	
0,00011000 (24)	1,11101000 (−24)	

(a) +3 × 8 = +24   *(b) −3 × 8 = −24*   *(c) +3 × 10 = 30*

Should the sign bit change polarity, then a magnitude bit has overflowed. Some computers/MPUs have an Arithmetic Shift Left process that signals this situation, as opposed to the standard Logic Shift Left used in unsigned number shifts.

Multiplication by non-powers of 2 can be implemented by a combination of shifting and adding. Thus, as shown in (c) above, 3×10 is implemented as $(3 \times 8) + (3 \times 2) = (3 \times 10)$ or $(3 << 3) + (3 << 1)$.

In a similar fashion, division by powers of 2 is implemented by shifting right n places. Thus $1100(12) >> 0110(6) >> 0011(3) >> 0001.1(1.5)$. This process also works for signed numbers:

0,1111.000	(+15)	1,0001.000	(−15)	0001.1
>>		>>		1010 ⟌ 1111.0
0,0111.100	(+7.5)	1,1000.100	(−7.5)	−1010
>>		>>		0101
0,0011.110	(+3.75)	1,1100.010	(−3.75)	−101.0
>>		>>		000.0
0,0001.111	(+1.875)	1,11110.001	(−1.875)	

(a) +15/8 = 1.875   (b) −15/8 = −1.875   (c) 15/10 = 1.5

Notice that rather than always shifting in 0s, the sign bit should be propagated in from the left. Thus positive numbers shift in 0s and negative numbers shift in 1s. This is known as **Arithmetic Shift Right**, as opposed to **Logic Shift Right** which always shifts in 0s.

Division by non-powers of 2 is illustrated in (c) above. This shows the familiar long division process used in decimal division. This is an analagous process to the shift and add technique for multiplication, using a combination of shifting and subtracting.

Arithmetic is not the only way to manipulate binary patterns. George Boole[8] in the mid-nineteenth century developed an algebra dealing with symbolic processing of logic propositions. This **Boolean algebra** deals with variables which can be true or false. In the 1930s it was realised that this mathematical system could equally well be used to analyze switching networks and thus binary logic systems. Here we will confine ourselves to looking at the fundamental logic operations of this switching algebra.

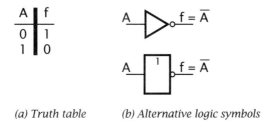

A	f
0	1
1	0

$f = \overline{A}$

$f = \overline{A}$

(a) Truth table   (b) Alternative logic symbols

Figure 1.1 *The NOT operation.*

The inversion or **NOT** operation is represented by overscoring. Thus $f = \overline{A}$ states that the variable f is the inverse of A; that is if A = 0 then f = 1 and if A = 1 then f = 0. In Fig. 1.1(a) this transfer characteristic

[8]The first professor of mathematics at Queen's College, Cork.

is presented in the form of a **truth table**. By definition, inverting twice returns a variable to its original state; thus $\bar{\bar{f}} = f$.[9]

Logic function implementations are normally represented in an abstract manner rather than as a detailed circuit diagram. The **NOT gate** is symbolized as shown in Fig. 1.1(b). The circle *always* represents inversion in a logic diagram, and is often used in conjunction with other logic elements, such as in Fig. 1.2(c).

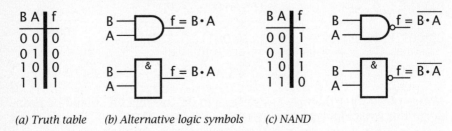

| (a) Truth table | (b) Alternative logic symbols | (c) NAND |

Figure 1.2 *The AND function.*

The **AND operator** gives an *all or nothing* function. The outcome will only be true when *every* one of the n inputs is true. In Fig. 1.2 two input variables are shown, and the output is symbolized as $f = B \cdot A$, where $\cdot$ is the Boolean AND operator. The number of inputs is not limited to two, and in general $f = A(0) \cdot A(1) \cdot A(2) \cdots A(n)$. The AND operator is sometimes called a logic product, as ANDing (cf. multiplying) any bit with logic 0 always yields a 0 output.

If we consider B as a control input and A as a stream of data, then consideration of the truth table shows that the output follows the data stream when $B = 1$ and is always 0 when $B = 0$. Thus the circuit can be considered to be acting as a valve, gating the data through on command. The term **gate** is generally applied to any logic circuit implementing a fundamental Boolean operator.

Most practical AND gate implementations have an inverting output. The logic of such implementations is NOT AND, or NAND for short, and is symbolized as shown in Fig. 1.2(c).

The **OR operator** gives an *anything* function. Here the outcome is true when *any* input or inputs are true (hence the ≥ 1 label in the logic symbol). In Fig. 1.3 two inputs are shown, but any number of variables may be ORed

---

[9]In days of yore when logic circuits were built out of discrete devices, such as diodes, resistors and transistors, problems due to sneak current paths were rife. In one such laboratory experiment the output lamp was rather dim, and the lecturer in charge suggested that two NOTs in series in a suspect line would not disturb the logic but would block off the unwanted current leak. On returning sometime later, the students complained that the remedy had had no effect. On investigation the lecturer discovered two knots in the offending wire — obviously not tied tightly enough!

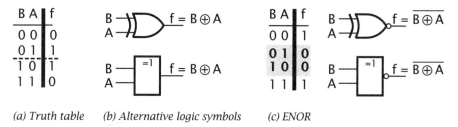

B A	f
0 0	0
0 1	1
1 0	1
1 1	1

$f = B + A$

$f = B + A$

B A	f
0 0	1
0 1	0
1 0	0
1 1	0

$f = \overline{B + A}$

$f = \overline{B + A}$

(a) Truth table   *(b) Alternative logic symbols*   *(c) NOR*

Figure 1.3 *The OR operation.*

together. ORing is sometimes referred to as a logic sum, and the + used as the mathematical operator; thus $f = B + A$. In an analogous manner to the AND gate detecting all 1s, the OR gate can be used to detect all 0s. This is illustrated in Fig. 2.16 on page 29 where an eight-bit zero outcome brings the output of the NOR gate to 1.

Considering B as a control input and A as data (or vice versa), then from Fig. 1.3(a) we see that the data is gated through when B is 0 and inhibited (always 1) when B is 1. This is a little like the inverse of the AND function. In fact the OR function can be expressed in terms of AND using the duality relationship $\overline{A + B} = \overline{B} \cdot \overline{A}$. This states that the NOR function can be implemented by inverting all inputs into an AND gate.

AND, OR and NOT are the three fundamental Boolean operators. There is one more operation commonly available as an electronic gate; the **Exclusive-OR operator (EOR)**. The EOR function is true if *only one* input is true (hence the =1 label in the logic symbol). Unlike the inclusive-OR, the situation where both inputs are true gives a false outcome.

B A	f
0 0	0
0 1	1
1 0	1
1 1	0

$f = B \oplus A$

$f = B \oplus A$

B A	f
0 0	1
0 1	0
1 0	0
1 1	1

$f = \overline{B \oplus A}$

$f = \overline{B \oplus A}$

(a) Truth table   *(b) Alternative logic symbols*   *(c) ENOR*

Figure 1.4 *The EOR operation.*

If we consider B as a control input and A as data (they are fully interchangeable) then:

- When B = 0 then $f = A$; that is the output follows the data input.

- When B = 1 then $f = \overline{A}$; that is the output is the inverse of the data input.

Thus an EOR gate can be used as a programmable inverter.

Another useful property considers the EOR function as a logic differentiator. The EOR truth table shows that the gate gives a true output if the two inputs differ. Alternatively, the ENOR truth table of Fig. 1.4(c) shows a true output when the two inputs are the same. Thus an ENOR gate can be considered to be a one-bit equality detector. The equality of two n-bit words can be tested by ANDing an array of ENOR gates (see Fig. 2.7 on page 21), each generating the function $\overline{B_k \oplus A_k}$; that is:

$$f_{B=A} = \sum_{k=0}^{n-1} \overline{B_k \oplus A_k}$$

As a simple example of the use of the EOR/ENOR gates, consider the problem of detecting sign overflow (see page 9). This occurs if both the sign bits of word B and word A are the same $(\overline{S_B \oplus S_A})$ AND the sign bit of the outcome word C is not the same as either of these sign bits, say $S_B \oplus S_C$. The logic diagram for this detector is shown in Fig. 1.5 and implements the Boolean function:

$$(\overline{S_B \oplus S_A}) \cdot (S_B \oplus S_C)$$

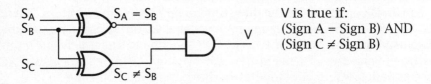

V is true if:
(Sign A = Sign B) AND
(Sign C ≠ Sign B)

Figure 1.5 *Detecting sign overflow.*

Finally, the EOR function can be considered as detecting when the number of true inputs is odd. By cascading $n + 1$ EOR gates, the overall parity function is true if the n-bit word has an odd number of 1s. Some measure of error protection can be obtained by adding an additional bit to each word, so that overall the number of bits is odd. This oddness can be checked at the receiver, any deviation indicating corruption (see page 105).

CHAPTER 2

Logic circuitry

We have noted that digital processing is all about transmission, manipulation and storage of binary word patterns. Here we will extend the concepts introduced in the last chapter as a lead into the architecture of the computer and microprocessor. We will look at some relevant logic functions, their commercial implementations and some practical considerations.

After reading this chapter you will:

- *Understand the properties and use of active pull-up, open-collector and three-state output structures.*
- *Appreciate the logic structure and function of the natural decoder.*
- *Comprehend the function of a highest-priority encoder.*
- *See how a medium-scale integration implementation of an array of ENOR gates can compare two words for equality.*
- *Understand how a one-bit adder can be constructed from gates, and can be extended to deal with the addition of two n-bit words.*
- *Appreciate how the function of an arithmetic logic unit is so important to a programmable system.*
- *Be aware of the structure and utility of read-only memory.*
- *Understand how two cross-coupled gates can implement a R S latch.*
- *Appreciate the difference between a D latch and D flip flop.*
- *Understand how an array of D flip flops or latches can implement a register.*
- *See how an ALU/PIPO register can implement an accumulator processor unit.*
- *Appreciate the function of random-access memory.*

The first integrated circuits, available at the end of the 1960s, were mainly NAND, NOR and NOT gates. The most popular family of logic functions was, and still is, the 74 series transistor-transistor logic (TTL), introduced by Texas Instruments and soon copied by all the major semiconductor manufacturers.

The 74LS00[1] comprises four 2-input NAND gates in a 14-pin package. The integrated circuit (IC) is powered with a 5 ± 0.25 V supply between

---

[1]The LS stands for "Low-power Schottky transistor". There are very many other versions, such as ALS (Advanced LS), AS (Advanced Schottky) and HC (High-speed Complementary metal-oxide transistor — CMOS). These family variants differ in speed and power consumption, but for a given number designation have the same logic function and pinout.

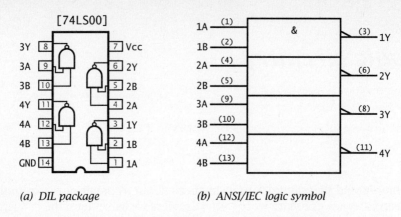

(a) DIL package   (b) ANSI/IEC logic symbol

Figure 2.1 The 74LS00 quad 2-I/P NAND package.

V_{CC}[2] (usually about 5 V) and **GND**. The logic outputs are 2.4–5 V for High and 0–0.4 V for Low. Most IC logic families require a 5 V supply, but 3 V versions are becoming available, and some CMOS implementations can operate with a range of supplies between 3 V and 15 V.

The 74LS00 IC is shown in Fig. 2.1(a) in its Dual In-Line (DIL) package. Strictly it should be described as a positive-logic quad 2-input (I/P) NAND gate, as the electrical equivalent for the two logic levels 0 and 1 are Low (L is around ground potential) and High (H is around **Vcc**. If the relationship $0 \rightarrow H$; $1 \rightarrow L$ is used (negative logic) then the 74LS00 is actually a quad 2-I/P NOR gate. The ANSI/IEC[3] logic symbol of Fig. 2.1(b) denotes a Low electrical potential by using the polarity ◣ symbol. The ANSI/IEC NAND symbol shown is thus based on the *real* electrical operation of the circuit. In this case the logic coincides with a positive-logic NAND function. The & operator shown in the top block is assumed applicable to the three lower gates.

The output structure of a 74LS00 NAND gate is **active pull-up**. Here both the High and Low states are generated by connection via a low-resistance switch to **Vcc** or **GND** respectively. In Fig. 2.2(a) these switches are shown for simplicity as metallic contacts, but they are of course transistor derived.

Logic circuits, such as the 74LS00, change output state in around 10 nanoseconds.[4] To be able to do this, the capacitance of any intercon-

---

[2]For historical reasons the positive supply on logic ICs are usually designated as V_{CC}; the C referring to a bipolar's transistor Collector supply. Similarily field-effect circuitry sometimes use the designation V_{DD} for Drain voltage. The zero reference pin is normally designated as the ground point (GND), but sometimes the V_{EE} (for emitter) or V_{SS} (for Drain) label is employed.

[3]The American National Standards Institution/International Electrotechnical Commission.

[4]A nanosecond is 10^{-9} s, so 100,000,000 transitions can occur each second.

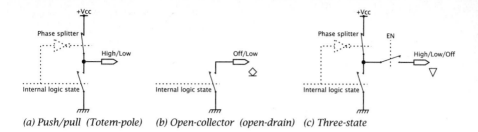

(a) Push/pull (Totem-pole) (b) Open-collector (open-drain) (c) Three-state

Figure 2.2 *Output structures.*

necting conductors and other logic circuits' inputs must be rapidly discharged. Mainly for this reason, active pull-up (sometimes called totem-pole) outputs are used by most logic circuits. There are certain circumstances where alternative output structures have some advantages. The **open-collector** (or open-drain) configuration of Fig. 2.2(b) provides a 'hard' Low state, but the High state is in fact an open circuit. The High-state voltage can be generated by connecting an external resistor to either Vcc or indeed to a different power rail. Non-orthodox devices, such as relays, lamps or light-emitting diodes, can replace this pull-up resistor. Output transistors with higher than usual current or voltage ratings are often provided for this purpose. As an example, the 74LS05 hex inverting open-collector buffer is shown in Fig. 15.3 on page 254.

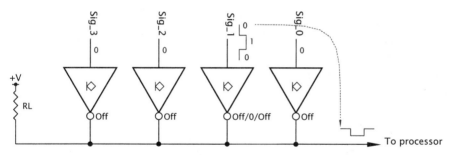

Figure 2.3 *Open-collector buffers driving a party line.*

The application of most interest to us here is illustrated in Fig. 2.3. Here four open-collector gates share a *single* pull-up resistor. Note the use of the ⌂ symbol to denote an open-collector output. Assume that there are four peripheral devices, any of which may wish to attract the attention of the processor (e.g. computer or microprocessor). If this processor has only one Attention pin, then the four Signal lines must be **wire-ORed** together as shown. With all Signals inactive (logic 0) the outputs of all buffer NOT gates are off (state H), and the party line is pulled up to +V by RL. If *any* Signal line is activated (logic 1), as in Sig_1, then the output of the corresponding buffer gate goes hard Low. This pulls the party line Low, irrespective of the state of the other signal lines, and thus interrupts the processor.

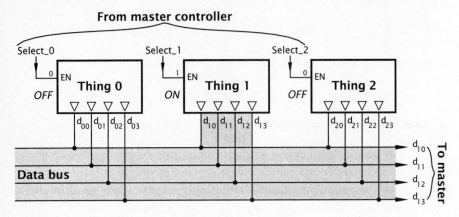

Figure 2.4 *Sharing a bus.*

The **three-state** structure of Fig. 2.2(c) has the properties of both the preceeding output structures. When enabled, the two logic states are represented in the usual way by high and low voltages. When disabled, the output is open circuit irrespective of the activities of the internal logic circuitry and any change in input state. A logic output with this three-state is indicated by the ∇ symbol.

As an example of the use of this structure, consider the situation depicted in Fig. 2.4. Here a master controller wishes to read one of several devices, all connected to this master over a set of party lines. As this data highway or **Data bus** is a common resource, so only the selected device can be allowed access to the bus at any one time. The access has to be withdrawn immediately the data has been read, so that another device can use the resource. As shown in the diagram, the three-state outputs of each Thing are connected to the bus in tandem. When selected, *only* the active logic levels will drive the bus lines. The 74LS244 octal ($\times 8$) three-state buffer shown in Fig. 13.2(a) on page 214 has high-current outputs (designated by the $\triangleright$ symbol) specifically designed to charge/discharge the capacitance associated with long bus lines.

Integrated circuits with a complexity of up to 12 gates are categorized as Small-Scale Integration (SSI). Gate counts upwards to 100 on a single IC are Medium-Scale Integration (MSI), up to 1000 are known as Large-Scale Integration (LSI) and over this, Very Large-Scale Integration (VLSI). Memory chips and MPUs are examples of this latter category.

The NAND gate networks shown in Fig. 2.5 are typical MSI-complexity ICs. Remembering that the output of a NAND gate is logic 0 only when

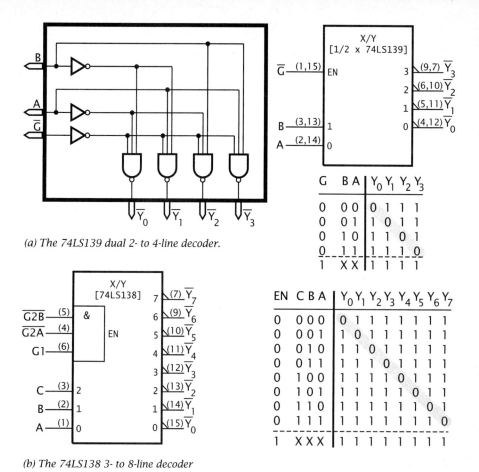

(a) The 74LS139 dual 2- to 4-line decoder.

G	B A	Y_0 Y_1 Y_2 Y_3
0	0 0	0 1 1 1
0	0 1	1 0 1 1
0	1 0	1 1 0 1
0	1 1	1 1 1 0
1	X X	1 1 1 1

(b) The 74LS138 3- to 8-line decoder

EN	C B A	Y_0 Y_1 Y_2 Y_3 Y_4 Y_5 Y_6 Y_7
0	0 0 0	0 1 1 1 1 1 1 1
0	0 0 1	1 0 1 1 1 1 1 1
0	0 1 0	1 1 0 1 1 1 1 1
0	0 1 1	1 1 1 0 1 1 1 1
0	1 0 0	1 1 1 1 0 1 1 1
0	1 0 1	1 1 1 1 1 0 1 1
0	1 1 0	1 1 1 1 1 1 0 1
0	1 1 1	1 1 1 1 1 1 1 0
1	X X X	1 1 1 1 1 1 1 1

Figure 2.5 *The 74LS138 and 74LS139 MSI natural decoders.*

all its inputs are logic 1 (see Fig. 1.2(c) on page 12) then we see that for any combination of the *Select* inputs B A (2^1 2^0) in Fig. 2.5(a) only *one* gate will go to logic 0. Thus output $\overline{Y_2}$ will be activated when B A = 10. The associated truth table shows the circuit *decodes* the binary address B A so that address n selects output $\overline{Y_n}$. The 74LS139 is described as a dual 2- to 4-line **natural decoder** — dual because there are two such circuits in the one chip. The symbol X/Y denotes converting code X (natural binary) to code Y (unary — one of n). The Enable input $\overline{G}$ is connected to all gates in parallel. Thus the decoder function only operates if $\overline{G}$ is Low (logic 0). If $\overline{G}$ is High, then irrespective of the state of B A (the X entries in the truth table denote a 'don't care' situation) all outputs remain deselected — logic 1. An example of the use of the 74LS139 is given in Fig. 12.1 on page 198.

The 74LS138 of Fig. 2.5(b) is similar, but implements a 3-to 8-line decoder function. The state n of the three address lines C B A (2^2 2^1 2^0) selects the corresponding *one only* of the eight outputs $\overline{Y_n}$. The 74LS138 has three Gate inputs which generate an internal Enable signal $\overline{G2B} \cdot \overline{G2A} \cdot G1$. Only if both $\overline{G2A}$ and $\overline{G2B}$ are Low and G1 is High will the device be enabled. The 74LS138 is used several times in Chapter 12 to decode MPU Address lines, for example Fig. 12.3 on page 201.

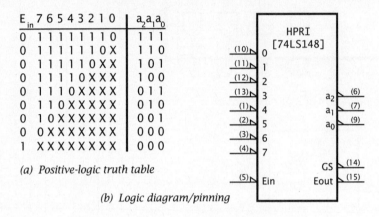

E_{in} 7 6 5 4 3 2 1 0	$a_2 a_1 a_0$
0 1 1 1 1 1 1 1 0	1 1 1
0 1 1 1 1 1 1 0 X	1 1 0
0 1 1 1 1 1 0 X X	1 0 1
0 1 1 1 1 0 X X X	1 0 0
0 1 1 1 0 X X X X	0 1 1
0 1 1 0 X X X X X	0 1 0
0 1 0 X X X X X X	0 0 1
0 0 X X X X X X X	0 0 0
1 X X X X X X X X	0 0 0

(a) Positive-logic truth table

(b) Logic diagram/pinning

Figure 2.6 *The 74LS148 highest-priority encoder.*

The **priority encoder** illustrated in Fig. 2.6 is a sort of reverse decoder. Bringing one of the eight input lines Low results in the active-Low three-bit binary equivalent appearing at the output. Thus if $\overline{5}$ is Low, then $\overline{a_2}\,\overline{a_1}\,\overline{a_0} = 010$ (active low 101).

If more than one input line is active, then the output code reflects the highest. Thus if both $\overline{5}$ and $\overline{3}$ are low, the output code is still 010. Hence the label HPRI for Highest PRIority. The device is enabled when Enable_In ($\overline{E_{in}}$) is Low. Enable_Out ($\overline{E_{out}}$) and Group_Strobe ($\overline{GS}$) are used to cascade 74LS148s to expand the number of lines. Figure 14.3 on page 241 gives an application of this function.

A large class of ICs implement arithmetic operations. The gate array illustrated in Fig. 2.7 detects when the eight-bit byte P7...P0 is identical to the byte Q7...Q0. Eight ENOR gates each give a logic 1 when their two input bits Pn, Qn are identical, as described on page 14. Only if *all* eight bit pairs are the same will the output NAND gate go Low. The 74LS688 **Equality comparator** also has a direct input $\overline{G}$ into this NAND gate, acting as an overall Enable signal.

The ANSI/IEC logic symbol, shown in Fig. 12.1, uses the COMP label to denote the arithmetic comparator function. The output is prefixed with the numeral 1, indicating that its operation P=Q is dependent on any input qualifying the same numeral; that is G1. Thus the active-Low Enable input G1 gates the active-Low output, 1P=Q.

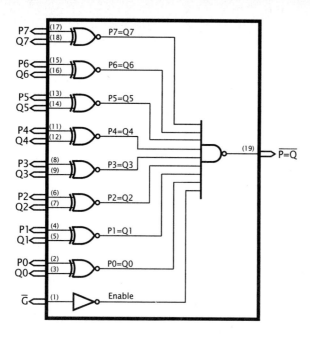

Figure 2.7 *The 74LS688 octal equality detector.*

One of the first functions beyond simple gates to be integrated into a single IC was that of addition. The truth table of Fig. 2.8(a) shows the Sum (S) and Carry-Out (C_1) resulting from the addition of the two bits A and B and any Carry-In (C_0). For instance row 6 states that adding two 1s with a Carry-In of 0 gives a Sum of 0 and a Carry-Out of 1 ($1 + 1 + 0 = {}^1 0$). To implement this row we require to detect the pattern 1 1 0; that is $A \cdot B \cdot \overline{C_0}$; which is gate 6 in the logic diagram. Thus we have, by ORing all applicable patterns together for each output:

$$S = (\overline{A} \cdot \overline{B} \cdot C_0) + (\overline{A} \cdot B \cdot \overline{C_0}) + (A \cdot \overline{B} \cdot \overline{C_0}) + (A \cdot B \cdot C_0)$$
$$C_1 = (\overline{A} \cdot B \cdot C_0) + (A \cdot \overline{B} \cdot C_0) + (A \cdot B \cdot \overline{C_0}) + (A \cdot B \cdot C_0)$$

Using such a circuit for *each* column of a binary addition, with the Carry-Out from column $k-1$ feeding the Carry-In of column k, means that the addition of *any* two n-bit words can be simultaneously implemented. As shown in Fig. 2.8(b), the 74LS283 adds two 4-bit nybbles in 25 ns. In practice the final Carry-Out C_4 is generated using additional circuitry to avoid the delays inherent on the carries rippling though each stage from the least to the most significant digit. n 74LS283s can be cascaded to implement addition for words of $4 \times n$ width. Thus two 74LS283s perform

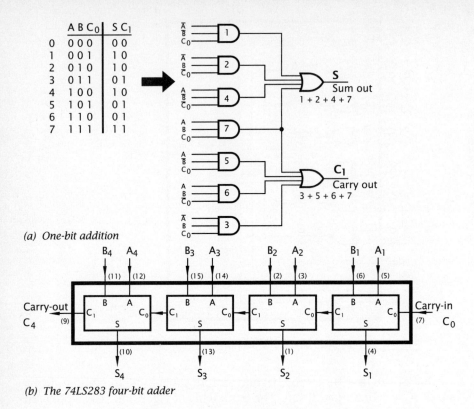

(a) One-bit addition

(b) The 74LS283 four-bit adder

Figure 2.8 *Addition.*

a 16-bit addition in 45 ns, the extra time being accounted for by the carry propagation between the two units.

Adders can of course be coaxed into subtraction by inverting the minuend and adding 1, that is 2's complementation. An Adder/Subtractor circuit could be constructed by feeding the minuend word through an array of EOR gates acting as programmable inverters (see Fig. 1.4(a) on page 13). The Mode line $\overline{Add}/Sub$ that controls these inverters also feeds the Carry-In, effectively adding one when in the Subtract mode.

Extending this line of argument leads to the **Arithmetic Logic Unit** (**ALU**). An ALU is a circuit which can undertake a selection of arithmetic and logic processes on input data as controlled by Mode inputs. The 74LS382 in Fig. 2.9 processes two 4-bit operands in eight ways, as controlled by the three Select bits $S_2 S_1 S_0$ and tabulated in Fig. 2.9(a). Besides addition and subtraction, the logic operations of AND, OR and EOR are supported. The 74LS382 even generates the 2's complement overflow function (see page 9).

As we shall see, the ALU is the heart of the computer and MPU ar-

$S_2S_1S_0$	Operation	
0 0 0	Clear	(F=0000)
0 0 1	Subtract	(B-A)
0 1 0	Subtract	(A-B)
0 1 1	Add	(A+B)
1 0 0	EOR	(A ⊕ B)
1 0 1	OR	(A + B)
1 1 0	AND	(A • B)
1 1 1	Preset	(F=1111)

Word A   Word B   Mode Select S

Carry-In

(17) (19) (1) (3)   (16) (18) (2) (4)   (7) (6) (5)   (15)

A3 A2 A1 A0   B3 B2 B1 B0   S2 S1 S0   C(n)

ALU

[74LS382]

C(n+4)   OVR   F3 F2 F1 F0

(14)   (13)   (12) (11) (9) (8)

Carry-Out

Overflow   Function Output F

(a) Function table   (b) Logic diagram/pinning

Figure 2.9 The 74LS382 ALU.

chitectures. By feeding the Select inputs with a series of mode words, a program of operations can be performed by the ALU. Such operation codes are stored in an external memory, and are accessed sequentially by the computer's control circuits.

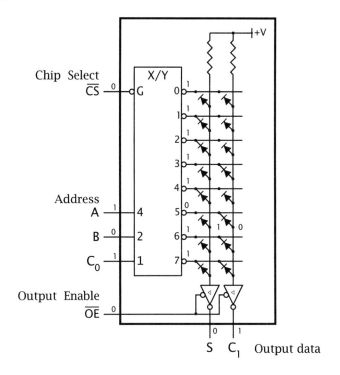

Figure 2.10 A ROM-implemented one-bit adder.

Sequences of program operation codes are normally stored in an LSI **Read-Only Memory** (**ROM**). Consider the architecture shown in Fig. 2.10. This is essentially a 3- to 8-line decoder driving an 8×2 array of diodes. The three-bit address selects only row n for each input combination n. If a diode is connected to this row, then it conducts and brings the appropriate column Low. The inverting three-state output buffer consequently gives a High for each connected diode and Low where the link is broken. The pattern of diode links then defines the output code for each input. For illustrative purposes, the structure has been programmed to implement the one-bit full adder of Fig. 2.8(a), but any two functions of three variables can be generated.

The diode matrix look-up table shown here is known as a Read-Only Memory, as its 'memory' is in the diode pattern, which is programmed in when the device is manufactured. Early devices, which were typically decoder/32×8 matrices, usually came in user-programmable versions in which the links were implemented with fuses. By using a high voltage, a selection of diodes could be taken out of contact. Such devices are called **Programmable ROMs** (**PROMs**).

Fuses are messy when implementing the larger sizes of VLSI PROM necessary to store computer programs. For example, the 2764 device shown

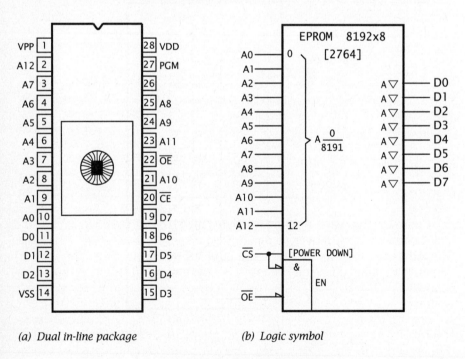

(a) Dual in-line package   (b) Logic symbol

Figure 2.11 *The 2764 Erasable PROM.*

in Fig. 2.11 has the equivalent of 65,536 fuse/diode pairs, and this is a relatively small device capable of storing 8192 bytes of memory. The 2764 uses electrical charge on the floating gate of a metal-oxide field-effect transistor (MOSFET) as the programmable link, with another MOSFET to replace the diode. Charge can be tunnelled on to this isolated gate by, again, using a high voltage. Once on the gate, the electric field keeps the link MOSFET conducting. This charge takes many decades to leak away, but this can be dramatically reduced to about 30 minutes by exposure to intensive ultra-violet radiation. For this reason the 2764 is known as an **Erasable PROM (EPROM)**. When an EPROM is designed for reusability, a quartz window is integrated into the package, as shown in Fig. 2.11. Programming is normally done externally with special equipment, known as PROM programmers, or colloquially as PROM blasters. Versions without windows are referred to as One-Time Programmable ROMs (OTPROMs), as they cannot easily be erased once programmed. They are, however, much cheaper to produce and are thus suitable for small- to medium-scale production runs.

There are PROM structures which can be erased electrically, often in situ in the circuit. These are known as Electrically Erasable PROMs (EEPROMs) or flash memories.

Most modern EPROM/EEPROMs are fairly fast, taking around 150 ns to access and read. Programming is slow, at perhaps 10 ms per word, but is an infrequent activity.

All the circuits shown thus far are categorized as **combinational logic**. They have no memory in the sense that the output simply depends only on the present input, and not the sequence of events leading up to that input. Logic circuits such as latches, counters, registers and read/write memories are described as **sequential logic**. Their output not only depends on the current input, but also the sequence of prior inputs.

Consider a typical doorbell push switch. When you press such a switch the bell rings, and it stops as soon as you release it. This switch has no memory.

Compare this with a standard light switch. Set the switch and the light comes on. Moreover, it remains on when you remove the stimulus (usually your finger!). To turn the light off you must reset the switch. Again it remains off when the input is taken away. This type of switch is known as a **bistable**, as it has two stable states. Effectively it is a one-bit memory cell, that can store either an on or an off state indefinitely.

A read/write memory, such as the 6264 device of Fig. 2.17, implements each bistable cell using two cross-coupled transistors. Here we are not concerned with this microscopic view. Instead, consider the two cross-coupled NOR gates of Fig. 2.12. Remembering from Fig. 1.3(c) on page 13

R S	Q
0 0	Q (no change)
0 1	1 (set)
1 0	0 (reset)

(a) Defining RS latch truth table

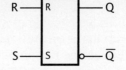

(b) Logic symbol with true/complement outputs

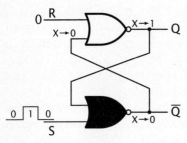

(c) Setting the latch

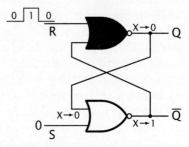

(d) Resetting the latch

Figure 2.12 *The R S latch.*

that any logic 1 into a NOR gate will always give a logic 0 output irrespective of the state of the other inputs, allows us to analyze the circuit:

- If the S input goes to 1, then output $\overline{Q}$ goes to 0. Both inputs to the top gate are now 0 and thus output Q goes to 1. If the S input now goes back to 0, then the lower gate remains 0 (as the Q feedback is 1) and the top gate output also remains unaltered. Thus the latch is *set* by pulsing the S input.
- If the R input goes to 1, then output Q goes to 0. Both inputs to the bottom gate are now 0 and thus output $\overline{Q}$ goes to 1. If the R input now goes back to 0, then the upper gate remains 0 (as the $\overline{Q}$ feedback is 1) and the bottom gate output also remains unaltered. Thus the latch is *reset* by pulsing the R input.

In the normal course of events — that is, assuming that the R and S inputs are not both active at the same time[5] then the two outputs are always complements of each other, as indicated by the logic symbol of Fig. 2.12(b).

There are many bistable implementations. For example, replacing the NOR gates by NAND gives an $\overline{R}\overline{S}$ latch, where the inputs are active on

---

[5]If they were, then both Q and $\overline{Q}$ would go to 0. On relaxing the inputs, the latch will end up in one of its stable states, depending on the relaxation sequence. The response of a latch to simultaneous active Set and Reset inputs is not part of the latch definition, shown in Fig. 2.12(a), but depends on its implementation. For example, trying to turn a light switch on and off together could end in splitting it in two!

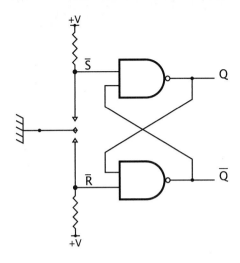

Figure 2.13 *Using an $\overline{R}\,\overline{S}$ latch to debounce a switch.*

a logic 0. The circuit illustrated in Fig. 2.13 shows such a latch used to debounce a mechanical switch. Manual switches are frequently used as inputs to logic circuits. However, most metallic contacts will bounce off the destination contact many times over a period of several tens of milliseconds before settling. For instance, using a mechanical switch to interrupt a computer/microprocessor will give entirely unpredictable results.

In Fig. 2.13, when the switch is moved up and hits the contact the latch is set. When the contact is broken, the latch remains unchanged, provided that the switch does not bounce all the way back to the lower contact. The state will remain Set no matter how many bounces occur. By symmetry, the latch will reset when the switch is moved to the bottom contact, and remain in this Reset state on subsequent bounces.

The **D latch** is an extension of the R S latch, where the output follows the D (Data) input when the C (Control) input is active (logic 1 in our example) and freezes when C is inactive. The D latch can be considered to be a one-bit memory cell where the datum is retained at its value at the end of the sample pulse.

In Fig. 2.14(b) the dependency of the Data input with its Control is shown by the symbols C1 and 1D. The 1 prefix to D shows that it depends on any signal with a 1 suffix, in this case the C input.

A flip flop is also a one-bit memory cell, but the datum is only sampled on an *edge* of the control (known here as the Clock) input. The **D flip flop** described in Fig. 2.14(c) is triggered on a rising edge $\_\!\!\!\!\diagup\!\!\!\!\overline{}$ (as illustrated in the truth table as ↑), but falling-edge ($\overline{}\!\!\!\!\diagdown\_$) clocked flip flops are common. The edge-triggered activity is denoted as $>$ on a logic diagram, as shown in Fig. 2.14(d).

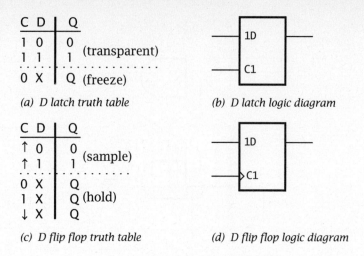

(a) D latch truth table   *(b) D latch logic diagram*

(c) D flip flop truth table   *(d) D flip flop logic diagram*

Figure 2.14 *The D latch and flip flop.*

The 74LS74 shown in Fig. 14.2 on page 239 has two D flip flops in the one SSI circuit. Each flip flop has an overriding Reset ($\overline{R}$) and Set ($\overline{S}$) input, which are asynchronous — that is not controlled by the Clock input. MSI functions include arrays of four, six and eight flip flops all sampling simultaneously with a common Clock input.

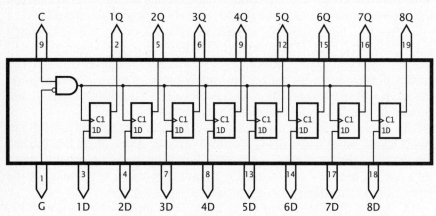

Figure 2.15 *The 74LS377 octal D flip flop array.*

The 74LS377 shown in Fig. 2.15 consists of eight D flip flops all clocked by the same single Clock input C, which is gated by input $\overline{G}$. Thus the eight-bit data 8D...1D is clocked in on the _/⎺ of C if $\overline{G}$ is Low. In the ANSI/ISO logic diagram shown in Fig. 13.5 on page 218, this dependency is indicated as G1→1C2→2D, which states that $\overline{G}$ enables the Clock input, which in turn acts on the Data inputs.

Arrays of D flip flops are known as **registers,** i.e. read/write memories that hold a single word. The 74LS377 is technically known as a parallel-in parallel-out (PIPO) register, as data is entered in parallel (that is all in one go) and is available to read in one go. D latch arrays are also available; the 74LS373 octal PIPO register shown in Fig. 13.6 on page 220 is typical.

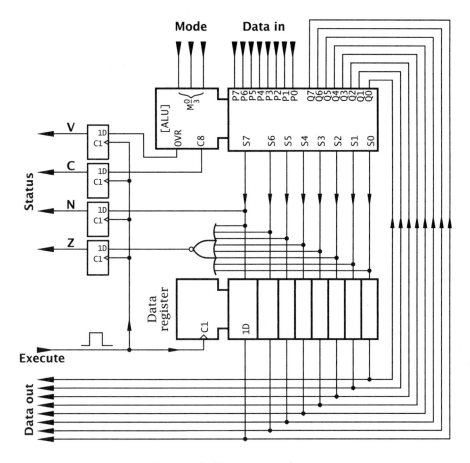

Figure 2.16 *An eight-bit ALU-accumulator processor.*

A pertinent example of the use of a PIPO register is shown in Fig. 2.16. Here an eight-bit ALU is coupled with an eight-bit PIPO register, accepting as its input the ALU output, and in turn feeding one input word back to the ALU. This register accumulates the outcome of a series of operations, and is sometimes called an **Accumulator** or **Working register.** To describe the operation of this circuit, consider the problem of adding two words A and B. The sequence of operations, assuming the ALU is implemented by cascading two 74LS382s, might be:

1. Program step.
   - Mode = 000 (Clear).
   - Pulsing Execute loads the ALU output (0000 0000) into the register.
   - Data out is zero (0000 0000).
2. Program step.
   - Fetch Word A down to the ALU input.
   - Mode = 011 (Add).
   - Pulse _/‾_ Execute to load the ALU output (Word A + zero) into the register.
   - Data out is Word A.
3. Program step.
   - Fetch Word B down to the ALU input.
   - Mode = 011 (Add).
   - _/‾_ Execute to load the ALU output (Word B + Word A) into the register.
   - Data out is Word B plus Word A.

The sequence of operation codes, that is $000 - 100 - 100$, constitutes the program. In practice each instruction would also contain the address (where relevant) in memory of the data to be processed; in this case the locations of Word A and Word B.

Each outcome of a process will have associated properties. For instance it may be zero, be negative (most significant bit is 1), have a carry-out or 2's complement overflow. Such properties may be significant in the future progress of the program. In the diagram four D flip flops, clocked by Execute, are used to grab this status information. In this situation the flip flops are usually known as **flags** (or sometimes semaphores). Thus we have **C**, **N**, **Z** and **V** flags, which form a Code Condition or Status register.

There are various other forms of register. The serial-in serial-out or shift register accepts its data in series, one bit at a time, and outputs it in the same manner. The data is shifted over one bit at a time on each clock pulse. An example is given in Fig. 12.6 on page 205. Combinations of architectures are possible, with data entry and exit being either serial or/and parallel. Counting registers (counters) increment or decrement on each clock pulse, according to a binary sequence. Typically an n-bit counter can perform a count of 2^n states.

The term register is commonly applied to a read/write memory that can store a single binary word, typically 4–64 bits. Larger memories can be constructed by grouping n such registers and selecting one of n. Such a

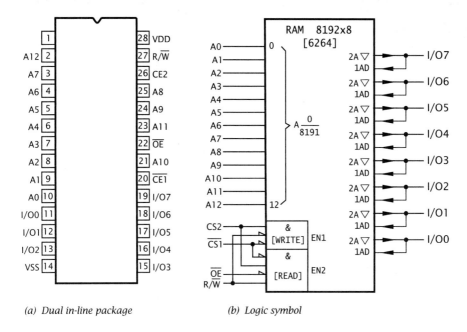

| (a) Dual in-line package | (b) Logic symbol |

Figure 2.17 *The 6264 8196 × 8 RAM.*

structure is sometimes known as a register file. For example, the 74LS670 is a 4 × 4 register file with a separate four-bit data input and data output and separate two-bit address. This means that any register can be read at any time, independently of any concurrent writing process.

Larger read/write memories are normally known as **read/write Random-Access Memories**, or **RAMs** for short. The term random-access indicates that any memory word may be selected with the same access time, irrespective of its position in the memory matrix.[6] This contrasts with a magnetic tape memory, where the reel must be wound to the sector in question — and if this happens to be at the end of the tape then access will take an inordinately long time!

For our example, Fig. 2.17 shows the 6264 RAM. This has a matrix of 65,536 (2^{16}) bistables organized as an array of 8192 (2^{13}) words of eight bits. Word n is accessed by placing the binary pattern of n on the 13-bit Address pins A12...A0.

When in the Read mode (Read/$\overline{\text{Write}}$ = 1), word n will appear at the eight data outputs (I/O7...I/O0) as determined by the state n of the address bits. The A symbol at the input/outputs (as was the case in Fig. 2.11) indicates this addressability. In order to enable the three-state output buffers, the

---

[6]Strictly speaking, ROMs should also be described as random access, but custom and practice have reserved the term for read-write memories.

$\overline{\text{Output Enable}}$ input must be Low.

The addressed word is written into if R/$\overline{\text{W}}$ is Low. The data to be written into word n is applied by the outside controller to the eight I/O pins. This bidirectional traffic is a feature of computer buses; for example see Fig. 11.1 on page 177.

In both cases, the RAM chip as a whole is enabled when $\overline{\text{CS1}}$ is Low and CS2 is High. Depending on the version of the 6264, this access from enabling takes around 100–150 ns. There is no upper limit to how long the data can be held, provided power is maintained. For this reason, the 6264 is described as static (SRAM). Rather than using a transistor pair bistable to implement each bit of storage, data can be stored as charge on the gate-source capacitance of a single field-effect transistor. Such charge leaks away in a few milliseconds, so needs to be refreshed on a regular basis. Dynamic RAMs (DRAMs) are cheaper to fabricate than SRAM equivalents and obtainable in larger capacities. They are usually found where very large memories are to be implemented, such as found in a personal computer. In such situations, the expense of refresh circuitry is more than amortized by the reduction in cost of the memory devices.

Both types of read/write memories are volatile, that is they do not retain their contents if power is removed. Some SRAMs can support existing data at a very low holding current and lower than normal power supply voltage. Thus a backup battery can be used in such circumstances to keep the contents intact for many months.

CHAPTER 3

Stored-program processing

If we take the ALU/data register pair depicted in Fig. 2.16 on page 29 and feed it with function codes, then we have in essence a programmable processing unit. These command codes may be stored in digital memory and constitute the system's **program**. By *fetching* these **instructions** down one at a time we can execute this program. Memory can also hold data on which the ALU operates. This structure, together with its associated data paths, decoders and logic circuitry, is known as a digital **computer**.

In Part II we will see that MPU architecture is modelled on that of the computer. As a prelude to this we will look at the architecture and operating rhythm of the computer structure and some characteristics of its programming. Although this computer is strictly hypothetical, it has been very much "designed" with our book's target MPU in mind.

After reading this chapter you will:

- *Appreciate the von Neumann structure, with its common Data highway connecting memory, input, output and processor.*

- *Understand the fetch and execute rhythm and its interaction with memory and the Central Processing Unit's internal registers.*

- *Understand the concept of an address as a pointer to where data or program code is stored in memory.*

- *Comprehend the structure of an instruction and appreciate that the string of instructions necessary to implement the task is known as a program.*

- *Have an understanding of a basic instruction set, covering data movement, arithmetic, logic and conditional branching categories.*

- *Understand how Immediate, Direct and Indirect address modes permit an instruction to target an operand for processing.*

- *To be able to write short programs using a symbolic assembly-level language and appreciate its one-to-one relationship to machine code.*

The architecture of the great majority of general-purpose computers and microprocesors is modelled after the **von Neumann** model shown in

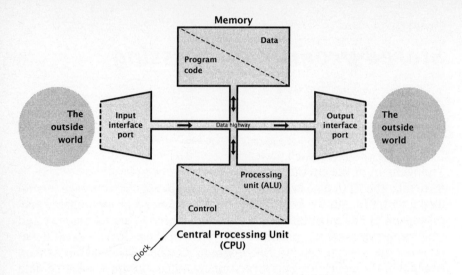

Figure 3.1 *An elementary von Neumann computer.*

Fig. 3.1.[1] The few electronic computers in use up to the late 1940s either only ever ran one program (like the wartime code-breaking Colossus) or else needed to be partly rewired to change their behavior (for example the ENIAC). The Web site entry for this chapter gives historical and technical details of these prehistorical machines.

Von Neumann's great leap forward was to recognize that the program could be stored in memory along with any data. The advantage of this approach is flexibility. To alter the program, simply load the bit pattern into the appropriate area of memory. In essence, the von Neumann architecture comprises a Central Processing Unit (CPU), a memory and a common connecting highway carrying data back and forth. In practice the CPU must also communicate with the environment outside the computer. For this purpose data to and from suitable interface ports is also funnelled through the data highway.

Let us look at these elements in a little more detail.

The Central Processing Unit
The CPU consists of the ALU/working register together with the associ-

---

[1] Von Neumann was a Hungarian mathematician working for the American Manhattan nuclear weapons program during the Second World War. After the war he became a consultant for the Moore School of Electrical Engineering at the University of Pennsylvania's EDVAC computer project, for which he was to employ his new concept where the program was to be stored in memory along with its data. He published his ideas in 1946 and EDVAC became operational in 1951. Ironically, a somewhat lower-key project at Manchester University made use of this approach and the Mark 1 executed its first stored program in 1948! This was closely followed by Cambridge University's EDSAC which ran its program in May 1949, almost two years ahead of EDVAC.

ated control logic. Under the management of the control unit, program instructions are fetched from memory, decoded and executed. Data resulting from, or used by, the program is also accessed from memory. This fetch and execute cycle constitutes the operating rhythm of the computer and continues indefinitely, as long as the system is activated.

Memory

Memory holds the bit patterns which define the program. These sequences of instructions are known as the **software**. The word is a play on the term hardware; as such patterns do not correspond to any physical rearrangement of the circuitry. Memory holding software should ideally be as fast as the CPU, and normally uses semiconductor technologies, such as that described in the last chapter.[2] This memory also holds data being processed by the program.

Program memories appear as an array of cells, each holding a bit pattern. As each cell ultimately feeds the single data highway, a decoding network is necessary to select only *one* cell at a time for interrogation. The computer must target its intended cell for connection by driving this decoder with the appropriate code or **address**. Thus if location 602Eh is to be read, then the pattern $\overset{6}{0110}\ \overset{0}{0000}\ \overset{2}{0010}\ \overset{E}{1110}$ b must be presented to the decoder. For simplicity, this address highway is not shown here, but see Fig. 11.1 on page 177.

This addressing technique is known as random access, as it takes the same time to access a cell regardless of where it is situated in memory. Most computers have large backup memories, usually magnetic or optical disk-based or magnetic tape, in which case access does depend on the cell's physical position. Apart from this sequential access problem, such media are normally too slow to act as the main memory and are used for backup storage of large arrays of data (e.g. student exam records) or programs that must be loaded into main memory before execution.

The Interface Ports

To be of any use, a computer must be able to interact with its environment. Although conventionally one thinks of a keyboard and screen, any of a range of physical devices may be read and controlled. Thus the flow of fuel injected into a cylinder together with engine speed may be used to control the instant of spark ignition in the combustion chamber of a gas/petrol engine.

Data Highway

All the elements of our computer are wired together with the one *common* data highway, or bus. With the CPU acting as the master controller,

---

[2]This wasn't always so; the earliest practical large high-speed program memories used miniature ferrite cores that could be magnetized in any one of two directions. Core memories were in use from the 1950s to the early 1970s, and program memory is still sometimes referred to as core.

all information flow is back and forward along these shared wires. Although this is efficient, it does mean that only one thing can happen at any time, and this phenomenon is sometimes known as the von Neumann bottleneck.

The fetch instruction down — decode it — execute sequence, the so called **fetch and execute cycle**, is fundamental to the understanding of the operation of the von Neumann computer and MPU. To illustrate this operating rhythm we look at a simple program that takes a variable called NUM_1, adds $65h$ ($101d$) to it and assigns the the resultant value to the variable called NUM_2. In the high-level language **C** this may be written as:[3]

```
NUM_2 = NUM_1 + 101;
```

A rather more detailed close-up of our computer, which I have named BASIC (for Basic All-purpose Stored Instruction Computer), is shown in Fig. 3.2. This shows the CPU and memory, together with the common data highway (or **bus**) and an Address bus. Let us look first at the individual components of the CPU.

Data Buffer
The DATA_BUF holds the last 16-bit word fetched from the Data bus. As shown here, this is the code for the first instruction move.w (MOVE Word to the Data register) $3038h$.

Instruction Register
The last fetched instruction code (usually termed **op-code**, short for operation code) is stored in the IR, feeding the Instruction Decoder (ID).

Instruction Decoder
The ID is the 'brains' of the CPU, deciphering the op-code and sending out the appropriate sequence of signals necessary to locate the operand and to configure the ALU to execute the operation.

Arithmetic Logic Unit
The ALU carries out an arithmetic or logic operation as commanded by its function code generated by the Instruction Decoder.

Data Register
Data register 0 (D0) is the ALU's working register. Most instructions use D0 to hold either the source or the destination operand; for example sub.w #6,d0 which subtracts the constant 06 from the Data register and then places the result back in D0.

Program Counter
Instructions are normally stored sequentially in memory, and the PC is the counter which keeps track of the current instruction word. This register

---

[3]If you are more familiar with PASCAL or Modula-2, then it would be expressed as NUM_2 := NUM_1 + 101

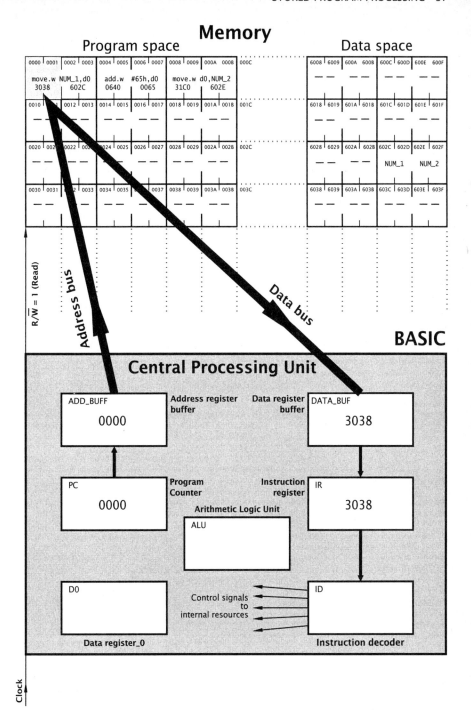

Figure 3.2 *A snapshot of the CPU fetching down the first instruction.*

is sometimes called (more sensibly) an Instruction Pointer. Loading the PC with a new value disrupts the orderly count and causes the execution sequence to jump or branch to another part of the program.

Address Buffer

When the CPU wishes to fetch an instruction word, it transfers the contents of the PC into the ADD_BUFF register. This directly addresses the memory via the Address bus. The resulting data is connected to the CPU via the Data bus and loaded into the DATA_BUF register. During this time the R/$\overline{\text{W}}$ direction control line is 1 to indicate a Read cycle. Where the CPU wishes to access data from memory (as opposed to an instruction), it places the appropriate address in ADD_BUFF. R/$\overline{\text{W}}$ is logic 1 where the CPU wishes to read data and 0 where data is to be written (from DATA_BUF to memory).

As shown in Fig. 3.2, I have depicted memory as an array of cells (or pigeon-holes), each with a unique address. This is shown divided into two sectors: one holding the **program code** (sometimes called text) and one the **data code**. Although these two sectors may physically be part of the same memory circuits, typically different memory technologies are used for the two functions. Thus program code (and indeed fixed tables of constants) may be located in ROM, whilst alterable data (i.e. variable objects) are in RAM. I have, quite arbitrarily, originated the program code at address 0000h and data at 6000h.

Each instruction in memory is 32 bits long, with a 16-bit word holding the op-code and a word relating to where in memory the operand is or sometimes the operand itself. The first instruction is stored as 3038-602Ch.[4] As the Data bus is only 16 bits wide, *two* read actions are required to fetch down each instruction. The first of these fetches is shown in the diagram in which the op-code 3038h (or 0011 0000 0011 1000b if you prefer) has been brought down through DATA_BUF into IR. The memory cell involved is shown shaded.

As depicted in Fig. 3.2, each memory cell is subdivided into two eight-bit bytes, each with its own address, even though the Data bus can swallow a 16-bit word in one gulp. This is because the computer can deal with eight-bit data bytes as single entities (of course only using half the Data bus), so each *byte* needs its own unique address (see Fig. 11.5 on page 189). A word address is simply the byte address, but going up in even steps of two. This is because the least significant binary bit of the address ($a_0 = 2^0$) is ignored, and $2^0 = 1$ is the only power of 2 that is not even. For example NUM_2 in the diagram has the address 602Eh (0110 0000 0010 111$X$$b$).

---

[4]Remember that we are only using hexadecimal notation as a human convenience. If you took an electron microscope and looked inside these cells you would 'see' 0011 0000 0011 1000 0110 0000 0010 1100.

So much for the CPU and memory. Let us look at the program itself. There are three instructions in our illustrative software, and, as we have already observed, the task is to copy the value of a word-sized variable NUM_1 plus 101d (65h) into a variable called NUM_2, i.e.

NUM_2 = NUM_1 + 101;

We see from our diagram that the variable named NUM_1 is simply a symbolic representation for "the contents of 602C:Dh", and similarly NUM_2 is a much prettier way of saying "the contents of 602E:Fh".

Now as far as the computer is concerned, our program is, starting at location 0000h:

```
00110000001110000110000000101100
00000110010000000000000001100101
00110001110000000110000000101110
```

Unless you are a CPU this is not much fun![5]

Using hexadecimal is a little better:

```
3038602C
06400065
31C0602E
```

but is still instantly forgettable. Furthermore, the CPU still only understands binary, so you are likely to have to use a translator program running on, say, a PC to translate from hexadecimal to binary.

If you are going to use computer aid, it makes sense to go the whole hog and express the program using symbolic representations of the various instructions (e.g. clr.b for "CLeaR Byte", sub.w for "SUBtract Word") and for variables' addresses. Doing this, our program becomes:

```
move.w   NUM_1,d0   ; Copy the word-sized variable NUM_1 down to D0
add.w    #101,d0    ; Add to it the constant 101 decimal (65h)
move.w   d0,NUM_2   ; Copy NUM_1+65h into NUM_2
```

where text after a semicolon is comment.

Chapter 7 is completely devoted to the process of translation from this **Assembly-level** source code to machine-readable binary. Here it is only necessary to look at the general symbolic form of an instruction which is:

```
instruction mnemonic   <src operand's address>,<destn operand's address>
```

Most instructions, including our three here, have both a source and a destination field. Thus we cannot just say add.w, we need to say "add something to something else", for example add.w 06000h,d0 means "add the word contents of 6000:1h to the contents of the Data register and place the outcome back in the destination". This could be written as: (d0) <- (6000:1) + (d0), where the parentheses mean "contents of" and <- means "becomes". This notation is called **Register Transfer Language (RTL)**. Some instructions have only one operand address field, for example clr.b 06002h which means "CLeaR the Byte at 6002h", or in RTL

---

[5]I know; I was programming this way back in the primitive mid-1970s.

(6000h) <- 00. Here the operand address specifies a destination; there is no point having an instruction only specifying a source. A few instructions have no operand fields; for example the nop instruction (for "No OPeration") that does not act on data.

All our three instructions have source and destination. All use the Data register D0 *directly* as one of these. The first and last specify an *absolute* address, which is the actual location in memory of the data. It is easier for us humans to give these variables symbolic names, such as NUM_1, but actually they are addresses. The middle instruction adds a *constant* number rather than a variable in memory. This constant is indicated thus as #65h, where the hash symbol (known as the pound symbol in North America) signifies a constant in assembly language. The constant word itself really is stored in memory, as the second word of the instruction. If you leave the # out[6] then the instruction add.w 65h,d0 will be translated as "add the word-sized contents of 0065:6h to D0", rather than "add the *constant* 65h to D0". In RTL (d0) <- (0065:6h) + (d0) instead of (d0) <- 0065h + (d0).

In writing programs using assembly-level symbolic representation, it is important to remember that each instruction has a one-to-one correspondence to the underlying machine instructions and its binary code. In Chapter 10 we will see that high-level languages loose that close relationship.

The essence of computer operation is the rhythm of the **fetch and execute cycle**. Here, each instruction is sucessively brought down from memory (fetched), interpreted and then executed. In order to illustrate this let us trace through our example program. We assume that our computer, that is the Program Counter, is reset to 0000h.

Fetch 1(a) ....Fig. 3.3
- Program Counter (0000h) to ADD_BUFF and on to Address bus.
- First op-code (Move word to D0) in memory then appears on the Data bus, through to DATA_BUF and IR.
- Program Counter incremented by 2 (one word is two bytes).

Fetch 1(b)
- Program Counter (0002h) to ADD_BUFF and on to Address bus.
- The address of the variable NUM_1 (602Ch) in memory then appears on the Data bus, through to DATA_BUF.
- Program Counter incremented by 2.

Execute 1
- The operand address 602Ch to ADD_BUFF and on to Address bus.
- Resulting data (NUM_1) is read on to the Data bus (R/$\overline{W}$ = 0). through to DATA_BUF.
- The ALU is configured to Pass Through mode, which feeds NUM_1 through to the Data register D0.

---

[6]As you surely will do on occasion!

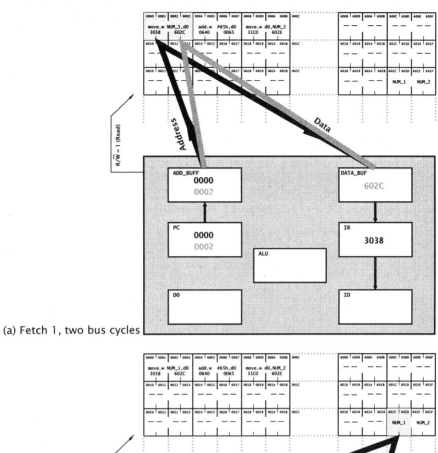

(a) Fetch 1, two bus cycles

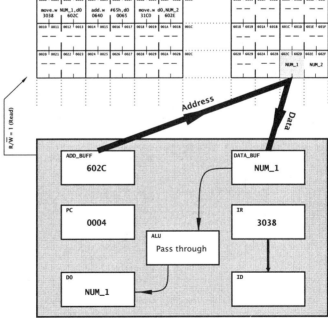

(b) Execute 1

Figure 3.3 *Fetch and execute the first instruction.*

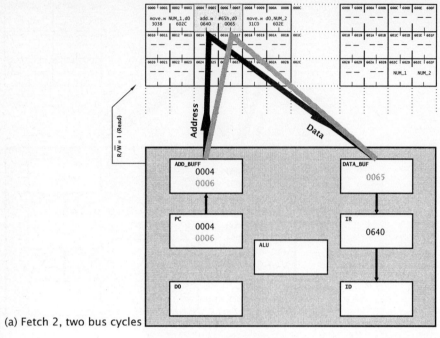

(a) Fetch 2, two bus cycles

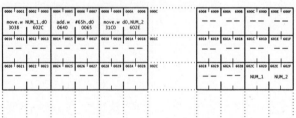

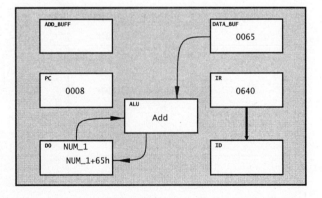

(b) Execute 2

Figure 3.4 *Fetch and execute the second instruction.*

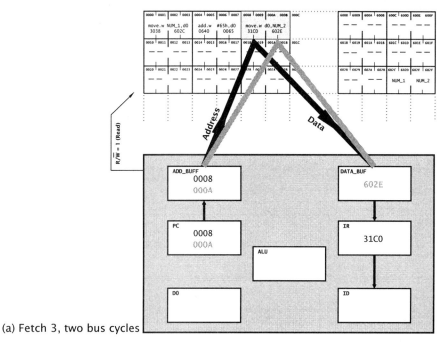

(a) Fetch 3, two bus cycles

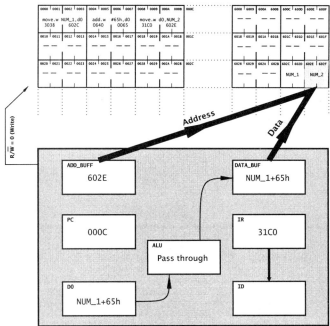

(b) Execute 3

Figure 3.5 *The final fetch and execute cycle.*

Fetch 2(a) ....Fig. 3.4

- Program Counter (0004h) to ADD_BUFF and on to Address bus.

- Second op-code (Add *constant* word to D0) in memory then appears on the Data bus, through to DATA_BUF and IR.

- Program Counter incremented by 2.

Fetch 2(b)

- Program Counter (0006h) to ADD_BUFF and on to Address bus.

- The constant operand (0065h) in memory then appears on the Data bus and through to DATA_BUF.

- Program Counter incremented by 2.

Execute 2

- The ALU is configured to Add mode, the outcome of which (NUM_1+65h) is placed in D0.

Fetch 3(a) ....Fig. 3.5

- Program Counter (0008h) to ADD_BUFF and on to Address bus.

- Third op-code (Move word from D0 to memory) in memory then appears on the Data bus, through to DATA_BUF and IR.

- Program Counter incremented by 2.

Fetch 3(b)

- Program Counter (000Ah) to ADD_BUFF and on to Address bus.

- The address of the variable NUM_2 (602Eh) in memory then appears on the Data bus, through to DATA_BUF.

- Program Counter incremented by 2.

Execute 3

- The operand address 602Eh to ADD_BUFF and on to Address bus.

- The ALU is configured to Pass Through mode, which feeds the contents of D0 through to DATA_BUF and to the Data bus. The data is stored in memory by bringing R/$\overline{W}$ to logic 0 for a write action.

Notice how the Program Counter is automatically advanced during each fetch cycle. This sequential advance will continue indefinitely until an instruction to modify the PC occurs, such as jmp 0200h. This would place the address 0200h into the PC, overwriting the normal incrementing process, and effectively causing the CPU to jump to whatever instruction was located at 0200h. Thereafter, the linear progression would continue.

Although our program doesn't do very much, it only takes around 1 μs to execute each instruction. A million unimpressive operations each second can amount to a great deal! Nevertheless, it hardly rates highly in the annals of software, so we will wrap up our introduction to computing by looking at some slightly more sophisticated examples.

Writing a program is somewhat akin to building a house. Given a known range of building materials, the builder simply puts these together in the right order. Of course there are tremendous skills in all this; poor building techniques lead to houses that leak, are draughty and eventually may fall down!

It is possible to design a house at the same time as it is being built. Whilst this may be quite feasible for a log cabin, it is likely that the final result will not remain rainproof very long, nor will it be economical, maintainable, ergonomic or very pretty. It is rather better to employ an architect to design the edifice before building commences. Such a design is at an abstract level, although it is better if the designer is aware of the technical and economic properties of the available building materials.

Unfortunately much programming is of the "on the hoof" variety, with little thought of any higher-level design. In the software arena this means devising strategies and designing data structures in memory. Again, it is better if the design algorithms keep in mind the materials of which the program will be built: in our case the machine instructions.

At the level of our examples in this chapter, it will be this coding (building) task that we will be mostly concerned with. Later chapters will cover more advanced structures which will help this process, and we will get more practice at devising strategies and data structures.

In order to code software we must have a knowledge of the register architecture of the computer/MPU and of the individual instructions. Figure 3.6 shows the **programming model** we will use for our exercises. This shows all registers that can be 'got at' by the program. I have added two registers to the previous complement. An **Address register A0** complements the Data register and is primarily meant to point to an object in memory. The Code Condition Register **CCR** comprises three flip flops or flags which are used to tell the software something about the outcome from an instruction. Thus the **C** flag is primarily the Carry bit from the last addition (or borrow from a subtraction). The **Z** flag is set if the operation result is zero, and the **N** flag is set if the operation result has its most significant bit set to 1 (which is the sign bit if the object is treated as a signed 2's complement number).

Table 3.1 shows all the instructions supported by the BASIC computer. Before looking at these, let us discuss the concept of the **address mode**. Most instructions act on data, which may be in internal CPU registers or out in memory. Thus the location of such operands must be part of the instruction. It isn't sufficient to simply state clr — Clear what? There

Instruction	Address modes for [ea]					Flags		
	#	d0	a0	(a0)	Abs	N	Z	C
Arithmetic								
add [ea],d0	*	*	*	*	*	√	√	√
adda [ea],a0	*	*	*	*	*	•	•	•
addq #d_3,[ea]		*	*	*	*	√	√	√
clr [ea]		*		*	*	0	1	0
sub [ea],d0	*	*	*	*	*	√	√	√
suba [ea],a0	*	*	*	*	*	•	•	•
subq #d_3,[ea]		*	*	*	*	√	√	√
Movement								
move [ea],[ead]	*S	*	*S	*	*	√	√	0
movea [ea],a0	*	*	*	*	*	•	•	•
Logic								
and [ea],d0	*	*		*	*	•	•	0
not [ea]		*		*	*	•	•	0
or [ea],d0	*	*		*	*	•	•	0
lsl #d_3,d0						√	√	√
lsr #d_3,d0						√	√	√
Testing								
cmp [ea],d0	*	*	*	*	*	√	√	√
cmpa [ea],a0	*	*	*	*	*	√	√	√
Branch								
bra						•	•	•
beq						•	•	•
bne						•	•	•
bcc/bhs						•	•	•
bcs/blo						•	•	•
bpl						•	•	•
bmi						•	•	•

*	: Available	√	: Flag operates normally
S	: Source only	•	: Not affected
[ea]	: Effective address	0	: Flag cleared
[ead]	: Destination effective address	1	: Flag set
#d_3	: Constant 1-8		

Table 3.1 *Our BASIC computer's instruction set.*

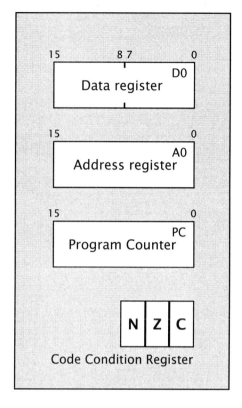

Figure 3.6 *Programmers' model.*

are different ways of specifying the operand location; for instance clr d0 and clr 6000h are legitimate manifestations of the same clr instruction. In the first case the target is the Data register, and in the second out in memory at the fixed address 6000*h*. The different ways of pointing out an operand's location are the address modes. Which address mode an instruction is to use is specified by some of the bits in its operation code. They are:

Immediate
This is used when the operand is *fixed* data; for example:

add.w #120,d0   ; Add the constant 120 decimal to D0

Remember the use of the # symbol to denote that the following number is *constant data*. If we leave this out, e.g. add.w 120,d0, then this is interpreted as "add the contents of *address* 0120 to D0". The actual constant is usually located in memory following the op-code, i.e. is it is part of the instruction.

Data Register Direct

Here the operand is to be found in the Data register. For example:

```
clr.w  d0      ; Clear the data in the Data register
```

The Data Register Direct mode is also that used for the destination of the previous example, which shows that source and destination operands need not use the same address mode.

Keeping operands in internal Data registers is faster and yields shorter code. As we shall see, our MPU has eight of these registers.

Address Register Direct

This address mode specifies that the operand is to be found in the Address register. For example:

```
adda #1,a0   ; Increment the Address register
```

The Address register normally holds an address, not data, and for this reason special instructions (such as adda as opposed to plain add) are used where the Address register can be altered. Such instructions do not affect the CCR flags.

Absolute

Here the absolute address of the operand follows the op-code. For instance:

```
clr.b  6050h  ; Clear the byte at memory address 6050h
```

The characteristic of this address mode is that the *location* of the operand is fixed as an integral part of the program, and this cannot be changed as execution progresses.[7]

Although directly specifying its address may seem to be the obvious way to locate an object in memory, this technique is rather inflexible. Suppose we wished to clear an area of memory between 6000h and 61FFh,

---

Program 3.1 *Clearing memory the linear way.*

```
CLEAR_ARR:   clr.b   6000h   ; Clear Array[0]
             clr.b   6001h   ; and Array[1]
             clr.b   6002h   ; Each clr occupies four bytes
             clr.b   6003h   ; of program memory
             clr.b   6004h   ; Keep on going
             .....   .....

             clr.b   61FEh   ; Clear Array[510]; nearly there
             clr.b   61FFh   ; Clear Array[511]; Phew!
```

---

say to hold an array of 512 byte elements Array[0]...Array[511]. The obvious way to do this is shown in Program 3.1, which uses a clr.b instruction for each byte. This program needs 512 four-byte instructions,

---

[7]If the code is stored in RAM, in theory the program can change itself, but self-modifying code is a somewhat hair-raising practice!

totalling 2 Kbyte of program memory for storage! Although it works, this is highly inefficient, and the mind boggles if you wanted to clear a 4 Kbyte memory space! There has got to be a better way.[8]

Address Register Indirect

Here the Address register *points to* the location in memory. The term indirect is used as the register does not hold the data itself, only a location pointer. The terminology is to say the **effective address** (**ea**) is the contents of the Address register. All the instruction has to do is to specify this address mode, for example:

```
clr.b  (a0)        ; Clear the byte pointed to by A0
```

This seems rather an obscure way of doing things, but let us revisit our array clearing example. Repeating the same thing 512 times on successive memory locations is a dubious way of doing this. Why not use a pointer into the array, and increment the pointer each time we do a Clear? This is just what we have done in Program 3.2. The linear structure of the previous program has been folded into a **loop**, shown shaded. The execution path keeps circulating around the clr.b instruction which is "walked" through the array by advancing the pointer on each pass through the loop. Eventually the pointer moves out of the desired range and the program then exits the loop.

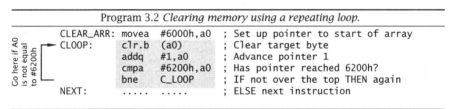

Program 3.2 *Clearing memory using a repeating loop.*

```
           CLEAR_ARR: movea  #6000h,a0  ; Set up pointer to start of array
           CLOOP:     clr.b  (a0)       ; Clear target byte
                      addq   #1,a0      ; Advance pointer 1
                      cmpa   #6200h,a0  ; Has pointer reached 6200h?
                      bne    C_LOOP     ; IF not over the top THEN again
           NEXT:      .....  .....      ; ELSE next instruction
```

Go here if A0 is not equal to #6200h

Program 3.2 has many new features, especially as we haven't yet reviewed the instruction set.

1. Line 1 initializes the Address register by moving the *constant* 6000h (the location of Array[0]) into it. Note the use of movea rather than the ordinary move instruction. Nearly all loop structures involve some setting up before entry.

2. The actual Clear instruction uses the Indirect Address Register mode. This line has a label associated with it; it is called CLOOP. The assembler knows this is a label and not an instruction by the appended colon.

3. Each pass around the loop involves an incrementation of the pointer. This is done here by simply adding 1 to the Address register with the

---

[8]Can you figure out a simple way of halving the number of instructions?

ADD Quick instruction.

4. Almost every loop needs a mechanism so it can eventually exit, otherwise it will become an endless loop. In our case this is done by comparing the contents of the Address register with the constant 6200*h*. If they are *not* equal then the code execution path transfers back up to the beginning of the loop. This transfer uses the Branch if Not Equal (bne) instruction. Note the use of the label CLOOP in this instruction; this is why we labelled this entry point earlier. If the comparison test fails (when A0 = 6200*h*) then the branch back is ignored and execution passes to the next instruction after the loop.

Having covered the address modes, let us look briefly at the instruction set in Table 3.1. Instructions that can target memory or the Data register come in two sizes, namely byte .b and word .w. No byte-size alterations on the Address register are allowed. Instructions have been divided into five groups as follows.

Arithmetic

This covers addition, subtraction and clearing operations. The former two put their result into a register, whilst clr can operate directly on memory. The addq/subq pair also can operate on memory, and can add/subtract constants between 1 and 8. Thus addq.b #1,6000h increments the contents of memory location 6000*h*. The terminology "quick" results from a comparison with the alternative of using three instructions to bring down the data, add/subtract and put back again. Furthermore, if the contents of D0 are important, this will have to be saved before and retrieved after the operation. The three-bit binary code for the constant range 1–8 is embedded in the op-code, so these are one-word instructions and thus fetch more quickly. Quick instructions can also act on an Address register, but in this case the CCR flags are unaffected.

Movement

These instructions *copy* data from source to destination. The majority of operations involve moving data, so move is the most flexible of the instructions. Data can be copied directly from one memory location to another without going via the Data register. Thus the instruction move.w 6000h,6700h is legitimate.

Logic

The not instruction inverts all bits in the target location. The and instruction bitwise ANDs the source with the destination; for example if the contents of D0 were 0101 0110 1001 0111*b*, then and.w #00FFh will give **0000 0000** 1001 0111*b* in D0. In a similar manner or.w #8000h gives 1101 0110 1001 0111*b*.

Two instructions are provided that can shift the contents of the Data register from one to eight places either left or right, e.g. lsl.w #6,d0. As shown in Fig. 3.7, the last bit shifted out ends up in the Carry flag.

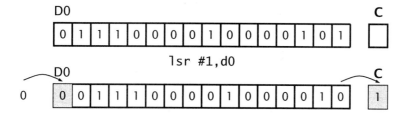

Figure 3.7 *Shifting data one place to the right.*

Testing

Mathematically the way to compare the magnitude of two numbers is to subtract them, NUM_1 − NUM_2. If they are *equal* then the outcome will be zero, that is the **Z** flag will be set. If NUM_1 is *higher than* NUM_2 then there will be no borrow generated, **C** is clear. If NUM_1 is *lower than* NUM_2 then a borrow will be generated and the **C** flag will be set. If NUM_1 is in the Data register then Table 3.2 summarizes the situation.

D0 *higher than* NUM: D0 − NUM → no Carry and non-Zero   C=0, Z=0 ($\overline{C+Z}$=1)
D0 *equal to*   NUM: D0 − NUM → gives Zero   Z=1
D0 *lower than*   NUM: D0 − NUM → gives a Carry   C=1

Table 3.2 *Comparing two unsigned numbers.*

If we are only interested in the relative magnitude of two quantities, e.g. "Is the temperature lower than 10?" and not by how much they differ, then using the sub instruction is overkill, in that the operand in D0 will be destroyed (replaced by the difference). The cmp instruction uses the ALU to perform the subtraction and sets the appropriate flags but then throws away the answer (i.e. does not put it in D0). Compare can be thought of as a non-destructive subtract.

Branch

Branch instructions make the Program Counter skip *xx* places forwards or backwards, usually based on the state of the CCR flags. Thus the instruction bcc .+8 means "add eight to the *current* state of the PC if the **C** flag is clear". Notice the terminology .+8 to mean "from the current place". Remember, from Figs 3.3(b), 3.4(b) and 3.5(b), that by the time an instruction is executed the PC is already pointing to the *next* instruction. Thus this instruction actually lands the execution point 12 bytes further along from the Branch instruction. Backward skips, e.g. bcs .−16, use a 2's complement offset following the op-code. With a word-sized offset, a range of +32,770 to −32, 764 bytes[9] is possible.

---

[9]Remember that the Program Counter has advanced to the following instruction 4 bytes on before it is augmented by the offset, which ranges from 7FFF*h* to 8000*h*.

Rather than calculating these offsets by hand, use labels and allow the assembler to do the sums. Thus in Program 3.2 we have bne CLOOP instead of bne .0F8h. Eight Branch instructions are listed. Branch Always (bra) is unconditional, i.e. the offset is *always* added to the PC. The bcc:bcs pair have the alternative mnemonic bhs:blo for Branch if Higher or Same and Branch if LOwer than, which is more meaningful after a Comparison operation. Branch if EQual to zero/Not Equal to zero similarly check the **Z** flag. Although Conditional Branch instructions frequently come after a Compare operation (as in Program 3.2), they can follow any operation that affects the appropriate flags, such as a move instruction.

Examples

Example 3.1
The ASCII code for the character '0' is 30h. Write a program that fills an area of memory from 6000h through to 601Fh with '0's.

Solution
This is exactly the same as Program 3.2 but with line 2 replaced by move.b #30h,(a0). Remember that the move instruction can target memory locations directly.

Example 3.2
A data logger samples temperature every 5 minutes. After 24 hours, 288 byte-sized temperatures are stored in memory from 2000h upwards. Write a program to scan through this array and find the maximum temperature. This is to be stored in location 6000h.

Solution

Program 3.3 *Finding the maximum in an array.*

```
1            .define MAXIMUM = 6000h; Maximum value
2            .define TEMP    = 2000h; Temperature array
3   SCAN:  movea  #TEMP,a0         ; Point A0 to the const address TEMP[0]
4          clr.b  MAXIMUM          ; MAXIMUM = 0
5   MLOOP: move.b (a0),d0          ; Get TEMP[i]
6          cmp.b  MAXIMUM,d0       ; TEMP[i] > MAXIMUM?
7          blo    CONT             ; IF not THEN no update
8          move.b d0,MAXIMUM       ; ELSE new MAXIMUM
9   CONT:  addq.b #1,a0            ; Move to next sample (i=i+1)
10         cmpa   #(TEMP+288),a0   ; Over the top yet?
11         bne    MLOOP            ; IF not THEN again
12 NEXT:
```

Again this involves a loop, in which the array is walked through (Program 3.3). Each temperature is compared with the value in 6000h and if lower than this no action is taken. Otherwise the value in 6000h is updated with the temperature under inspection. The procedure can be formulated as:

1. $MAXIMUM = 0$

2. FOR $i = 0$ to $i = 287$ DO:

     • IF $TEMP[i] > MAXIMUM$ THEN $MAXIMUM = TEMP[i]$

     • $i = i + 1$

In the program listing I have given the memory location 6000h the name MAXIMUM to clarify the program text. Similarly, the address 2000h was assigned to the name TEMP in line 2, that is the beginning of the temperature array. This allows line 10 to use the label expression TEMP+288, rather than have the programmer calculate 2000h + 288d = 2120h. All assemblers are capable of doing simple calculations like this, and the resulting program is easier to read and therefore less error-prone. Although hardly worth the effort for small programs like this, for any real program the use of labels and names is crucial. Notice how the Address register was initialized in line 3 by copying in the *constant* 2000h — that is the label TEMP.

The body of the program closely follows our task list. If the comparison of line 6's outcome is that the contents of D0 (i.e. TEMP) are lower than MAXIMUM, then the following blo simply steps over the instruction updating MAXIMUM with TEMP[i]. The loop exits in the normal way when A0 goes over the top of the array. We have of course assumed that the temperatures are unsigned quantities, that is not 2's complement with a sign bit.

Example 3.3

A simple technique of noise reduction is to sample an input n times and take the average. If the noise is random, then the signal to noise ratio is improved by a factor of $\sqrt{n}$.

Write a routine to apply this technique to an eight-bit analog to digital converter located at 8000h to give an improvement factor of 16.

Solution

In essence, this simply requires adding the byte at 8000h 256 times and then dividing by 256 (Program 3.4). This is summarized by the task list.

1. Clear SUM

2. FOR $i = 0$ to $i = 255$ DO:

- Add data to *SUM*
- $i = i + 1$

3. $AVERAGE = SUM/256$

Program 3.4 *Noise reduction by averaging.*

```
1              .define COUNT     = 6000h; Keep count of times round the loop
2              .define TEMPORARY = 6002h; Room to extend byte sample to word
3              .define ANALOG_IN = 8000h; The A/D converter
4   FILTER: clr.b COUNT              ; Loop count i = 0
5           clr.w TEMPORARY         ; Word workspace zeroed
6           clr.w d0               ; SUM = 0
7   N_LOOP: move.b ANALOG_IN,TEMPORARY+1
8   ; Extend ANALOG_IN byte to 16-bit TEMPORARY
9           add.w  TEMPORARY,d0     ; SUM = SUM + data
10          addq.b #1,COUNT         ; i = i + 1
11          bne    N_LOOP           ; REPEAT UNTIL i returns to 0 (=256)
12          lsr.w  #8,d0            ; ELSE AVERAGE = SUM/256
13  NEXT:
```

Dividing by 256 is no problem, simply shift right eight times, as inplemented in line 12. However, addition is more problematical! This is because the sum total in D0 is a 16-bit word whilst the A/D converter at 8000h is only eight-bit byte size. Thus the instruction add.w ANALOG_IN,d0 would actually add 8000:1h to D0. To get around this problem I have reserved a word in memory (why did I choose 6002h for this rather than 6001h?). If the upper byte of TEMPORARY is cleared (line 5) and the eight-bit data from location 8000h is copied to the lower byte, we get

TEMPORARY	TEMPORARY+1
00	data

. This is a 16-bit **extension** of the original value and may be added to D0.W in line 9. The 16-bit D0.W is large enough to hold any combination of 256 bytes.

Rather conveniently, the eight-bit variable i will wrap around $255 \rightarrow 0$ after 256 passes through the loop. Line 11 detects this event by branching whenever the **Z** flag is set. No Compare instruction is needed.

Example 3.4
Write a routine that will convert a binary byte in location 6000h to three BCD digits in locations 6020h – 6022h. For example

11111111$b \rightarrow$ 0010 0101 0101 (255).

Solution
This example is really asking "How many hundreds are there in the number; how many tens and how many units?". This approach gives us the following task list:

1. $HUNDS = 0$

2. $TENS = 0$

3. WHILE $BINARY \geq 100$

  • $BINARY = BINARY - 100$
  • $HUNDS = HUNDS + 1$

4. WHILE $BINARY \geq 10$

  • $BINARY = BINARY - 10$
  • $TENS = TENS + 1$

5. $UNITS = BINARY$

Program 3.5 *Binary to BCD conversion.*

```
1                  .define BINARY = 6000h ; Where the binary byte is
2                  .define HUNDS  = 6020h ; Where hundreds BCD digit will be
3                  .define TENS   = 6021h ; Where tens BCD digit will be
4                  .define UNITS  = 6022h ; Where units BCD digit will be
5   BIN_2_BCD: clr.b   HUNDS         ; Hundreds = 0
6              clr.b   TENS          ; Tens = 0
7              move.b  BINARY,d0     ; Get binary byte
8   H_LOOP:    sub.b   #100,d0       ; Binary - 100
9              bcs     NEXT_TEN      ; IF undershoot THEN go to tens
10             addq.b  HUNDS         ; ELSE one more hundred
11             bra     H_LOOP        ; and take another hundred away
12  NEXT_TEN:  add.b   #100,d0       ; Restore the one hundred too many
13  T_LOOP:    sub.b   #10,d0        ; Binary - 10
14             bcs     NEXT_UNIT     ; IF undershoot THEN go to units
15             addq.b  #1,TENS       ; ELSE one more ten
16             bra     T_LOOP        ; and take another ten away
17  NEXT_UNIT: add.b   #10,d0        ; Restore the ten too many
18             move.b  d0,UNITS      ; The residue is the units!
19  NEXT:
```

Implementation follows the task list closely (Program 3.5). In lines 8–11 the constant 100 is continually subtracted form the binary number until a borrow (carry) is produced. Each successful subtraction is recorded by incrementing the hundreds slot. Once this phase is terminated, the last subtraction (which failed) is cancelled by adding 100 (line 12) and the process repeated but in tens (lines 13–16). When this terminates, whatever is left is the units.

Self-assessment questions

3.1 Why is `bra .+123` illegal?

3.2 Write a routine that will multiply a byte located in memory at $6001h$ by ten, putting the word product in D0.

3.3 Parity is a simple technique protecting digital data from corruption by noise. Odd parity adds a single bit to a word in such a way as to ensure the overall packet has an odd number of 1s. Write a routine that takes a 16-bit word stored at 6000:1h and alters its most significant bit to comply with this specification. You can assume that bit 15 is always 0 before the routine begins. Hint: Determine if the word is odd or even by counting the number of 1s using the shift instruction for the appropriate number of times and examining the **C** flag.

3.4 Write a routine that tests RAM between 6000h – 7FFFh and finishes with the fail address in A0. The test is to be implemented by placing a test pattern in each location in a loop and checking that it was stored correctly.

3.5 A simple digital low-pass filter can be implemented using the algorithm:

$$\text{Array[i]} = \frac{S_n}{4} + \frac{S_{n-1}}{2} + \frac{S_{n-2}}{4}$$

where S_n is the nth sample from an eight-bit analog to digital converter located at 8000h.

Write a routine using three byte memory locations to store S_n, S_{n-1} and S_{n-2} to continually generate Array[i] after each sample and send it out to a digital to analog converter at 9000h.

3.6 Repeat the last example but assuming that the processor has eight Data registers D0 to D7. Comment on the efficiency improvement over the single register implementation. Note that instructions that do not target a memory location only require a single word of storage.

PART II

The software

In Part I we developed the concept of the von Neumann stored program architecture, ending up with our somewhat simplified BASIC computer. Although BASIC was entirely fictitious, it was designed with an eye to the MPU that forms the basis for the rest of this book.

This part of the text looks mainly at the software aspects of our chosen MPU, the Motorola 68000 series. We will be covering:

- *The internal structure of the MPU.*
- *The instruction set.*
- *Address modes.*
- *The assembly translation process.*
- *Subroutines and modular program design.*
- *Software and hardware interrupts.*
- *The high-level language* **C***.*

The 68000 microprocessor

In this chapter we introduce the 68000 MPU, which we will use as our illustrative device for the rest of the text. Here we will primarily look at the internal structure, reserving external hardware considerations for later.

After reading this chapter you should:

- *Understand that the 68000 MPU has eight general purpose Data registers, all of which are interchangeable.*

- *Know that most instructions involving a Data register can affect either the lower eight bits (.b), the lower 16 bits (.w) or all 32 bits (.1), and that in the first two cases, all unused upper bits are unaltered.*

- *Realize that the 68000 is a 16-bit device by virtue of its 16-bit ALU and Data buses, but supports a 32-bit architecture by virtue of its internal 32-bit registers.*

- *Understand that the 68000 has eight 32-bit Address registers, all of which are interchangeable except for **A7** which is used as the Stack Pointer.*

- *Know that most instructions referencing an Address register come in two sizes, namely word (.w) and long-word (.1), but that all 32 bits are affected in both cases. In the former case the 16-bit word address is sign-extended to a 32-bit address.*

- *Realize that the location of word and long-word data and of instruction words should always be at an even address.*

- *Understand the function of the **C, N, Z, V** and **X** flags in the Code Condition register.*

- *Appreciate the difference between the User and Supervisor states as set by the **S** bit in the Control register.*

What exactly is an MPU? This question is best approached from a historical perspective. In 1968, Robert Noyce (one of the inventors of the integrated circuit), Gordon Moore[1] and Andrew Grove left the Fairchild

---

[1] Moore's law stated in 1964 that the number of elements on a chip would double every 18 months, although this was subsequently revised to 2 years.

Corporation and founded their own company, which they called Intel.[2] Within three years, Intel had developed all the basic types of semiconductor memories used today — dynamic and static RAMs and EPROMs.

As a sideline Intel also designed large-scale integrated circuits to customers' specifications. In 1971 they were approached by a Japanese maker of electronic calculators called Busicom, and asked to manufacture a suitable chip set. At that time calculators were a fast-evolving product and any LSI devices were likely to be superseded within a few years. This of course would reduce an LSI product's profitability and increase its cost. Engineer Ted Hoff — reputedly while on a topless beach in Tahiti — came up with a revolutionary way to tackle this project. Why not make a simple von Neumann CPU on silicon? This could then be programmed to implement the calculator functions, and as time progressed these could be enhanced by developing this software. Besides giving the chip a longer and more profitable life, Intel were in the business of making memories — and computer-like architectures need lots of memory. Truly a brain wave. Busicom endorsed the Intel design for its simplicity and flexibility in late 1969, rather than the conventional implementation.

Federico Faggin joined Intel in spring 1970[3] and by the end of the year had produced working samples of the first chip set. This could only be sold to Busicom, but by the middle of 1971, in return for a price reduction, Intel were given the right to sell the chip set to anyone for non-calculator purposes. Intel was dubious about the market for this device, but went ahead and advertised the 4004 "Micro-Programmable Computer on a Chip" in the *Electronic News* of November 1971. The term **MicroProcessor Unit** (**MPU**) was not coined until 1972. The 4004 created a lot of interest as a means of introducing intelligence into electronic products.

The 4004 MPU featured a four-bit Data bus, with direct addressing of 512 bytes of memory. Clocked at 108 kHz, it was implemented with a transistor count of 2300.[4] Within a year the eight-bit 200 kHz 8008 appeared, addressing 16 Kbytes and needing a 3500 transistor implementation. Four bits is satisfactory for the BCD digits used in calculators but eight bits is more appropriate for intelligent data terminals (like cash registers) which needed to handle a wide range of alphanumeric characters. The 8008 was replaced by the 8080[5] in 1974, and then the slightly modified 8085 in 1976. The 8085 is still the current Intel eight-bit device. Strangely, four-bit MPUs were to outsell all other sizes until the early 1990s.

The MPU concept was such a hit that many other electronic manufactures clambered on to the bandwagon. In addition, many designers

---

[2]Reputed to stand for INTELligence or INTegrated ELectronics.

[3]He was later to found Zilog.

[4]Compare with the Pentium Pro (also known as the P6 or 80686) at around 5.5 million!

[5]Designed by Masatoshi Shima, who went on to design the 8080-compatible Z80 for Zilog.

jumped ship and set up shop on their own, such as Zilog. By 1976 there were 54 different MPUs either available or announced. One of the most successful of these was the 6800 family produced by Motorola.[6] The Motorola 6800 had a clean and flexible architecture, could be clocked at 2 MHz and address up to 64 Kbyte of memory. The 6802 (1977) even had 128 bytes of on-board memory and an internal clock oscillator. By 1979 the improved 6809 represented the last in the line of eight-bit devices, competing mainly with the Intel 8085, Zilog Z80 and MOS Technology's 6502.

The MPU was not really devised to power conventional computers, but a small calculator company called MITS,[7] faced with bankruptcy, took a final desperate gamble in 1975 and decided to make and market a computer. This primitive machine, designed by Ed Roberts, was based on the 8080 MPU and interacted with the operator using front panel toggle switches and lamps — no keyboard and VDU. The Altair[8] was advertised for $500, and within a month MITS had $250,000 in the bank for advance orders.

This first **Personal Computer (PC)** spawned a generation of computer hackers. Thus an unknown 19-year-old Harvard computer science student, Bill Gates, and a visiting friend, Paul Allen, in December 1975 noticed a picture of the Altair[9] on the front cover of *Popular Electronics* and decided to write software for this primordial PC. They called Ed Robert with a bluff, telling him that they had just about finished a version of the BASIC programming language that would run on the Altair. Thus was the Microsoft Corporation born.

In a parallel development, 22 Altair owners in San Fransisco set up the Home-brew club. Two members were Steve Jobs and Steve Wozniak. As a club demonstration, they built a PC which they called the Apple.[10] By 1978 the Apple II made $700,000; in 1979 sales were $7 million, and then $48 million...

The Apple II was based around the low-cost 6502 MPU which was produced by a company called MOS Technology. It was designed by Chuck Peddle, who was also responsible for the 6800 MPU, and had subsequently left Motorola. The 6502 was one of the main players in PC hardware by the end of the 1970s, being the computing engine of the BBC series and Commodore PETs amongst many others.

What really powered up Apple II sales was the VisiCalc spreadsheet

---

[6]Motorola was set up in the 1930s to manufacture motor car radios, hence the name "motor" and "ola" (as in pianola).

[7]Located next door to a massage parlor in New Mexico.

[8]After a planet in *Star Trek*.

[9]The picture was just a mock up, they actually were not yet available; an early example of computer 'vaporware'!

[10]Jobs was a fruitarian and had previously worked in an apple orchard.

package. When the business community discovered that the PC was not just a toy, but could do 'real' tasks, sales took off. The same thing happened to the IBM PC. Introduced in 1981, the PC was powered by an Intel 8088 MPU clocked at 4.77 MHz and 128 Kbyte of RAM, a twin 360 Kbyte disk drive and a monochrome text-only VDU. The operating system was Microsoft's PC/MS-DOS version 1.0. The spreadsheet package here was Lotus 1-2-3.

Intel had introduced the 29,000-transistor 8086 MPU in 1978 as a 16-bit version of the 8085 MPU. It was designed to be compatible with its eight-bit predecessor in both hardware and software aspects. This was wise commercially, in order to keep the 8085's extensive customer base from looking at competitor products, but technically dubious. It was such previous experience that led IBM to use the 8088 version, which had a reduced eight-bit Data bus and 20-bit Address bus[11] to save board space.

In 1979 Motorola brought out its 16-bit offering called the 68000 and its eight-bit Data bus version, the 68008 MPU. However, internally it was 32-bit, and this has provided compatibility right up to the 68060 introduced in 1995. With a much smaller eight-bit customer base to worry about, the 68000 MPU was an entirely new design and technically much in advance of its 80X86 rivals.

The 68000 was adopted by Apple for its Macintosh series of PCs. However, the Apple Mac only accounts for less than 20% of PC sales. Motorola MPUs have been much more successful in the embedded microprocessor market, the area of smart instrumentation from egg timers to aircraft management systems. Of course, this is just the area which MPUs were developed for in the first place, and the number, if not the profile and value, of devices sold for this purpose exceeds those for computers by more than an order of magnitude.

A somewhat simplified view of the 68HC001 MPU[12] is shown in Fig. 4.1. Although we are dealing here with the innards of the beast, note that the Data bus has 16 lines whilst the Address bus has 24 lines. Thus, like our computer BASIC, the world is viewed in 16-bit word chunks, but now our address space has increased to $2^{24} = 16$ Mbyte. If the 68000's structure has more than a passing resemblance to our make-believe computer's architecture, then this is not a coincidence and you should first read Chapter 3's discussion of the function of the various blocks.

Of importance to the programmer are the Data and Address registers. Our BASIC computer had only one 16-bit Data register. Here we now have eight **Data registers**, D0...D7, which may be used interchangeably. That means that any instruction that can operate on a Data register can

---

[11]A 2^{20} address space is 1 Mbyte, and this is why for backwards compatibility MS-DOS is still limited to 1 Mbyte of conventional memory.

[12]This is virtually identical to the other members of the 68000 series: the 68EC000, 68HC000 and the original 68000 device. See Chapter 15.

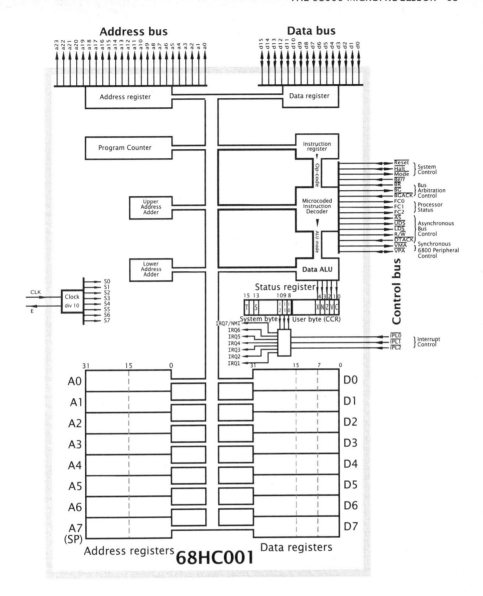

Figure 4.1 *Internal 68HC001 structure.*

target *any* such register in the same manner, e.g. clr.w d3 and clr.w
d7. This general-purpose property is sometimes known as orthogonality,
and contrasts with the Intel 80X86 family where most of the registers have
specialized functions.

The majority of instructions that use a Data register can deal with three
sizes of data, namely byte (.b), word (.w) and long-word (.1), which affect

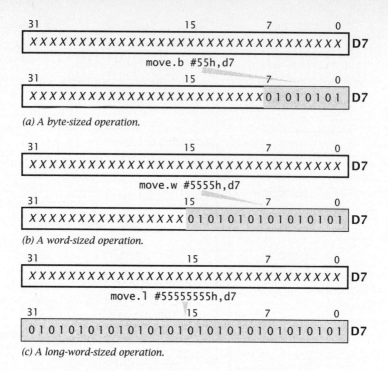

(a) A byte-sized operation.

(b) A word-sized operation.

(c) A long-word-sized operation.

Figure 4.2 *The three sizes of Data register instructions.*

the lower 8, 16 and 32 bits respectively. As shown in Fig. 4.2, in the former two cases the unused upper bits *remain unaltered*. Although this makes sense, sometimes the unwary can fall into the trap of assuming that the upper bits are zero. For example, consider the situation where a word-sized number n resides in D0.W and it is desired to work out the sum of the series:

$$n + (n - 1) + (n - 2) \cdots + 1 \text{ or } \sum_{i=0}^{i=(n-1)} n - i$$

Assuming that the 32-bit sum is to be in D7.L, a simple code fragment to do this is:

```
        clr.l   d7      ; The long sum is zeroed
LOOP:   add.l   d0,d7   ; sum = sum + n
        sub.w   #1,d0   ; n = n - 1
        bne     LOOP    ; Continue until n = 0
        .....   .....
```

This simply continually adds n to the precleared sum, decrementing n after each summation. As 32 bits must be reserved for the outcome, a long-sized addition must be used in line 2. However, we are really adding the word-sized n to the long-word-sized *sum* and thus are implicitly assuming that the upper 16 bits of D0 are zero. This is not a legitimate assumption, unless explicitly known. Adding the instruction `and.l #0FFFFh,d0` before the line labelled `LOOP:` will clear bits 31...16 (ANDed with 0) and leave the lower bits 15...0 unchanged (ANDed with 1).

When writing programs, the implications of using your chosen size for each instruction should be carefully considered. Most assemblers default to word size if a size is not explicitly given; thus `clr d3` and `clr.w d3` are the same. However, sloppy coding like this is not recommended — *give an explicit size for each instruction if there is more than one option.*

The 68000 series also has eight **Address registers**, A0...A7 which again are 32 bits long. Addresses in this family are represented as 32-bit entities, even though the Address bus is only 24 bits wide. The 68020 and subsequent members have a full 32-bit Address bus.

Again, like Data registers, the Address registers are interchangeable; for example `adda.l #2,a3` and `adda.l #2,a5` add 2 to A3[31:0] and A5[31:0] respectively. However, A7 is a little special, as it acts as the Stack Pointer — but we will leave this to Chapter 8. In general *handle* A7 *with kid gloves, and if in doubt keep away*!

Motorola intended the Address registers to hold pointers into memory and not to be used for other nefarious purposes. Because of this, only a rather limited repertoire of instructions can modify an Address register. Such instructions can come in two sizes only, word and long-word. There are *no byte-sized instructions* operating on an Address register. However, the situation is more complicated than for the Data registers in that any alteration to or reference to an Address register is *always to 32 bits*, even if word-sized. This can clearly be seen in Fig. 4.3(b), where the word-

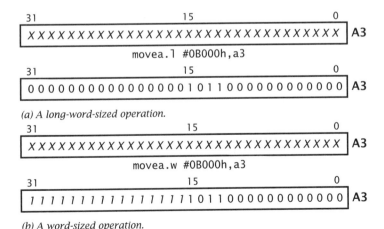

(a) A long-word-sized operation.

(b) A word-sized operation.

Figure 4.3 *The two sizes of Address register instructions.*

sized address B000*h* has been expanded to *FFFF*B000*h*. The expansion mechanism is to propagate the most significant bit upwards, which in this case is a 1. This sign bit extension (see page 10) is probably not what the programmer intended in this case. Generally speaking it is prudent to *only use the long-word size when dealing with Address registers*.

Another rule that must be observed is that *all addresses of word- or long-sized objects* **must** *lie at even addresses*. The processor treats any violation of this rule as a heinous crime and will cease to execute the user's program. What it then does is described on page 154.

Like the Address registers, the **Program Counter** (**PC**) also holds an address; this time the location of the current instruction. It is logical that it also should be 32 bits wide, and, as instructions are always multiples of words, that odd addresses are never allowed.

The 68000's 16-bit **Status register** (**SR**) is conceptually divided into a byte-sized **Code Condition Register** (**CCR**) — sometimes called the User byte — and the **Control register** or Control byte. The five flags in the CCR provide a status report on the ALU's activity. The Carry, Zero and Negative flags are standard, and are described on page 45.

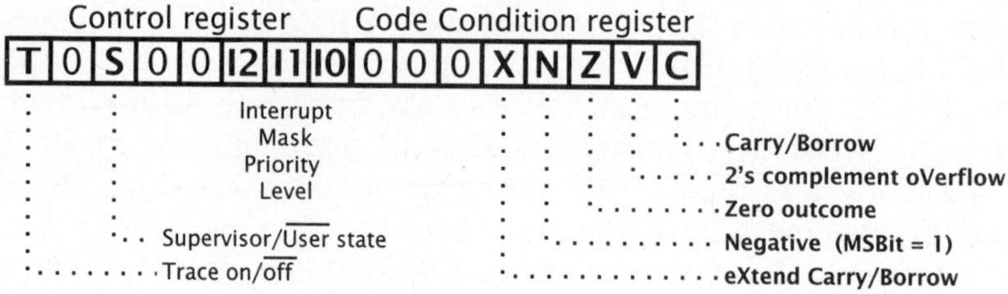

Control register   Code Condition register

| T | 0 | S | 0 | 0 | I2 | I1 | I0 | 0 | 0 | 0 | X | N | Z | V | C |

Interrupt Mask Priority Level · · · · Carry/Borrow

· · · · · · 2's complement oVerflow

· · · · · · · · Zero outcome

· · Supervisor/User state · · · · · · · · · Negative (MSBit = 1)

· · · · · · · · Trace on/off · · · · · · · · · · · · eXtend Carry/Borrow

Figure 4.4 *The* Status register.

Two flags are added to the complement that was available to our BASIC computer. The **V** flag is set when two numbers of the same sign (that is the MSBs are the same) are added or subtracted and give a different sign for the outcome. This oVerflow of the number into the sign position was described back on page 9.

The **X** flag needs some explanation. Where a higher-precision operation is required, this may be implemented by cascading. Thus a 64-bit addition can be implemented in two parts: firstly by adding the two lower 32-bit long-words and then the upper two 32-bit long-words *plus any carry from the lower addition*. This latter Add with Carry operation is implemented by the addx ADD with eXtend instruction (see Program 4.2). **X** is similar to the Carry flag but is affected by fewer operations; chiefly Add, Subtract and Shift. For example a Compare instruction, which of course affects the Carry flag, can be done in between multiple-precision operations without affecting the 'true' carry information (which is in **X**).

In summary we have:

- Carry (**C**): This flag is set if an Add operation generates a carry-out or a Subtract/Compare needs a borrow. Otherwise it resets. During a Shift operation it holds the last bit shifted out.
- oVerflow (**V**): If an arithmetic operation produces an incorrect result as seen from a signed 2's complement number perspective, this flag is set. Otherwise it is cleared.
- Zero (**Z**): If an operation has a zero outcome this flag is set; otherwise it is cleared.
- Negative (**N**): This shadows the most significant bit of the result of an Arithmetic or Shift operation. If the number is to be treated as a signed entity, then this may be interpreted as negative (= 1) or positive (= 0).
- eXtend (**X**): During an Arithmetic or Shift instruction this flag receives the carry or borrow status (in parallel with **C**). It is used as the carry or borrow bit in multiple-precision Arithmetic and Shift operations.

In all cases the flags operate correctly independently of the operand size of the instruction. Thus **C** reflects the carry from bit 7, bit 15 or bit 31 respectively for .b, .w or .l sizes respectively.

The several control bits occupy the upper byte of the Status register. The three bits I2 I1 I0 represent the Interrupt mask. The MPU will only respond to an interrupt request signalled externally on pins IPL2 IPL1 IPL0 if this active-low number is *above* the mask number (or number 7). This is described in Chapters 9 and 14.

When the 68000 is reset, or when an interrupt occurs, the **S** bit is set to 1. The processor is now in the **Supervisor state**. From the software aspect there are a few instructions[13] that will only run in this state. These so-called privileged instructions are mainly those that affect the bits in the Control register, such as the Interrupt mask level bits. Changes to these bits affect the overall operation or configuration of the processor. An example is move.w #0010010100000000b,sr which sets the IPL2 IPL1 IPL0 mask to level 5, turns off the **T** bit and clears all flags. The CCR flags alone can be altered by the non-privileged move.b #XXXXXXXXb,ccr instruction.

More significantly, when the **S** bit is set, the Function Code pin FC2 is high. The hardware engineer can arrange for this to switch in banks of memory circuits that are only active when the processor is in this state; see page 204.

By clearing **S** (for example and.w #0111111111111111b,sr), the processor will enter the **User state**. There are several differences between this User state and the Supervisor state.

---

[13]Mainly ignored in this book.

- The privileged instructions are illegal in the User state and thus the bits in the Control register cannot be altered. This means that once in this state, User programs cannot change the processor back to the Supervisor state. The only way back is to reset or interrupt the processor.
- The User state has its own separate A7. This is known as the **User Stack Pointer**, or USP. The private **Supervisor Stack Pointer** or SSP is sometimes designated A7'. The SSP cannot be accessed from the User state; however, the USP can be from the System state by using a privileged instruction.
- The FC2 pin goes low in the User state.

What is the point in having two distinct states? In a multitasking environment (more than one program running concurrently on the same machine) it is usual to have a master program, known as the operating system (OS). The OS provides resources to the user program, such as an interface to a magnetic disk store. Where more than one user program appears to run simultaneously, it may switch between these programs in a time-slice manner in a fairly complex way. As a simple example, consider an MPU development system to which software can be downloaded into RAM, whence it can be run and tested. The OS, here called a monitor, usually resides in ROM. Once control is passed from the monitor to the user program running in real time, the only way back to the OS is via an interrupt or reset. In all these situations it is important to ensure that user programs do not corrupt memory or other resources used by the OS. Both separate and mutually exclusive memory spaces and Stack Pointers make it difficult for the user program accidentally to corrupt the operating software. If the OS is corrupted then the system is likely to crash spectacularly.[14] Separate memory spaces are simple to implement in hardware; an example is shown in Fig. 12.5 on page 204.

In small dedicated embedded systems there often is no OS as a separate entity. In such naked cases, it is normal to stay in the Supervisor state and ignore the existence of the User state. We will do this for our project in Chapter 15. However, the security of two distinct states is important for the reliable operation of more sophisticated embedded systems, especially where an extensive interrupt-driven configuration is being used.

The programmer's model shown in Fig. 4.5 is that for the User state, and we will use this for the rest of the text. It does not show the Control byte of the Status register and depicts A7 as the Stack Pointer, but otherwise is identical to the Supervisor state programmer's model.

Finally, bit 15 of the Status register is the Trace bit. When set to 1, a Software interrupt/Trap (see Chapter 9) will occur at the end of each instruction execution. This can be used in conjunction with a suitable OS

---

[14]Like Microsoft's Windows 3 is wont to do — frequently!

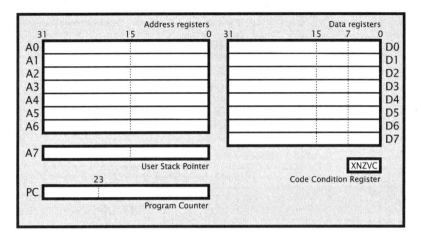

Figure 4.5 *Programmers' model for the 68000 MPU in the User state.*

routine to print out information, such as the register contents, after each step of the program. The **T** bit is turned off on reset.

Examples

Example 4.1
Using the instructions of Table 3.1, add together two 64-bit numbers in D0:D1 and D6:D7. The 65-bit total is to be in D2:D3:D4.

Solution
The Addition instructions are limited to 32-bit long-word size. Thus two additions will be required, the second more significant one adding any carry from the first least significant addition. Any carry

Program 4.1 *Adding two 64-bit numbers.*

```
DBL_ADDN: clr.l    d3       ; D3.L holds the middle sum long-word
          clr.l    d2       ; D2.l holds 65th bit
          add.l    d1,d7    ; Add least-significant (LS) long-words
          move.l   d7,d4    ; and make the LS sum long-word
          bcc      ADD_MS   ; IF no Carry THEN go on
          addq.b   #1,d3    ; ELSE effectively add Carry
ADD_MS:   add.l    d0,d6    ; Add the most-signif. (MS) long words
          add.l    d6,d3    ; and to the middle sum long-word
          bcc      CONTINUE ; Finished IF no Carry
          addq.b   #1,d2    ; ELSE make 65th bit = 1
CONTINUE: .....    .....
```

from this is the 65th bit.

The trick, here shown in Program 4.1, is to add 1 on to the appropriate precleared sum long-word if the addition produces a carry. Thus if the least significant (LS) addition has a carry, the second long-word of the sum (D3.L) is set to 1, otherwise it is 0. This will be subsequently added to the outcome of the second addition. If the outcome of this final addition yields a carry, the 65th bit is set to 1, otherwise it is 0.

Motorola have an Add with Carry instruction addx, which uses the **X** carry flag. Using this our program now becomes:

Program 4.2 *Using* addx *to add two 32-bit numbers.*

```
DBL_ADDN: clr.l   d5      ; D5.L will hold the 65th bit
          add.l   d1,d7   ; Add the least significant long-words
          addx.l  d0,d6   ; Add the MS long-words plus Carry
          addx.b  d5,d5   ; As D5.L is zero, just adds the Carry
          .....   .....
```

This time we simply leave the 65-bit sum in D5:D6:D7 as we do not have to resort to the strategy of using an image of the sum in order to simulate adding a carry. Despite the obvious increase in efficiency using addx, we will not use this or related instructions in subsequent chapters, as 32-bit operations will more than meet the requirements of the great majority of programs.

Example 4.2
A certain array contains 256 elements, each 24 bits in size and occupying three bytes in memory. For example ARRAY[0] in B000:1:2h, ARRAY[1] in B003:4:5h ...ARRAY[255] in B2FD:E:Fh. Using the instructions in Table 3.1, write a routine to add decimal 32 to *each* array element.

Solution
Superficially this seems a simple task — just use a long-sized Move for each element and zero the top eight bits. However, many of the long-word boundaries will have odd addresses and this is illegal for word- and long-word-sized instructions. The best strategy then is to build up a copy of the three-byte element by using three byte-sized Moves from memory into a Data register, shifting the contents of that register eight bits to the left after each fetch. This is shown in Program 4.3, lines 3–7.

Once in situ the addition can be made and the reverse process used to return the 24-bit data. Of course we are assuming that the outcome is never more than 24 bits!

Program 4.3 *Handling a 24-bit element array.*

```
         movea.l  #0B000h,a0   ; Point to bottom of array
GET_IT:  clr.l    d0           ; Build up a long-word in D0.L
         move.b   (a0),d0      ; Get MS byte
         lsl.w    #8,d0        ; Move over to the left
         addq.l   #1,a0        ; Pointer to next byte
         move.b   (a0),d0      ; and get it
         lsl.l    #8,d0        ; Again move over to the left
         addq.l   #1,a0        ; Pointer to LS byte
         move.b   (a0),d0      ; and get it
         add.l    #32,d0       ; Add 32 to element
; Now return the data in reverse
         move.b   d0,(a0)      ; Put away the LS byte
         subq.l   #1,a0        ; Pointer to middle byte
         lsr.l    #8,d0        ; Align this byte
         move.b   d0,(a0)      ; and put away in memory
         subq.l   #1,a0        ; Pointer to  MS byte
         lsr.w    #8,d0        ; Align MS byte in register
         move.b   d0,(a0)      ; Put it away
; Now move on to the next element
         addq.l   #3,a0        ; Move pointer to next element
         cmpa.l   #0B300h,a0   ; Over the top?
         blo      GET_IT       ; IF not THEN next element
         .....    .....
```

Can you devise a higher-speed stratagem at the expense of additional memory to store the array?

Example 4.3

A data logging system has stored 256 byte samples in memory between 0B000*h* and 0B0FF*h*. Devise a software strategy that does *not* use the cmpa instruction that will *continually* sequentially access this data, sending each byte out to a modem at 09000*h*. In addition to the instructions of Table 3.1 on page 46, you can use the exg (EXchanGe registers) instruction, which swaps over the entire contents of any two Data/Address registers, e.g. exg a0,d0.

Solution

The conventional method of doing this is shown in Program 4.4. Line 4 is the active code, the rest of the program is simply the loop handling overhead. Any reduction in this code will substantially

Program 4.4 *Using the conventional approach to loop control.*

```
           .define  0B000h = Array
           .define  Modem  = 9000h
MAIN:      movea.l #Array,a0     ; Point to array bottom #3, 12~
OUT_LOOP:  move.b  (a0),Modem    ; Copy to modem @ 9000h #3, 20~
           addq.l  #1,a0         ; Increment pointer #1,      8~
           cmpa.l  #Array+256,a0 ; Has pointer overshot? #3,  6~
           bne     OUT_LOOP      ; IF not THEN next byte #2, 10~
           bra     MAIN          ; ELSE begin again #2,      10~
```

increase the rate of data throughput.

As the array is located between 0B0<u>00</u>h and 0B0<u>FF</u>h a simple way of stepping through the array would be to increment the lower byte of the pointer only, as shown underlined. But there is no .b instruction permitted on an Address register.

A sneaky way of fiddling with the contents of an Address register is to exchange it with a Data register, do whatever with it, and then return it. Doing this gives the code of Program 4.5. Although this still takes six instructions, a closer look reveals a decrease in both program length and loop execution time. Beside each instruction, I have listed the instruction length in words; thus movea.l #0B000h,a0 is three words long and takes 12 cycles (indicated in the listing as #12˜) to execute. To get the actual time in microseconds just divide the number of cycles by the clock speed in megahertz. This gives 1.5 µs at 8 MHz. The total length of Program 4.4 is 14 words against 11 words; an improvement of 21%. The improvement in loop execution time is 54˜ against 46˜, a 16% improvement in throughput.

How do you think you could use this technique for a 1024-byte array?

Program 4.5 *A devious approach to loop control.*

```
          .define  0B000h = Array
          .define  Modem  = 9000h
MAIN:     movea.l  #Array,a0   ; Point to array bottom #3,       12˜
OUT_LOOP: move.b   (a0),Modem  ; Copy to modem at 9000h #3,      20˜
          exg      d0,a0       ; A0.L <-> D0.L interchange #1,  6˜
          addq.b   #1,d0       ; Increment bytewise #1,          4˜
          exg      d0,a0       ; A0.L <-> D0.L interchange #1,  6˜
          bra      OUT_LOOP    ; Next byte ad infinitum #2,     10˜
```

Self-assessment questions

4.1   Given that there is no Clear Address register instruction, can you deduce at least two ways of zeroing an Address register?

4.2   The 68000's ALU has only a 16-bit capacity. How do you think it implements long-word-sized instructions and what speed implication does this have in using .l against .w or .b data formats?

4.3   What is wrong with the following?

```
          movea  #0B000h,a0
LOOP: clr    (a0)
          adda   #1,a0
          bne    LOOP
```

CHAPTER 5

Address modes

The majority of instructions act on data. This data may lie either in an internal register or out in memory. Thus the location of such operands must be part of the instruction. There are several different ways of specifying the **effective address** (**ea**) of an operand. The various address modes have characteristics which are advantageous in appropriate situations. In this chapter we will look at the more common of these address modes, their properties and application areas.

We have already covered many of these back in Chapter 3 on pages 45–50 in conjunction with our BASIC computer, and now would be a good time to review this material. As we will not formally look at the 68000's instruction set until the next chapter, we will use BASIC's instructions listed in Table 3.1 on page 46 for our illustrative examples.

After reading this chapter you will:

- *Know that an address mode is the way an instruction pin-points its data.*
- *Appreciate that where instructions have two operands, the source and destination address modes can be different, e.g.* add.l #1,d7.
- *Know that constant operands are specified using the Immediate address mode, e.g.* addq.l #8,d3.
- *Know that operands located in an internal register are specified using one of the Register Direct modes.*
  - ***Data Register Direct*** *addressing is used for operands located in a Data register, e.g.* clr.l d2.
  - ***Address Register Direct*** *addressing is used for operands located in an Address register, e.g.* movea.l a2,a5.
- *Know that operands sited out in memory can be pointed to using one of the following address modes:*
  - ***Absolute*** *addressing, where the fixed address itself pin-points the data's fixed location, e.g.* clr.b 06000h.
  - ***Address Register Indirect*** *addressing, where the Address register points to the operand, e.g.* clr.b (a2).

- *Address Register Indirect with Pre-Decrement* addressing, where the pointer Address register is automatically decremented before it is used to target the operand, e.g. clr.w -(a2). Decrementation is 1 for .b, 2 for .w and 4 for .l-sized instructions.

- *Address Register Indirect with Post-Increment* addressing, where the pointer Address register is automatically incremented after it has been used to target the operand, e.g. clr.l (a3)+. As in the previous mode, incrementation is size-dependent, 1,2 or 4.

- *Address Register with Offset* addressing uses a fixed signed 16-bit offset to augment the Address register pointer, e.g. clr.b 64(a3) has an ea of 64 above the base address held in A3.

- *Address Register with Index* calculates the ea as the sum of the base address in an Address register plus a variable offset in any Address/Data register (the Index register) plus a fixed signed 8-bit offset, e.g. clr.b -4(a3,d7.l) calculates the ea as 4 below the address held in A3 plus the contents of D7.L. The Index register can be .w-sized, but will be sign-extended to the full 32 bits.

- *Know that a few instructions, known as Inherent, have no operand and therefore no address mode, e.g.* nop.

The general symbolic form of a two-operand 68000 instruction is:

```
instruction mnemonic   <source's address>,<destination's address>
```

For example, move.l d0,d7 means copy the 32-bit contents (.l) from Data Register 0 (the source operand's address) to Data register 7 (the destination operand's address). In RTL (see page 39) this is represented as (d7[31:0] <- d0[31:0]).

A significant number of instructions have only a destination operand, symbolized as:

```
instruction   <destination operand's address>
```

Thus clr.w d0 clears the lower 16 bits in D0 ((d0[15:0] <- 00h).

A very few so-called **inherent** instructions have no operand to specify explicitly, such as rts (ReTurn from Subroutine).

Where an instruction is to access an operand, the programmer must specify its location or ea. Operand variables will be located either in a processor register or out in memory. A constant operand, known as a **literal**, can alternatively be specified as a source, for example addq.b #2,d0 adds the literal 2 (symbolized as #2) to the eight-bit contents of D0.B; (d0[7:0] <- 2). The address modes used to specify the location of the source operand (if any) and destination are part of the instruction's operation code (see page 38). Thus the op-code for clr.b d3 is:

Code for clr   .b   Data reg. 3

0100001000000011

whereas clr.b 0E000h is:

Code for clr   .b Absolute mode   Absolute address   0000 E000 *h*

0100001000111001	0000000000000000	1110000000000000

In both cases the top eight bits 0100 0010*b* represent the operation Clear, the following two the size (00*b* for .b, 01*b* for .w and 10*b* for .l) and the last six the address mode code (000*b* for Data Register Direct and 111001*b* for Absolute).

The various address modes have differing properties. For instance, from the above we see that locating an operand in a Data register is clearly much more efficient than locating it in a memory location: the latter takes six bytes of program memory to store whilst the former only two. This is reflected in an execution time of 20 clock cycles against four (using an 8 MHz crystal, 2.5 μs against 0.5 μs — see page 184). Clearly a knowledge of the different address modes is important when writing programs. Here we will look at ten of the most important of these.

Immediate

The **Immediate** address mode is used where the source is a *constant* (a literal), for example:

```
add.w  #1234,d3    ; Add the constant 1234 decimal to D3[15:0]
```

Note the use of the # symbol to denote that the following is a *constant* and not an address.[1] A constant can *never* be a destination, for example clr.b #6 is obviously nonsense — you cannot clear 6!

The literal data normally follows the op-code in memory, as shown below, but there are three **quick instructions**, namely addq, subq and moveq, that embed the literal inside a single op-code word. As can be seen from the diagram, op-code bits 9–11 are used in the addq op-code to carry immediate data from 1 to 8 (8 is coded as 000*b*). The effect of the example addq.l #4,d3 is to add 4 to the 32 bits in D3, leaving the result in D3, i.e. (d3[31:0]) <- (d3[31:0]) + 4. This takes 1 μs at 8 MHz. For values above 8 the literal follows the op-code in program memory in either a single word (for .b- and .w-sized literals) or two words (for a .l literal). The latter takes 2 μs to execute, double the time, hence the terminology 'quick'.

---

[1] One of the more frequent errors you will make is to leave out the #. The instruction add.w 1234,d3 would be interpreted as "add the word contents of memory locations 1234:5 to the lower word of D3" — a perfectly legitimate construction, but very different from what was desired. Another frequent error is mismatch of size; for example add.b #500,d2. The literal 500 cannot fit in a byte — you cannot put a quart into a pint pot!

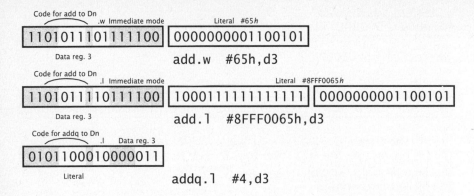

As we shall see in the next chapter, most double-operand instructions, such as add, must have at least one operand in a register. Thus with an immediate source, the destination in our examples was a Data register. addq and subq can also target an Address register or a memory location; for example addq.b #1,0E000h increments the contents of address 0E000h, i.e. (0E000h) <- (0E000h)+1. For literals outside the range 1–8 the Immediate Add/Subtract instructions (addi and subi) can target a memory location, e.g. addi.b #26,0E000h ((0E000h) <- (0E000h)+26).

Register Direct Modes

The following two modes target data in internal CPU registers.

Data Register Direct

Here the operand is to be found in a Data register. For example:

```
clr.l  d3    ; Clear all bits in Data register D3
```

The 68000 family has eight 32-bit Data registers. Given that data stored in internal registers does not require fetching from memory and that the register(s) are specified in the op-code word itself, it makes sense to locate as much data in these registers as possible. The diagram on page 75 compares the use of **Data Register Direct** addressing with that where data is stored in external RAM. Not only is there a space saving of 3:1, but execution time is reduced from 1.25 μs to 0.5 μs!

Many double-operand instructions require that at least one operand be located in a Data register. This was the case for the defining example for the Immediate mode where the literal #1234 was added to the lower 16 bits of D3, designated as D3[15:0]. This example (and the following one) shows that source and destination operand need not use the same address mode.

Address Register Direct

Operands located in an Address register are targeted using **Address Register Direct** addressing. For example:

```
adda.l  #20,a3   ; Increment Address register 3 by 20
```

Address registers are really supposed to hold address data rather than general-purpose data. For this reason, only a few special instructions can alter data in such registers. Thus in our example I used `adda` instead of plain `add`. However, `addq` and `subq` can target Address registers and are useful in lieu of an Increment or Decrement instruction, for example `adda.l #1,a3` and `suba.l #1,a4`.

   We have already observed on page 65 that instructions using Address Register Direct addressing only come in .w and .l sizes, and that the former always affects all 32 bits by sign extension, as shown in Fig. 4.3.

External Memory Modes

These address modes are used to locate operands in external memory.

Absolute

Where an operand lies at a *fixed known location*, for instance a port, then its address may be specified directly using the **Absolute** address mode. For example:

```
clr.b  6050h   ; Clear byte at fixed memory address 6050h
```

   There are two forms of Absolute addressing, namely short and long.

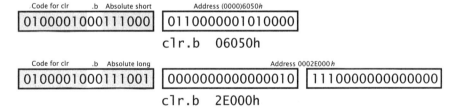

In the former only the lower word of the address follows the op-code word. The MPU, in the normal address way, *sign-extends* this internally to a full two-word address. Thus address $6050h \rightarrow 00006050h$, and address $8050h \rightarrow FFFF8050h$. Short Absolute addressing can thus be used to specify addresses between $0000\ 0000h$ and $0000\ 7FFFh$ and also between FFFF 8000 and FFFF FFFFh. Long Absolute addressing follows the op-code word with the full two-word address. This is slower, but can be used for any address in the MPU's address space.

Some assemblers allow the programmer to specify which version of Absolute addressing to use,[2] but the majority of packages choose the correct type automatically. If they cannot, they default automatically to long.

Although directly specifying its address may seem to be the obvious way of locating an object in memory, this technique is rather inflexible. Suppose we wanted to scan through an array of 256 bytes in memory located between $6000h$ and $60FFh$ and evaluate the maximum value. We could do this by using a convenient Data register to store this maximum and comparing each byte array element with the current maximum as described in the task analysis on page 52. Where an element is above the maximum, then its value becomes the new maximum. Program 5.1 shows how this could be done using only Absolute addressing.

Program 5.1 *Scanning memory looking for the maximum.*

```
MAXIMUM:  clr.b   d0          ; Use D0[7:0] to hold the maximum
          cmp.b   6000h,d0    ; Compare Array[0] with the maximum
          blo     NEXT1       ; IF LOwer THEN leave alone
          move.b  6000h,d0    ; ELSE update maximum
NEXT1:    cmp.b   6001h,d0    ; Compare Array[1] with the maximum
          blo     NEXT2       ; IF LOwer THEN leave alone
          move.b  6001h,d0    ; ELSE update maximum
NEXT2:    cmp.b   6002h,d0    ; Compare Array[2] with the maximum
          blo     NEXT3       ; IF LOwer THEN leave alone
          move.b  6002h,d0    ; ELSE update maximum
NEXT3:    .....   .....
          .....   .....
          .....   .....
NEXT255:  cmp.b   60FFh,d0    ; Compare Array[255] with maximum
          blo     EXIT        ; IF LOwer THEN leave alone
          move.b  60FFh,d0    ; ELSE update maximum
EXIT:     .....   .....       ; Finished. Phew!
```

This program needs 1281 words (2562 bytes) of storage and takes around 1 ms to execute at 8 MHz. Although this program works, there has got to be a better way! See Program 3.1 on page 48 for another program using the same absolute technique.

Address Register Indirect Modes

The following modes use an Address register to *point to* an operand in memory. The term indirect is used as the register does not hold the operand itself, only the *address* of the operand.

---

[2]Not the assembler used this text.

Address Register Indirect

The simplest indirect address mode is where the specified Address register holds the effective address. **Address Register Indirect** addressing is symbolized by placing the Address register in parentheses; for example:

```
clr.b  (a3)    ; Clear the byte pointed to by A3
```

This seems a rather obscure way of doing things, but let us revisit our maximum scan program. Repeating the same Compare-Branch-Update sequence 256 times on successive memory locations is a dubious way of doing things. Why not use a pointer into the array and increment the pointer after each sequence?

This is just what we have done in Program 5.2. The linear structure of the previous program has been folded into a **loop**, shown shaded. The execution path keeps circulating around the Compare-Branch-Update trio of instructions, which is "walked" through the array by advancing the pointer held in A3. Eventually the pointer moves out of the desired range and the program then exits.

Program 5.2 *Scanning memory for the maximum using a repeating loop.*

```
        MAXIMUM: movea.l #06000h,a3  ; Set up pointer to start of array (n=0)
                 clr.b   d0          ; Use D0[7:0] to hold the maximum value
        M_LOOP:  cmp.b   (a3),d0     ; Compare Array[n] with maximum
                 blo     M_CONT      ; IF LOwer THEN leave maximum alone
                 move.b  (a3),d0     ; ELSE update maximum
        M_CONT:  addq.l  #1,a3       ; Advance pointer one (n=n+1)
                 cmpa.l  #6100h,a3   ; Has pointer gone over the top?
                 bne     M_LOOP      ; IF not THEN again
        EXIT:    .....   .....       ; ELSE exit loop
```

Go here if A3 is not equal to #6100h

Program 5.2 has many new features, especially as we haven't yet reviewed the instruction set.

Setting up

Line 1 initializes Address register 3 by moving the *constant* 6000*h* into it; the location of Array[0]. Note the use of movea rather than the ordinary move. Line 2 clears Data register 0, which will hold the maximum value. Nearly all loop structures have a preceding setup phase where variables are initialized.

Loop

The core of the loop involves the same three instructions as the linear version. This time the Indirect Address Register mode is used to pinpoint the data Array[n]. The first instruction of this trio has a **label** associated with it called M_LOOP. The assembler knows this is a label and not an instruction by the appended colon. Line 6 is also labelled and is used as the target for the Branch if LOwer instruction, which omits the update if true. A label is of course a symbolic representation of the address where that instruction is stored in memory.

Housekeeping

Each pass involves an incrementation of the pointer in order to step through the array. This is done here in line 6 by using the ADD Quick instruction. Exiting the loop is done in lines 7 and 8 by checking the contents of the pointer register against the upper bound 6100h. If it is not equal, execution will fall out of the loop, as the Branch if Not Equal test will fail to transfer back to the instruction labelled M_LOOP.

Except for some simple endless loops, a housekeeping phase is necessary to update any loop variables and exit on specified conditions. As this phase is executed on each loop pass it represents a time overhead which can be quite severe.

The program length is now 10 words, less than 0.8% of the original! However, execution time has nearly doubled to 1.9 ms, mainly due to the housekeeping overhead. See Program 3.2 on page 49 for a similar loop example.

Address Register Indirect with Post-Increment

The housekeeping of incrementing a pointer when repeating a loop is a common enough requirement to warrant an address mode that uses an Address register not only as a pointer but also automatically increments that pointer. For example:

```
clr.w  (a3)+   ; Clear the word pointed to and then increment A3
```

Program 5.3 uses the **Address Register Indirect with Post-Increment** mode to step automatically through the array 1 byte at a time, eliminating the need for the addq housekeeping instruction of the previous implementation. This reduces the size of the program to nine words and execution time to 1.6 ms.

Program 5.3 *Repeating loop using the Address Register Indirect with Post-Increment mode.*

```
MAXIMUM: movea.l  #6000h,a3  ; Set pointer to the element Array[0]
         clr.b    d0         ; Use D0[7:0] to hold the maximum
M_LOOP:  cmp.b    (a3)+,d0   ; Compare with Array[n] & then inc n
         blo      M_CONT     ; IF LOwer THEN leave alone
         move.b   -1(a3),d0  ; ELSE update maximum
M_CONT:  cmpa.l   #6100h,a3  ; Has pointer gone over the top?
         bne      M_LOOP     ; IF not THEN again
END:     .....    .....      ; ELSE exit loop
```

As the pointer has already been advanced by the time the maximum is updated in line 5, I have had to modify the ea to 1 below A3, by using an offset of −1 (see below).

Incrementation in this mode is intelligent, in that it automatically follows the size of the instruction using it; for example:

```
clr.b  (a2)+  ; Clear pointed-to byte,      then add 1 to A2
clr.w  (a2)+  ; Clear pointed-to word,      then add 2 to A2
clr.l  (a2)+  ; Clear pointed-to long-word, then add 4 to A2
```

ensuring that the step should match the size of the object. Thus the term increment really means "augment by one object".

Address Register Indirect with Pre-Decrement

This is similar to the previous mode but the pointer register is decremented by the object size *before* the Address register is used. **Address Register Indirect with Post-Increment** addressing is symbolized by preceding the indirect parentheses by a minus; for example:

```
clr.l  -(a1)  ; Decrement A1 and then clear the long-word pointed to by A1
```

Address Register Indirect with Offset

Rather than systematically walking through a data array, it can be useful to access any data object at random. The **Address Register Indirect with Offset** mode allows the programmer to use a *fixed* 16-bit signed offset to augment the pointer in an Address by between +32,767 and −32, 768; for example:

```
clr.b  26(a3)  ; Clear the byte at 26 above the address in A3
```

Note that the contents of the Address register are not altered in this mode.

As an example consider three data words stored in memory as shown in Fig. 5.1. The A3 has been set to point to the bottom of the pile, and each word then can be pin-pointed as an offset above this pointer. The

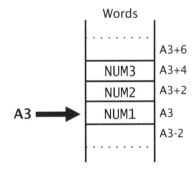

Figure 5.1 *Data stored in a frame.*

scheme also works downwards (see line 5 in Program 5.3). This type of structure is sometimes called a **frame** and the pointer a **frame pointer**.

Consider a program to calculate:

$$F = \frac{NUM1}{4} + \frac{NUM2}{2} + \frac{NUM3}{4}$$

which is known as the three-point low-pass filter algorithm (see also self-assesssment question 3.5). Each of these data words can be accessed using an offset from the frame pointer thus:

NUM1 → (a3)
NUM2 → 2(a3)
NUM3 → 4(a3)

This is the technique used in Program 5.4, in lines 4 and 8, to fetch data.

Program 5.4 *A three point filter using Address Register Indirect with Offset addressing.*

```
FILTER:  clr.l   d2          ; Zero working register 1
         clr.l   d3          ; Zero working register 2
         move.w  (a3),d2     ; Get NUM1, extended to long
         move.w  2(a3),d3    ; Get NUM2, extended to long
         lsl.l   #1,d3       ; Multiply by 2
         add.l   d3,d2       ; Add giving NUM1 + 2*NUM2
         clr.l   d3          ; Zero working register 2
         move.w  4(a3),d3    ; Get NUM3, extended to long
         add.l   d3,d2       ; Add giving NUM1 + 2*NUM2 + NUM3
         lsr.l   #2,d2       ; Divide by 4
```

Rather than divide the data words when fetched, the sum

$$NUM1 + 2 \times NUM2 + NUM3$$

is calculated and then the whole is divided by 4. Notice how multiplication and division are implemented by shifting left and right respectively (see page 10). Working with the largest possible numbers until the last moment increases accuracy by reducing the effect for fractional truncation, as bits are thrown away when shifting right. To cope with these larger numbers, the data words are extended to long-word precision by moving into a long-word precleared Data register.[3] Thus long additions and shifts can be used. The final filtered outcome can be found in D2.W.

Address Register with Index

This is the most elaborate of all the address modes. **Address Register with Index** addressing pin-points memory data as located in the effective

---

[3]This assumes that the data words are not signed.

address calculated as the sum of a base address plus the *variable* contents of any long[4] Address or Data register (the Index register) plus a *fixed* signed offset; for example:

```
clr.b  6(a0,d7.1)   ; Clear the memory byte at 6+(A0)+(D7.L)
```

This mode is useful where it is necessary to access any specified element *n* in a block of data at random. Unlike the fixed offset of the last mode, *n* is a *variable*. The Address register is pointed to the base of the block and the index *n* in, say, a Data register.

As our example we need to introduce the concept of the subroutine, which we will meet formally in Chapter 8. Here it is sufficient to note that a subroutine is a stand-alone software module to which you 'send' data, which is then processed and returned in some modified form.

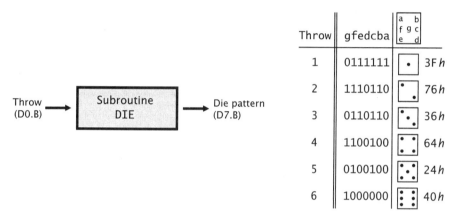

Figure 5.2 *The active-low die patterns.*

Our problem, outlined in Fig. 5.2, is to generate the appropriate pattern on an array of active-low light-emitting diodes to simulate an electronic game die.[5] The 'throw' enters the subroutine as a number between 1 and 6 in D0.B and the die pattern is available on exit in D7.B. As there is no mathematical pattern to this mapping, this is most easily done by storing the patterns in memory as a **look-up table**. Assuming this table is already in memory from location 00500*h* upwards:

0500*h*	0501*h*	0502*h*	0503*h*	0504*h*	0505*h*	0506*h*
FF*h*	3F*h*	76*h*	36*h*	64*h*	24*h*	40*h*

---

[4]It is possible to specify a word-sized Index register (see Program 5.5) but — as with all dealings with Address registers — it will be sign-extended to a full 32 bits (see Fig. 4.3 on page 65) before being added. So it is probably better to keep to .1 unless you know what you are doing!

[5]Although I have shown seven bits corresponding to the seven 'pips', a close look at the patterns shows that this could be reduced to only four.

(we will see how to do this on page 121) then the subroutine could be coded as shown in Program 5.5.

Program 5.5 *The DIE subroutine.*

```
DIE: movea.l  #0500h,a0     ; Point a0 to the table bottom
     and.w    #0111b,d0     ; Clear all but the lower three bits
     move.b   0(a0,d0.w),d7 ; Move table[n] to D7.B
     rts                    ; Return from subroutine
```

Address register A0 is used as a pointer to the start of the table and with D0.W used as the Index register, then the effective address is calculated as 0500h + (D0.W), which is 050nh. For example, if the throw were 3, then the data in location $0503h$ (that is $36h$ or $0110110b$) is moved in line 3 to D7.B.

Notice how all bits but the lower three of D0.W are cleared using the and instruction — remembering that ANDing with a 0 clears that bit and ANDing with a 1 leaves the corresponding bit unchanged. As we shall see, all subroutines are terminated by a ReTurn from Subroutine instruction.

Examples

Example 5.1

Modify the scan for maximum program of page 80 to find the minimum, but this time using the Address Register Indirect with Pre-Decrement address mode.

Solution

The structure of this program is similar, but this time the minimum is set to the highest possible value (in line 2) and we walk downwards through the array. As decrementation takes place *before* the Address register is used to reference the operand, we start our pointer in line 1 one above the top of the array.

Program 5.6 *Scanning for the minimum.*

```
MINIMUM: movea.l #6100h,a3 ; Set pointer to just over array top
         move.l  #0FFh,d0   ; Use D0[7:0] to hold minimum value
MIN_LOOP:cmp.b   -(a3),d0   ; Dec pointer, then compare Array[n]
         bhi     MIN_CONT   ; IF HIgher than minimum, leave alone
         move.b  (a3),d0    ; ELSE update minimum
MIN_CONT:cmpa.l  #6000h,a3  ; Has pointer reached the bottom?
         bne     MIN_LOOP   ; IF not THEN again
         .....   .....      ; ELSE exit loop
```

As the Pre-Decrement mode takes two clock cycles longer than the Post-Increment mode to execute, we have a total time deficit of 2×256 clock cycles, or $\frac{512}{8} = 64\,\mu s$ at 8 MHz, over the corresponding walk-up approach.

Example 5.2
Write a program to add two 256 byte-element arrays to give a single 256 word-element array. The arrays follow each other in memory, the first beginning at 0E000h.

Solution
Again this is a walking-array problem. I have used a single pointer in A0 to reference both the augend and addend array elements, making use in line 5 of the fact that they are spaced 256 bytes apart. Line 6 both fetches Array2[n] and also steps the pointer by one (.b-sized instruction). The same pointer cannot be used for the sum array, as each element here is a word (two bytes) and therefore is not a fixed distance from the primary arrays. Using A1 as the pointer to this array in conjunction with the Post-Increment address mode in line 8 steps up two at a time (.w-sized instruction).

Program 5.7 *Adding two arrays.*

```
ADD_ARRAY: movea.l  #0E000h,a0  ; Point A0 to start of arrays
           movea.l  #0E200h,a1  ; Point A1 to start of sum array
A_LOOP:    clr.w    d0          ; Word-sized space for Array1[n]
           clr.w    d1          ; Word-sized space for Array2[n]
           move.b   256(a0),d0  ; Get Array2[n] byte -> word
           move.b   (a0)+,d1    ; Get Array1[n] & THEN inc n
           add.w    d0,d1       ; Array1[n] + Array2[n]
           move.w   d1,(a1)+    ; Put away Array3[k] & THEN inc k
           cmpa.l   #0E100h,a0  ; Over the top yet?
           bne      A_LOOP      ; IF not THEN next addition
           .....    .....       ; ELSE finished
```

Example 5.3
The Address Register Indirect with Index address mode is useful where a byte n up from the base address is to be pin-pointed. What modification would have to be made if each element were word- or long-word-sized?

Solution
Where each element is a word then the contents of the Index register should be doubled, and quadrupled for long-word elements. For Data register indices this is conveniently done by shifting left once or

twice respectively. The 68020 and later family devices (designated as 68020+) have a variation of this mode, known as Scaled Index, which augments the base address by a scaled Index register to overcome this problem, e.g. move.w (0,a0,d7.1*2) for word elements.

Self-assessment questions

5.1 Line 1 of Program 5.3 has been entered as movea.1 06000h,a3 by mistake. What will happen?

5.2 Modify Program 5.3 to exit prematurely if maximum is FFh. Would this be useful?

5.3 By mistake a student writing a die subroutine has replaced line 3 in Program 5.5 by move.b 0(a0,d0.1),d7. Why does this only work sporadically and how could you rectify this situation without changing the defective subroutine?

5.4 The die subroutine of Program 5.5 is not robust in that no notice is taken of the possibility that numbers above 6 can be sent out. What would happen if, say, the number 36 were sent out and how could you indicate this erroneous state? Why did I make the first table entry FFh?

5.5 Write a program to evaluate the average of a 256 byte-element array. What modifications would you have to make for a 1024 byte-element situation?

5.6 Show how you could improve the accuracy of the three-point filter of Program 5.4 by rounding up if the remainder after dividing by 4 is 2 or more.

CHAPTER 6

The instruction set

If you like to think of writing a program as analogous to preparing an elaborate meal, then the address modes discussed in the last chapter are the various ingredients available to the cook. For any given cooking appliance, such as a microwave oven or electric stove (the hardware) there are a range of processes: steaming, frying, boiling etc. Each process will be listed with properties in the appliance's manual, and in our frame of reference translate to the **instruction set**.

The 68000 MPU has 143 different instructions, but fortunately many of these are rarely used or are variations on a common theme. Up to the moment we have survived quite well on the diet of ten instructions listed in Table 3.1 on page 46. Taking variations into account increased that repertoire to 23. As these instructions are directly usable for our MPU, now would be a good time to review this material.

Here we will look at a few dozen frequently used instructions together with their common permutations. We will postpone those instructions mainly associated with subroutines and exceptions to later chapters. A convenient table of commonly used instructions is given in Appendix B.

After reading this chapter you will:

- *Know that Movement instructions, copying data in-between registers and memory, are the most used and flexible of the instruction categories.*

- *Appreciate that the processor can directly implement the common arithmetic operations of Addition, Subtraction, with some limited Multiplication and Division.*

- *Know that data can be shifted — logically or arithmetically — or rotated — straight or through the* **X** *flag — in memory; or in a Data register by a fixed or variable number of places.*

- *Understand how to use the four basic logic instructions to set, clear, toggle, bit test and differentiate data.*

- *Know how to compare or test signed or unsigned data for differences and relative magnitude, and take appropriate action.*

- *Recognize that different Conditional Branches must be used depending on whether the compared data is signed or unsigned.*

- *Know that Branch instructions specify their destination as an offset to be added to the Program Counter, sometimes known as Relative addressing, e.g.* `bra .+8` *(BRanch Always to the instruction eight bytes on).*

The 68000's instruction set can conveniently be divided into six groups as follows.

Movement Operations

Around one in three instructions move data around without alteration between registers and/or memory.[1] With this in mind, Motorola made the Move operations the most flexible in its repertoire.

Table 6.1 *Move instructions.*

Operation		Mnemonic		X	N	Z	V	C	Description
Move									Data, source to destination
	data	move.s3	ea1,ea2	•	√	√	0	0	(ea2) <- (ea1)
	to Address reg.	movea.s2	ea,an	•	•	•	•	•	(An) <- (ea)
	quick	moveq	# ± K8,Dn	•	√	√	0	0	(Dn) <- # ± K8
	to CCR	move	ea,ccr	√	√	√	√	√	(CCR) <- (ea)
	to SR	move	ea,sr	√	√	√	√	√	(SR) <- (ea), privileged
Exchange									Switch two registers
		exg.l	R1,R2	•	•	•	•	•	(R2) <--> (R1)
Swap									Switch lower/upper words
		swap	dn	•	√	√	0	0	(D[31:16]) <--> (D[15:0])

0	Flag always reset	Rn	Data or Address register n
1	Flag always set	an	Address register n
•	Flag not affected	dn	Data register n
√	Flag operated in the expected way	dn[x:y]	Data register n, bits x to y
s3	Three sizes, .b, .w, .l	# ± K8	Signed eight-bit value
s2	Two sizes, .w, .l	[ ]	Contents of
ea	Effective Address or immediate data	<-	Becomes

Thus the basic move can copy data from any memory location to any other; for instance line 1 below, which *copies* the long-word in 00508:9:A:Bh into 0E200:1:2:3h. Data in the source remains *unchanged*. No other dual-operand instruction can have both source and destination out in memory; usually a register is involved in at least one operand, or perhaps an immediate source is permissible.

```
move.l  00508h,0E200h   ; 1: (0E200:1:2:3h) <- (00508:9:A:Bh)
move.b  d0,0E000h       ; 2: Copy the lower eight bits of D0 into 0E000h
move.w  0E000h,d7       ; 3: Copy the contents of 0E000:1h into D7[15:0]
move.l  d1,d7           ; 4: Copy all bits of D1 into D7
move.b  #55h,0E000h     ; 5: Copy the constant 55h into 0E000h
```

---

[1]A straw poll of the programs in the last chapter produced a figure of around 36%.

```
moveq    #0FFh,d3         ; 6: Copy the constant FFFFFFFFh into D0[31:0]
move.l   a0,d0            ; 7: Copy A0[31:0] into D0[31:0]
movea.l  d0,a0            ; 8: Copy D0[31:0] into A0[31:0]
move     #00010000b,ccr ; 9: Set the X flag, clear all others
```

There are two variations of move listed here. movea must be used where an Address register is the *destination*, as in line 8 above. As with all instructions that reference Address registers, only .w and .l sizes are allowed. The former sign extends to affect all 32 bits, as shown in Fig. 4.3 on page 65. As usual with instructions that alter an Address register, the Code Condition flags are not altered.

The moveq instruction is a quick form where an eight-bit constant is *sign-extended* to 32 bits and then copied exclusively into a Data register. Line 6 above takes four clock cycles to execute as compared to 12 cycles for the equivalent move.l #0FFFFFFFFh,d3.[2]

It is also possible to copy a constant into the Code Condition register (CCR), which can be used to alter any of the flags. Although the mnemonic move is normally used,[3] this is in fact a separate instruction. Similarly, the Status register can be altered if sr is the destination. However, Move to SR is privileged; that is, only legal in the Supervisor mode.

The exg instruction exchanges the full 32-bit contents of *any* Data or/and Address register (Rn ↔ Rm), as shown in lines 1–3 below. swap switches over the upper and lower words of any *Data register*. As we shall see, this is useful in conjunction with the Divide instructions. Another example is given on page 228.

```
exg      d0,d3            ; 1: Interchange D0[31:0] with D3[31:0]
exg      d0,a0            ; 2: D0[31:0]   <--> A0[31:0]
exg      a2,d7            ; 3: A2[31:0]   <--> D7[31:0]
swap     d7               ; 4: D7[31:16] <--> D7[15:0]
```

Arithmetic operations

The 68000 MPU can add, subtract, multiply and divide, as well as performing the auxiliary operations of clearing, sign extension and 2's complement negation, as listed in Table 6.2.

The plain add instruction needs at least one operand to be in a Data register, as shown in the examples below. As in all double-operand instructions, the outcome is deposited at the destination effective address. Thus in line 4 the sum of the constant 20h is added to the contents of D4.L and the answer left in D4.L. Both source and destination operand must be of the same size; if not, the smallest must be promoted to the larger size before performing the operation.

---

[2]Most assemblers will pick the correct form of Move instruction (movea or moveq) for you if you are sloppy and just enter move, but this is not good practice.

[3]I have seen the mnemonic mtccr #kk used as an alternative.

```
add.b   d0,0E000h   ; 1: (0E000h)     <- (D0[7:0]) + (0E000h)
add.w   0E020h,d7   ; 2: (D7[15:0])   <- (0E020h) + (d7[15:0])
add.l   d1,d6       ; 3: (D6[31:0])   <- (D1[31:0]) + (D6[31:0])
add.l   #20h,d4     ; 4: (D4[31:0])   <- 20h + (D4[31:0])
sub.w   d2,0E000h   ; 5: (0E000:1h)   <- (0E000:1h) - (D2[15:0])
sub.b   0E020h,d3   ; 6: (D3[7:0])    <- (D3[7:0]) - (0E000h)
sub.b   #10h,d1     ; 7: (D1[7:0])    <- (D1[7:0]) - 10h
```

The plain sub instruction mirrors the corresponding add; the source being subtracted *from* the destination (the , can be read as 'from') and the difference overwrites the destination. Thus in line 7 above, $10h$ is subtracted *from* the lower byte of D1 and the outcome put into D1.B.

The variants adda and suba are used when an Address register is the destination, as in lines 1 and 2 below. As usual, the various flags are not

Table 6.2 *Arithmetic operations.*

Operation	Mnemonic	X	N	Z	V	C	Description
Add							Add source to destination
to Data reg.	add.s3 ea,dn	√	√	√	√	√	(Dn) <- (Dn) + (ea)
to memory	add.s3 dn,ea	√	√	√	√	√	(ea) <- (ea) + (Dn)
to Address reg.	adda.s2 ea,an	•	•	•	•	•	(An) <- (An) + (ea)
quick[1]	addq.s3 #K3,ea	√	√	√	√	√	(ea) <- (ea) + #K3[2]
immediate	addi.s3 #K,ea	√	√	√	√	√	(ea) <- (ea) + #K
Clear							Clears destination
	clr.s3 ea[3]	•	0	0	1	0	(ea) <- 00
Divide							Generates quotient and remainder (%)
signed	divs ea,dn	•	√	√	√	0	(Dn[15:0]) <-(Dn[31:0])÷(ea[15:0])
unsigned	divu ea,dn	•	√	√	√	0	(Dn[31:16])<-(Dn[31:0])%(ea[15:0])
Extend							Sign-extend Data register
word	ext.w dn	•	√	√	0	0	(Dn[15:0]) <- (SEX|(Dn[7:0]))
long	ext.l dn	•	√	√	0	0	(Dn[31:0]) <- (SEX|(Dn[15:0]))
Multiply							16×16 product
signed	muls ea,dn	•	√	√	0	0	(Dn[31:0])<-(Dn[15:0])×±(ea[15:0])
unsigned	mulu ea,dn	•	√	√	0	0	(Dn[31:0])<-(Dn[15:0])× (ea[15:0])
Negate							Reverses 2's complement sign
data	neg.s3 ea	√	√	√	√	√	(ea) <- 00 - (ea)
Subtract							Subtract source from destination
from Data reg.	sub.s3 ea,dn	√	√	√	√	√	(Dn) <- (Dn) - (ea)
from memory	sub.s3 dn,ea	√	√	√	√	√	(ea) <- (ea) - (Dn)
from Addr. reg.	suba.s2 ea,an	•	•	•	•	•	(An) <- (An) - (ea)
quick[1]	subq.s3 #K3,ea	√	√	√	√	√	(ea) <- (ea) - #K3[2]
immediate	subi.s3 #K,ea	√	√	√	√	√	(ea) <- (ea) - #K

Note 1: Only long and word with Address register destination. Also CCR unchanged.
Note 2: K_3 is a three-bit number from 1 to 8.
Note 3: Not Address register.

altered by these instructions, which come in the usual two sizes, i.e. .w and .l; the former being sign-extended to long.

```
adda.l  d0,a0       ; 1: Augment the Address register by D0.L
suba.l  #20h,a1     ; 2: Decrement A1.L by 20h
addq.w  #8,0E000h   ; 3: Increment the contents of E000:1h by 8
subq.w  #4,a2       ; 4: Decrement A2.L by 4
```

Where it is necessary to add or subtract a small constant, between 1 and 8, then addq or subq respectively is an efficient choice. The target operand can be either in a Data register, out in memory (line 3 above) or even in an Address register (line 4 above). In the customary way, all 32 bits of the latter are altered irrespective of which of the two sizes is used and the CCR flags are not altered. As we saw on page 76, three bits in the op-code are used to code the immediate data and thus Quick instructions are shorter and execute faster than the normal equivalents. There are no Increment or Decrement instructions; these Quick instructions act as a more flexible alternative.

Although this pair of instructions can target operands directly out in memory, execution is actually implemented by fetching the operand into an internal temporary register, performing the operation and returning the modified data. This mechanism is known as **read–modif–write**, and any instruction appearing to act directly on memory uses this technique.

Where a literal above 8 is to be added or subtracted from a memory location, we could use something like this sequence:

```
move.b   <mem>,d7    ; Copy byte (or word or long-word) from memory
add.b    #KK,d7      ; Add literal KK
move.b   d7,<mem>    ; and copy it back
```

The alternative is:

```
addi.b   #KK,<mem>  ; Augment the byte in memory by KK
```

Not only is addi (or subi) shorter and quicker, but it does not disturb a Data register. These Immediate instructions are read–modify–write when the destination is a memory location. Data (but not Address) registers can also be modified as an alternative to using their plain add/sub cousins.

It is possible to multiply any two words together, provided that the destination datum is in a Data register, but the source can be anywhere in memory, a Data register or a literal. For example:

```
mulu   0E020h,d7   ; 1: (D7[31:0]) <- (0E020:1h) x (D7[15:0])
muls   #-7,d0      ; 2: (D0[31:0]) <- -7 x (D0[15:0])
mulu   d1,d6       ; 3: (D6[31:0]) <- (D1[15:0]) x (D6[15:0])
```

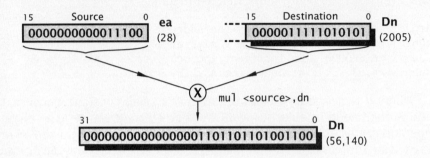

Figure 6.1 *The* mulu/muls *instruction.*

As the example in Fig. 6.1 shows, all 32 bits of the destination are over-written by the 32-bit product of the 16×16-bit multiplication.

There are two varieties of this instruction. mulu performs the process on the basis of unsigned arithmetic, whereas muls treats the operands as signed numbers. For example:

```
Multiplicand              1,111 1111 1111 1001  (-7)
Multiplier            X   0,000 0000 0000 1010  (+10)
                          _____
Product    1,111 1111 1111 1111 1111 1111 1011 1010  (-70)
```

The 68020+ MPUs have a Long Multiply instruction which gives a $32 \times 32 = 64$-bit operation.

The Divide instructions also come in signed and unsigned versions. divu and divs treat their data as unsigned and signed respectively. In both cases the long-word dividend *must* be a Data register and is the destination. The word-sized divisor source can be in memory, in a Data register or an immediate constant, e.g.:

```
divs  #-5000,d0  ; 1: Divide the contents of D0.L by -5000
                 ;     The quotient is to be found in D0[15:0]
                 ;     The remainder is to be found in D0[31:16]

divu  0E020h,d7  ; 2: Divide (D7.L) by the contents of 0E020:1h
                 ;     The quotient is put in D7[15:0]
                 ;     The remainder is put in D7[31:16]
```

One problem with integer division is of course there are two answers: a quotient and a remainder. For example, $65,536 \div 20 = 3276r16$, i.e. a quotient of 3276 with a remainder of 16.

The div instructions produce both answers at once, putting the quotient in the bottom word of the destination Data register and the remain-

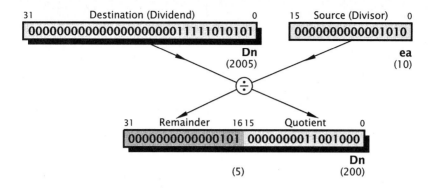

Figure 6.2 *Division; showing* 2005 ÷ 10 = 200*r*5.

der word in the the top 16 bits of the *same* register,[4] as shown in Fig. 6.2. If you need to examine the remainder, then the `swap` instruction interchanges the remainder/quotient pair, and any word-sized instruction on this Data register will act on the remainder. Another `swap` will return things back again. An example of this is given in Program 6.3.

As an example of the use of multiplication and division, consider the conversion from degrees Celsius to degrees Fahrenheit:

$$°F = \left(\frac{°C \times 9}{5} \right) + 32$$

If we assume that the Celsius datum is in D0.W, the Fahrenheit equivalent is to be generated in D7.W and the original is to be preserved, then we have:

```
move.w  d0,d7   ; Copy Celsius into D7 for safekeeping
mulu    #9,d0   ; (D0[31:0]) = C x 9
divu    #5,d0   ; (D0[15:0]) = (C x 9)/5
add.w   #32,d0  ; (D0[15:0]) = ((C x 9)/5) + 32 = F
exg     d0,d7   ; Fahrenheit to D7.W, Celsius back to D0.W
```

This code fragment will work for inputs ranging from 0 to 36, 390°C (32° to 65, 535°F). If you wish to deal with signed quantities in which the Celsius input is a signed word, then simply change the `divu` to `divs` and `mulu` to `muls` above. Given that the word capacity limits the °F range to +32, 767 to − 32, 768, then the modified routine can successfully convert from the range +18, 186°C to − 18, 222°C.

If you are going to use the `div` instructions, then you must keep in mind the following points.

---

[4]The 68020+ MPUs have additional instructions that can divide two 32-bit numbers or a 64-bit dividend by 32-bit divisor, giving a 32-bit quotient/remainder pair.

- The dividend must be in a 32-bit Data register. If your datum is only byte- or word-sized then you must extend it to long-word size before use.

- The divisor is only 16 bits long.

- The quotient outcome of the division is the bottom word of the Data register and therefore must fit into a 16-bit word. If this is not the case, then the **V** flag will be set to show quotient overflow.

- Never divide by zero. Mathematically this results in ∞, which obviously cannot be represented by 16 bits. The 68000 MPU regards this as a fatal error (exceptional condition) and ceases execution of the program forthwith. How this is handled is discussed on page 154.

We have frequently used the clr instruction in the past. As a quirk, when memory is targeted it is implemented as a read–modify–write instruction, even though the actual value of the operand does not affect the outcome. This was changed in the 68020+ MPUs.

The remaining two instructions listed in Table 6.2 are relevant where the operand is to be treated as a signed 2's complement number. neg 2's complements the operand, i.e. inverts all bits and adds 1 (see page 8). For example -1 converts to $+1$:

11111111		00000001	
D0 (−1)	neg.b d0 $\longrightarrow$		D0 (+1)

neg can operate directly on memory using the read–modify–write mechanism, for example neg.w 0E020h.

ext.w[5] extends a byte-sized signed 2's complement number in a Data register to a word-sized equivalent. For example:

01111111		0000000001111111	
D7 (+127)	ext.w d7 $\longrightarrow$		D7 (+127)

11111111		1111111111111111	
D7 (−1)	ext.w d7 $\longrightarrow$		D7 (−1)

ext.l similarly sign-extends a word in a Data register to the equivalent signed 2's complement long-word. In both cases the most significant bit, the sign bit, is propagated to the upper bits, as described on page 10.

Shift operations

The 68000 MPU has four categories of instructions which can shift a datum one or more places either left or right. Each of the eight instructions listed in Table 6.3 can specify the number of shifts on the target operand in three ways. As our illustration we will take the lsr (Logic Shift Right) and lsl (Logic Shift Left) instructions described in Fig. 3.7 on page 51.

---

[5]The designers of the 6809 MPU, conceived at about the same time as the 68000 MPU, had more of a sense of humor in calling this instruction sex for "Sign EXtension".

Table 6.3 *Shifting instructions.*

Operation	Mnemonic	X	N	Z	V	C	Description
Arithmetic Shift Right							Linear Shift Right keeping the sign
memory	asr.w ea	b_0	$\sqrt{}$	$\sqrt{}$	[1]	b_0	
static Data reg.	asr.s3 #K$_3$,dn	b_0	$\sqrt{}$	$\sqrt{}$	[1]	b_0	
dynamic Data reg.	asr.s3 dx,dy	b_0	$\sqrt{}$	$\sqrt{}$	[1]	b_0	
Logic Shift Right							Linear Shift Right
memory	lsr.w ea	b_0	$\sqrt{}$	$\sqrt{}$	0	b_0	
static Data reg.	lsr.s3 #K$_3$,dn	b_0	$\sqrt{}$	$\sqrt{}$	0	b_0	
dynamic Data reg.	lsr.s3 dx,dy	b_0	$\sqrt{}$	$\sqrt{}$	0	b_0	
Arithmetic Shift Left							Linear Shift Left
memory	asl.w ea	b_m	$\sqrt{}$	$\sqrt{}$	[1]	b_m	
static Data reg.	asl.s3 #K$_3$,dn	b_m	$\sqrt{}$	$\sqrt{}$	[1]	b_m	
dynamic Data reg.	asl.s3 dx,dy	b_m	$\sqrt{}$	$\sqrt{}$	[1]	b_m	
Logic Shift Left [2]							Linear Shift Left
memory	lsl.w ea	b_m	$\sqrt{}$	$\sqrt{}$	0	b_m	
static Data reg.	lsl.s3 #K$_3$,dn	b_m	$\sqrt{}$	$\sqrt{}$	0	b_m	
dynamic Data reg.	lsl.s3 dx,dy	b_m	$\sqrt{}$	$\sqrt{}$	0	b_m	
ROtate Right							Circular Shift Right
memory	ror.W ea	•	$\sqrt{}$	$\sqrt{}$	0	b_0	
static Data reg.	ror.s3 #K$_3$,dn	•	$\sqrt{}$	$\sqrt{}$	0	b_0	
dynamic Data reg.	ror.s3 dx,dy	•	$\sqrt{}$	$\sqrt{}$	0	b_0	
ROtate Left							Circular Shift Left
memory	rol.w ea	•	$\sqrt{}$	$\sqrt{}$	0	b_m	
static Data reg.	rol.s3 #K$_3$,dn	•	$\sqrt{}$	$\sqrt{}$	0	b_m	
dynamic Data reg.	rol.s3 dx,dy	•	$\sqrt{}$	$\sqrt{}$	0	b_m	
ROtate Right with eXtend							Circular Shift Right through X
memory	roxr.w ea	b_0	$\sqrt{}$	$\sqrt{}$	0	b_0	
static Data reg.	roxr.s3 #K$_3$,dn	b_0	$\sqrt{}$	$\sqrt{}$	0	b_0	
dynamic Data reg.	roxr.s3 dx,dy	b_0	$\sqrt{}$	$\sqrt{}$	0	b_0	
ROtate Left with eXtend							Circular Shift Left through X
memory	roxl.w ea	b_m	$\sqrt{}$	$\sqrt{}$	0	b_m	
static Data reg.	roxl.s3 #K$_3$,dn	b_m	$\sqrt{}$	$\sqrt{}$	0	b_m	
dynamic Data reg.	roxl.s3 dx,dy	b_m	$\sqrt{}$	$\sqrt{}$	0	b_m	

Note 1: Set IF most significant bit, b_m, changes, ELSE cleared.
Note 2: Identical with asl except **V** flag cleared.

• Where the operand is located out in memory, only a word-sized shift is allowed, one place left or right; for instance, lsl.w 0E020h shifts the *word* content of 0E020:1*h* left *one* place. Using RTL (see page 39) we have (0E020:1h) <- (0E020:1h) « 1, where the << operator denotes "Shift Left".

• Where the operand is located in a Data register, then a *fixed* number of places between 1 and 8 can be statically specified; for instance, lsr.b #2,d7 shifts the eight bits at the bottom of D7.B right *two* places, i.e. (D7[7:0]) <- (D7[7:0]) >> 2, where >> denotes "Shift Right". All three sizes are available.

• Where the operand is located in a Data register, then a *variable* number of shifts can be specified dynamically by the count held in the lower six bits of a Data register. For instance, lsl.l d0,d7 shifts all 32 bits in D7 left by the number held in D0[5:0]. If this happened to be 12 at the time of execution, then (D7[31:0]) <- (D7[31:0]) « (D0[5:0]) results in the contents of D7.L shifting left by 12 places. Dynamic mode shifting is used where shifts of more than eight places are needed in one instruction, or where a variable number of shifts as calculated by the program execution, that is at run-time, is required.

The four shifting categories are:

Logic
This is the basic lsl/lsr linear shift described in Fig. 3.7 on page 51. Here zeros are shifted in from the near side and the last shifted-out bit is lodged in the **C** and also **X** flag.

Arithmetic
Shifting is often used to multiply (left) or divide (right) a number by a power of 2, as described on page 10. As shown there, where a signed 2's complement number is to be divided by shifting right then the sign bit must be propagated along rather than always shifting in zeros. For example:

1,0100 (−12) ⟹ **0**,1010 (+10) !!! .... Logic Shift Right
1,0100 (−12) ⟹ **1**,1010 (−6) etc. .... Arithmetic Shift Right

The asr instruction differs from lsr in this particular but is otherwise the same.

The asl is virtually identical to its Logic stablemate, except that the **V** flag is set if the most significant bit changes. This would indicate an overflow condition if the data is being treated as a signed 2's complement number (see also page 10).

Rotate
The plain circular rotates, ror and rol feed each bit, as it is shifted out, back into the other end. In the case shown in Fig. 6.3(a) the bits are ejected

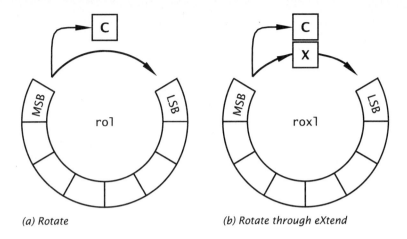

(a) Rotate   *(b) Rotate through eXtend*

Figure 6.3 *Circular shifts.*

from the most significant bit into the least significant bit. As usual, the C flag holds the last bit ejected. For example, `ror.b #4,d0` effectively swaps the lower and upper nybbles in D0.B.

Rotate through X

The `roxl` and `roxr` pair are also circular, but this time shifting is through the interposed **X** flag.

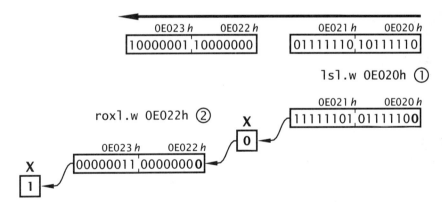

Figure 6.4 *Performing a 32-bit shift out in memory.*

Although this seems rather perverse, one use is shown in Fig. 6.4, where a multiple-precision shift is performed using a `roxl` to catch the previously ejected bit and inject it into the next shifted word. In this manner, shifts of any length can be implemented as a cascade. See Program 6.2 for another example of this instruction.

Table 6.4 *Logic Instructions.*

Operation		Mnemonic		X	N	Z	V	C	Description
AND									Logic bitwise AND
	to Data register	and.s3	ea,dn	•	$\sqrt{}$	$\sqrt{}$	0	0	(dn) <- (dn) · (ea)
	to memory	and.s3	dn,ea	•	$\sqrt{}$	$\sqrt{}$	0	0	(ea) <- (ea) · (dn)
	immediate	andi.s3	#K,ea[1]	•[2]	$\sqrt{}$[2]	$\sqrt{}$[2]	0[2]	0[2]	(ea) <- (ea) · #K
EOR									Logic bitwise Exclusive-OR
	to Data register	eor.s3	ea,dn	•	$\sqrt{}$	$\sqrt{}$	0	0	(dn) <- (dn) ⊕ (ea)
	immediate	eori.s3	#K,ea[1]	•[2]	$\sqrt{}$[2]	$\sqrt{}$[2]	0[2]	0[2]	(ea) <- (ea) ⊕ #K
NOT		not.s3	ea	•	$\sqrt{}$	$\sqrt{}$	0	0	(ea) <- $\overline{(ea)}$
OR									Logic bitwise OR
	to Data register	or.s3	ea,dn	•	$\sqrt{}$	$\sqrt{}$	0	0	(dn) <- (dn) + (ea)
	to memory	or.s3	dn,ea	•	$\sqrt{}$	$\sqrt{}$	0	0	(ea) <- (ea) + (dn)
	immediate	ori.s3	#K,ea[1]	•[2]	$\sqrt{}$[2]	$\sqrt{}$[2]	0[2]	0[2]	(ea) <- (ea) + #K

Note 1: Any alterable memory location, Data register, CCR or SR (privileged).
Note 2: With destination CCR or SR, all flags altered accordingly.

Logic

All four basic logic operations are provided, as shown in Table 6.4.

not is a single-operand instruction that inverts (or complements) all bits in either a Data register or out in memory. For example:

$$\boxed{10001110}_{D7} \xrightarrow{\text{not.b d7}} \boxed{01110001}_{D7}$$

The and instruction bitwise ANDs the source with the destination operand. ANDing an input with a 0 always gives a 0 output, whilst with a 1 does not change the logic value. At least one of the operands must lie in a Data register. For example:

$$\boxed{10001110}_{D7} \xrightarrow{\text{and.b \#0Fh}} \boxed{\textbf{0000}1110}_{D7}$$

which clears the upper nybble of D7.B.

ANDing is normally used to *clear* any bit or bits in the destination operand. Thus and.1 #0FFh,d3 clears the upper 24 bits in D3.L and leaves the lower byte untouched. This is a convenient way of extending an unsigned byte to long-word size. Another use of ANDing is to check the state of any bit or bits in a datum; for example:

```
and.b   #0100b,d7   ; Check bit 2 of D7.b
beq     FRED        ; IF EQual to zero THEN go to FRED
```

By ANDing D7.B by 0000 0*1*00*b*, the outcome will be either all zero or not if bit 2 of D7.B is 0 or 1 respectively. In the latter case, the **Z** flag will be set and the following Branch if EQual to zero will be taken. Similarly, a Branch may be executed if a *group* of bits are all zero; for example, and.w #0111b,d7 will cause the **Z** flag to be set only if bits 2, 1 and 0 are *all* zero.

Instruction andi is the Immediate variant allowing an operand in memory to be directly ANDed with a constant; see line 1 below.

```
andi.b  #01111111b,0E020h     ; 1: Clear bit 7 of memory location 0E020h
andi    #11111110b,ccr        ; 2: Clear C flag
andi    #1111100011111111b,sr ; 3: Clear I2 I1 I0 interrupt mask bits
```

It is also possible to clear any flags by specifying the **CCR** as the destination; as in line 2 above. Again this instruction can change any bits in the Status register; for instance in line 3 above, but this instruction is privileged.

The or instructions work in the same way as for and. ORing with a 0 leaves the source bit unchanged whereas ORing with a 1 sets the bit to a 1 irrespective. Thus ORing is normally used to set any bit or bits in the destination operand. For example:

$$\boxed{10001110}\,_{\text{D7}} \quad \overset{\text{or.b \#01,d7}}{\longrightarrow} \quad \boxed{1000111\textbf{1}}\,_{\text{D7}}$$

Again there is an ori immediate variant that allows you to set bits out in memory or in the **CCR** or **SR** (privileged). For example:

```
ori.b  #10000000b,0E020h     ; 1: Set bit 7 of memory location 0E020h
ori    #00000001b,ccr        ; 2: Set C flag
ori    #0000001100000000b,sr ; 3: Set I1 I0 interrupt mask
```

The eor instruction provides for the Exclusive-OR operation. This is slightly limited in that a Data register *must* be the destination. However, the immediate variant eori is available to target memory, the **CCR** or (privileged) the **SR**.

You will recall from page 14 that EORing with a 0 leaves a data bit unchanged, whilst EORing with a 1 inverts (or toggles) that bit. Thus, for example if we wished to invert both bits 0 and 7 of D3.B:

$$\boxed{10001110}\,_{\text{D3}} \quad \overset{\text{eor.b \#81h,d3}}{\longrightarrow} \quad \boxed{0000111\textbf{1}}\,_{\text{D3}}$$

Another use for EOR is to isolate changes between two bit patterns. From the truth table on page 13 we see that only when the two input bits *differ* is the output 1. Consider as an example a program routine that continually monitors a memory location that reflects the state of eight control switches (see page 214 for how this is done). This routine is waiting until someone changes a switch.

```
        .define  SWITCH = 09000h ; Switch port is at 09000h
START:  move.b   SWITCH,d7       ; Get initial state of switches
S_LOOP: eor.b    SWITCH,d7       ; Check for alterations
        beq      S_LOOP          ; until a change occurs
```

Two possible scenarios are:

10011110	eor.b SWITCH,d7	10011110		00000000	
SWITCH	$\longrightarrow$		D7 =		D7 Z = 1
10001110	eor.b SWITCH,d7	10011110		000 1 0000	
SWITCH	$\longrightarrow$		D7 =		D7 Z = 0

The outcome in D7.B reflects any changes. In the first case there are no changes; in the second Switch 4 has just been thrown from 1 to 0. You can determine which switch changed by shifting the outcome (the change bit) right, counting until the 1 pops out into the **C** flag. You can also determine the type of change (0 → 1 or 1 → 0) by ANDing the change byte to the new settings. If the outcome at bit 4 is a 0, then the change must have been from 1, and vice versa.

Data Testing operations

The simplest test on a datum is whether it is zero. The `tst` instruction of Table 6.5 can check that the contents of any memory location or Data register are zero (by setting the **Z** flag if they are) or negative (by setting the **N** flag if the MSB is 1); for example:

```
tst.b  0E020h ; Check contents of 0E020h for zero or negative
tst.l  d7      ; Check contents of D7[31:0] for zero or negative
```

Table 6.5 *Data testing instructions.*

Operation	Mnemonic		X	N	Z	V	C	Description
					Flags			
Bit TeST								Test bit n
dynamic	btst dx,ea[1]		•	•	$\overline{b_n}$	•	•	No change except in **Z**
static	btst #kk,ea[1]		•	•	$\overline{b_n}$	•	•	No change except in **Z**
Compare								Non-destructive (destn) − (src)
Data reg. with	cmp.s3[2]	ea,dx	•	√	√	√	√	(Dx) − (ea)
Addr. reg. with	cmpa.s2	ea,ax	•	√	√	√	√	(ax) − (ea)
Mem. with const.	cmpi.s3	#K,ea	•	√	√	√	√	(ea) − #K
Test for Zero or Minus								Non-destructive (destn) − 0
	tst.s3 ea[3]		•	√	√	0	0	(ea)-00

Note 1: Only alterable memory and Data register, not Address register.
Note 2: Long if testing a Data register, Byte if in memory.
Note 3: Only word- and long-size if source is Address register.

In the more general case it is often necessary to compare the magnitude of two numbers. Mathematically, this can be done by subtracting the source from the destination. If the outcome is positive, then destination > source; a zero outcome means destination = source and a negative outcome means destination < source.

Where the actual magnitude of the difference between the operands is required, then the appropriate Subtract instruction can be used. However, in most cases it is sufficient to determine the relative magnitude of the quantities. The three outcomes after a `sub <source>,<destination>` are in this situation:

destination *higher than* source .... No borrow, non-zero
destination *equal to* source .... Zero
destination *lower than* source .... Borrow, non-zero

In terms of our MPU, the **C** flag represents a borrow after subtraction and the **Z** flag is set on a zero outcome. Table 3.2 on page 51 sums up the effect on the flags.

Consider as an example a fuel tank with a capacity of 255 liters, with a sensor indicating the remaining volume of fuel. Assume that the sensor represents this as a byte that can be accessed from a read-only memory location called FUEL; see page 214 for how this could be done. We wish to write a routine that will light an 'empty' light if the remaining capacity is below 20 liters and ring an alarm bell if below 5 liters. This is how it could be done:

```
ALARM:  move.b  FUEL,d0    ; Read fuel gauge into D0.B
        move.b  d0,d1      ; Copy into D1.B for safekeeping
        sub.b   #5,d0      ; FUEL - 5 to compare
        blo     BUZZER     ; IF LOwer than 5 THEN sound BUZZER
        sub.b   #20,d1     ; FUEL - 20 to compare
        blo     EMPTY      ; IF LOwer than 20 THEN EMPTY lamp
NEXT:   .....   .....
```

The Branch if LOwer (`blo`) instruction skips if the **C** flag is set. This is an equivalent mnemonic to Branch if Carry Clear (`bcc`), but makes more sense in this context. Other Branches after a subtract of unsigned numbers, outlined in Table 6.6, are `bhs` for Branch if Higher or Same, `beq` for Branch if EQual and `bne` for Branch if Not Equal.

As we are only interested in the relative magnitude of the two quantities, then using the `sub` instruction is overkill, in that the destination operand will be destroyed — replaced by the difference. That is why I had to make a copy of FUEL into D1.B above, so that the second Subtract could be executed. The `cmp` instruction uses the ALU to perform the subtraction and set the appropriate flag and then throws away the answer, i.e. does not overwrite the destination. Compare can be thought of as a non-destructive subtract. Like the Subtract instructions, there are two common variants. `cmpa` is used on Address registers, often to check that a pointer is within its legitimate range in a loop; for example see Program 5.3 on page 80. `cmpi` allows the programmer to check the contents of memory directly against a literal. Using this[6] our code fragment becomes:

---

[6]Why couldn't I use `subi` previously?

```
ALARM:  cmpi.b  #5,FUEL      ; FUEL - 5 to compare
        blo     BUZZER       ; IF LOwer than 5 THEN sound BUZZER
        cmpi.b  #20,FUEL     ; FUEL - 20 to compare
        blo     EMPTY        ; IF LOwer than 20 THEN EMPTY lamp
NEXT:   .....   .....
```

Where the operands under the microscope are signed 2's complement quantities then the same sub or cmp instructions are used. However, their relative magnitude has to be gauged by "looking" at the **V** and **Z** flags, i.e. checking if the outcome is positive or negative, taking overflow into account (see page 9). For sub <source>,<destination> we have:

- If the signed destination is *Greater Than* the signed source, then

  –There will be a non-zero positive outcome with no overflow.
  ELSE

  –There will be an overflow with an apparently negative non-zero outcome.

  This can be expressed as $(N \oplus V) + Z = 0$.

- If the signed destination and source are *EQual* then the **Z** flag will be set.

- If the signed destination is *Less Than* the signed source, then:

  –There will be a negative outcome with no overflow.
  ELSE

  –There will be an overflow with an apparently positive outcome.

  This can be expressed as $N \oplus V = 1$.

Although this seems rather complicated, all the programmer has to remember is to use Conditional Branches with the words Higher (HI) or lower (LO) if the operands are unsigned, and greater (GT) or less (LT) if signed. Equality (or sameness) is the same irrespective.

As an example consider a severe-temperature warning system in an airplane. This comprises a temperature transducer which can be read by the MPU as a signed byte representing degrees Celsius. If the temperature is above $+5°$, then a green lamp is to be lit, below $-2°$ activates a flashing red lamp and otherwise an amber warning is issued. The code might be:

```
ALARM:  cmpi.b  #+5,TEMPERATURE  ; TEMP-5 to check
        bgt     GREEN            ; IF >5 then no problem
        cmpi.b  #-2,TEMPERATURE  ; TEMP-(-2) to check
        blt     FLASH_RED        ; IF <-2 then beware!
AMBER:  .....   .....            ; ELSE turn on amber lamp
```

It is possible to test a *single* bit in a long Data register or out in a memory byte. The actual target bit n can be specified as the source in two ways:

- As an immediate value, e.g. `btst #17,d3` to check bit 17 in D3.L.
- As a dynamic quantity in a Data register, e.g. `btst d0,d3` to check the bit in D3.L as specified by the content of D0. Thus if (D0) = 13 then bit 13 of D3.L is checked.

If the target bit is 0 then the Z flag is set to indicate zero, otherwise it is cleared. Thus `btst` is normally followed by a Branch if EQual to zero or Branch if Not Equal to zero instruction, see page 212 for an example. The target bit is unchanged by the test.[7]

Program Counter operations

As shown in Table 6.6 there are 14 Conditional Branches[8] which cause the offset to be added to the Program Counter (PC) if the indicated combination of flags is true.[9] Effectively this causes the program stream to skip forwards or backwards. There also is a BRanch Always `bra` which always skips.

In assembly language, the programmer can directly specify this offset; thus `beq .+16` means "Add 16 to the *current* state of the PC". The current state of the PC is actually pointing to the instruction op-code *after* the Branch instruction; see Fig. 3.3(b) on page 41. For the 68000 MPU, two sizes of Branch offset are possible. A short or byte Branch has a signed eight-bit offset, as an integral part of the op-code word, and can thus go forward by 128 or back by 126 from the Branch instruction. A word Branch has a signed 2's complement word offset following the op-code word and can go forward 32,770 bytes or back 32,764 bytes.[10]

Rather than calculating these offsets by hand, the destination instruction should be labelled, such as shown in Program 6.1, and the assembler will calculate both the necessary offset and the size (`.b` or `.w`) of the Branch instruction. If the program is subsequently altered, when it is reassembled all offsets will be automatically recalculated — a major advantage.

The `jmp` instruction is a go-to operation as compared to a relative skip. This can use any appropriate address mode and go directly anywhere in the address space.

---

[7] There are three read–modify–write versions that clear, set or change (toggle) the bit *after* the test: `bclr`, `bset` and `bchg` respectively.

[8] Although you may count 16, `blo` is an alternative mnemonic to `bcs` and `bhs` is equivalent to `bcc`.

[9] Although these usually follow a `sub`, `cmp` or `tst` instruction, they can follow any instruction that affects the appropriate flag(s); for example, `move.l MEM,d0` then `beq FRED`.

[10] The 68020+ MPUs have a long-word offset version that can go anywhere in the address space.

Table 6.6 *Instructions which affect the Program Counter.*

Operation	Mnemonic	Description
Unconditional Program Transfer		Always goto
Branch to Label	bra offset[1]	Offset always added to PC, relative goto
Jump to Label	jmp ea	[PC] <- ea, absolute goto
Conditional Program Transfer		Goto IF condition is TRUE
Conditionally Branch to Label	Bccf[2] Offset	Offset added on to PC IF condition is met
No Operation		Does nothing except increment PC by 2
	NOP	[PC] <- [PC] + 2, takes 4‾

Note 1: Normally a label is specified here and the assembler works out the offset.
Note 2: The Condition Codes Flags (*ccf*) are:

		True on			True on
HS	*dest* Higher or Same as *src*[3]	$C = 0$	VC	oVerflow Clear	$V = 0$
LO	*dest* LOwer than *src*[3]	$C = 1$	VS	oVerflow Set	$V = 1$
HI	*dest* HIgher than *src*[3]	$C+Z = 0$	PL	PLus	$N = 0$
LS	*dest* Lower or Same as *src*[3]	$C+Z = 1$	MI	MInus	$N = 1$
CC	Carry Clear	$C = 0$	GE	*dest* Greater or Equal to *src*[4]	$N \oplus V = 0$
CS	Carry Set	$C = 1$	LT	*dest* Less Than *src*[4]	$N \oplus V = 1$
NE	*dest* Not Equal to *src*[3,4]	$Z = 0$	GT	*dest* Greater Than *src*[4]	$\overline{N \oplus V \cdot \overline{Z}} = 1$
EQ	*dest* EQual to *src*[3,4]	$Z = 1$	LE	*dest* Less or Equal to *src*[4]	$\overline{N \oplus V \cdot \overline{Z}} = 0$

Note 3: After a Subtract or Compare of unsigned data.
Note 4: After a Subtract or Compare of 2's complement signed data.

Examples

Example 6.1
Parity is a simple technique for identifying digital data that has been corrupted by noise. Even parity adds a single bit to the word in such a way as to ensure that the overall packet has an even number of 1s. For example:

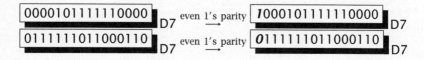

where the most significant bit is the parity bit, and is assumed to be zero before the parity operation. The receiver checks the packet for an even number of 1s, and if it finds an odd number then it assumes a one-bit error has occurred. Of course this is rather limited; however, more sophisticated error protection systems are often based on parity-type principles. Write a routine to add parity to a word stored in D7.W.

Solution

Two tasks can be identified here:

- •To determine if a binary number is even, check the least significant bit, which is worth $2^0 = 1$. All other bits ($2^n, n \geq 2$) are even multiples of 2; so if the LSB is 1 then the number is odd. Thus we must count the number of 1s in D7.W and check the LSB of this count.

- •If the number of 1s is odd, then the MSB of the word must be set to 1.

Program 6.1 *Even-parity word generator.*

```
PARITY:  move.w   d7,d0     ; Copy original word for safekeeping
; Now count the number of 1s in D7.W
         clr.b    d2        ; D2.B is the 1s count
P_LOOP:  lsr.w    #1,d0     ; Shift data into Carry flag
         bcc      P_CONT    ; IF C=0 don't increment count
         addq.b   #1,d2     ; ELSE count this 1
P_CONT:  tst.w    d0        ; Check for anymore 1s?
         bne      P_LOOP    ; IF there is THEN shift again
; Now check if LSB of count = 1 (i.e. odd)
         lsr.b    #1,d2     ; Shift LSB of count into C flag
         bcc      P_EXIT    ; IF =0 THEN data is already even
         or.w     #8000h,d7 ; ELSE set MSB by ORing
P_EXIT:  .....    .....     ; Even number of 1s in D7.W
```

In Program 6.1 the number of 1s is counted by repetitively shifting a copy of the word through the **C** flag and omitting the count increment of line 6 if this is zero. When no more 1s are left, as evidenced by the `tst` of line 7, then the resulting 1s' count in D2.B is checked for oddness by shifting its LSB into the **C** flag. If this is set, the count is odd and the MSB of the data word (the parity bit) is set to 1 by ORing with 1000 0000 0000 0000b in line 12.

As a self-assessment, extend the program to process a 256-word array of data in memory located from 0E000h upwards. How would you alter the specification to ensure that the number of 1s are always odd (odd 1s parity)?

Example 6.2

One rather simple way to security-encrypt data is to reverse the bit order of each data packet; for example:

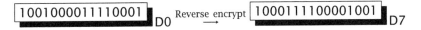

Write a routine to reverse-encrypt the lower word of D0 with the outcome being in D7.W.

Solution

From Program 6.2 we see that the technique (lines 2 and 3) is to shift the original data right bit by bit through the **X** flag and similarly rotate this left into the encrypted word. Doing this 16 times yields the reverse-encrypted version of the original word.

Program 6.2 *Reverse encryption.*

```
ENCRYPT: move.b  #16,d1  ; D1.B is the bit counter
E_LOOP:  lsr.w   d0      ; Shift data bit by bit right into X
         roxl.w          ; and rotate each bit in left from X
         subq.b  #1,d1   ; 16 times
         bne     E_LOOP
         .....   .....   ; Encrypted data in D7.W
```

Example 6.3

Write a routine that will convert a binary number in D7.L to a string of BCD digits (see page 6) in memory. Thus, as an example 9FFFFh transforms to 655,359 as:

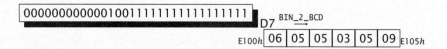

Solution

The principle of the base conversion used in Program 6.3 is to divide the binary number repetitively by 10. Each division yields a remainder between 0 and 9 which is a BCD digit, beginning with the unit digit which goes into 0E105h. The process is folded into a loop with a decrementing A0 pointing to the digit memory byte. As each digit (remainder) is moved out into memory, the remainder is zeroed and the residue from the last division — the quotient — is restored as the new *long* dividend.

The process continues until the pointer reaches down to the non-existent millionth digit, at which time the conversion is complete. The largest number that can be converted is 655,359, because the first quotient must fit into a word (maximum 65,535) and $655,359 \div 10 = 65,535r9$.

Program 6.3 *Converting from binary to BCD.*

```
         .define  BCD = 0E106h
BIN_2_BCD: movea.l  #BCD,a0    ; Point to just beyond BCD string
BCD_LOOP:  divu     #10,d7     ; Binary/10
           swap     d7         ; Remainder in D7.W
           move.b   d7,-(a0)   ; Store BCD nybble away
           clr.w    d7         ; Zero the remainder
           swap     d7         ; Long quotient -> new dividend
           cmpa.l   #BCD-6,a0  ; < the 10-thousand's digit yet?
           bne      BCD_LOOP
           .....    .....
```

Example 6.4

Many applications call for a random number. One way to generate a random sequence is shown in Fig. 6.5. Here a 16-bit shift register uses the EOR feedback $0 \oplus 2 \oplus 11 \oplus 15$ to generate its data input. Provided that the register is not in state $0000h$, then 65,535 random states will be generated before the cycle is repeated. Of course these 'random' signals are predictable if the circuit is known a priori, so the term **pseudo-random number generator** (**PRNG**) is used. Many combinations are possible,[11] the one shown here is based on a 16-bit shift register.

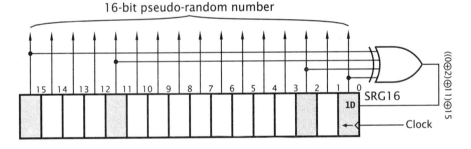

Figure 6.5 *A 16-bit pseudo-random number generator.*

Write a routine to simulate this hardware, with D7.W holding the number. Each number is to be sent to a 16-bit port at $09020:1h$.

Solution

The solution shown in Program 6.4 can be split into three phases.

1. Firstly, three copies of the current PRN are made, and each shifted to align the 'magic' bit to position zero. The only trick

---

[11] See S.J. Cahill's *Digital and Microprocessor Engineering*, 2nd edn., Prentice Hall, 1993, Fig. 4.71 for more details.

here is the use of Rotate Left instructions in lines 5 and 6 instead of Shift Right. As the number of fixed shifts for any one instruction is limited to 8, then going round left one place (line 5) is more efficient than going right 15 places!

2. With bits 0,2,11,15 aligned right, the series of three eors in lines 7,8,9 ends up with $0 \oplus 2 \oplus 11 \oplus 15$ in position zero.

3. Shifting this bit into the **X** flag (line 10) and then using the Rotate through X instruction of line 11 both shifts the PRN — still in D0.W — left and brings in the feedback bit as the new bit 0.

Program 6.4 *Generating the pseudo-random sequence.*

```
PRNG:  move.w   d7,d6       ; Copy 1 of PRN
       move.w   d7,d5       ; Copy 2 of PRN
       move.w   d7,d4       ; Copy 3 of PRN
       lsr.w    #2,d6       ; Align bit 2 with bit 0
       rol.w    #1,d5       ; Align bit 15 with bit 0
       rol.w    #5,d4       ; Align bit 11 with bit 0
       eor.w    d7,d6       ; 0 EOR 2
       eor.w    d6,d5       ; (0 EOR 2) EOR 15
       eor.w    d5,d4       ; ((0 EOR 2) EOR 15) EOR 11
       lsr.w    #1,d4       ; Move above into X flag
       roxl.w   #1,d7       ; and into the new PRN
       move.w   d7,09020h   ; Send out PRN to port
       bra      PRNG        ; Repeat forever
```

Self-assessment questions

6.1 An unsigned long-word datum is located in memory at $0E100:1:2:3h$. How could you add a *byte* datum located in D0.B to it?

6.2 If (D7.L) is 855,906, why will the instruction divu #5,d7 fail?

6.3 If the instruction ext were not available, how could you sign-extend a word-sized datum in D7.W?

6.4 A word received via a modem is located in D0.W. It has even parity. Write a routine to put FFh in D7.B if the parity has been violated, otherwise 00h.

6.5 The program on page 93 could be improved by rounding up the outcome if the remainder is at least $\frac{1}{2}$. Modify the listing to do this.

6.6 Write a program to convert from signed °F to °C. Assume that the former is in D0.W and the outcome is to be in D7.W.

6.7   Modify Program 6.3 to be able to convert a long-word of *any* size up to decimal 655,359,999 into a BCD string; for example:

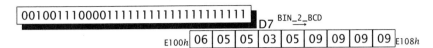

Hint: Divide by 10,000 and use the BIN_2_BCD routine twice.

6.8   Write a routine to convert a BCD string stored in memory — of maximum value 65,535 — to a binary word in D7.W; for example:

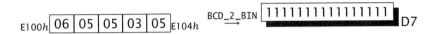

CHAPTER 7

Assembly language

We have now been writing programs with gay abandon since Chapter 3. For clarity these listings were written in a human-readable form. Thus, instructions are represented as a short mnemonic, such as add; the registers similarly have mnemonics, such as d7; lines have been labelled and comments attached. Such symbolic representations are only for human consumption. The MPU knows nothing beyond the binary codes making up operation codes and address modes, such as shown on page 39.

With the help of the programmer's manual supplied by the manufacturer, it is possible to translate from the human-readable symbolic form to machine-readable binary, and this was the method I used on page 76. However, it really isn't practical to do this for programs of more than a few instructions. As well as being excruciatingly slow and tedious, it is error-prone and difficult to maintain whenever there are changes to be made.

Computers are good at doing boring things quickly and accurately; and translating from symbolic to machine code definitely falls into this category. Here we will briefly look at the various software packages that aid in this translation process.

After reading this chapter you will:

- *Know what assembly-level language is and how it relates to machine code.*
- *Appreciate the advantages of a symbolic representation over machine-readable code.*
- *Understand the function of the assembler.*
- *Understand the difference between absolute and relocatable assembly.*
- *Understand the role of a linker.*
- *Appreciate the process involved in translating and locating an assembly-level language program to absolute machine code.*
- *Understand the structure of a machine-code file.*
- *Understand the role of a loader.*

The essence of the conversion process is shown in Fig. 7.1. Here the program is prepared by the tame human in symbolic form, digested by the computer and output in machine-readable form. Of course this simple statement belies a rather complex process, and we want to examine this in just enough detail to help you in writing your programs.

```
move.w   d0,d7
addq.w   #1,d7
mulu     d0,d7
lsr.l    #1,d7
rts
```

```
0011111000000000
0101001001000111
1100111011000000
1110001010001111
0100111001110101
```

Figure 7.1 *Conversion from assembly-level source code to machine code.*

The various translator and utility computer packages are written and sold by many software companies, and thus the actual details and procedures differ somewhat between the various commercial products. Here we will utilize Real Time Systems products[1] for illustrative purposes. Although most products are broadly similar, you will have to consult the documentation of the particular packages you are using for specific details.

Using the computer to aid in translating code from more user-friendly forms (source code) to binary machine code (object code) and loading this into memory began in the late 1940s for mainframe computers. At the very least it permitted the use of higher-order number bases, such as hexadecimal.[2] In this base the code fragment of Fig. 7.1 becomes:

```
3E00
5247
CEC0
E28F
4E75
```

A **hexadecimal loader** will translate this into binary and put the code in designated memory locations. This loader might be the software in your EPROM programmer or part of the operating system of the target computer.[3] Hexadecimal coding has little to commend it, except that the number of keystrokes is reduced — but there are more keys — and it is slightly easier to spot certain types of errors.

---

[1] Written by and available from RTS, M & G House, Head Road, Douglas, Isle of Man, British Isles. Details on http://mannet.mcb.net/rts/xa8.html.

[2] Actually base-8 (octal) was the popular choice for several decades.

[3] For example, MS-DOS or the monitor ROM in your trainer board.

As a minimum a symbolic translator, or **assembler,**[4] is required for serious programming. This allows the programmer to use mnemonics for the instructions and internal registers, with names for constants, variables and addresses. The symbolic language used in the source code is known as **assembly language.** Unlike high-level languages, such as **C** or PASCAL, assembly language has a *one-to-one relationship* with the generated machine code, i.e. one line of source code produces one instruction. As an example, Program 7.1 shows the source code of a module that will compute the average of an array of 24 data bytes (perhaps daily temperature sampled hourly) located in memory from 0F000*h* upwards. The program code itself begins at 00600*h*.

Program 7.1 *Absolute assembly-level source code for our averaging module.*

```
          .define NUMBER = 24       ; 1: Number of elements n=24
          .org    00600h            ; 2: Prog text begins @ 600h
AVERAGE:  movea.l #ARRAY,a0         ; 3: Point to start of array
          clr.l   d7                ; 4: Zero the sum total
LOOP:     move.b  (a0)+,d0          ; 5: Add array element n
          and.w   #0FFh,d0          ; 6: extended to word size
          add.w   d0,d7             ; 7: to grand total
          cmpa.l  #(ARRAY+NUMBER),a0 ; 8: Over the top yet?
          bne     LOOP              ; 9: IF not THEN again
          divu    #NUMBER,d7        ;10: Divide total by n
          rts

          .org    0F000h            ;12: Data area
ARRAY:    .byte   [NUMBER]          ;13: Reserve 24 data bytes
```

Giving names to addresses and constants is especially valuable for longer programs, which may easily exceed 10,000 lines. Together with the use of comments, this makes code easier to debug, develop and maintain. Thus, if we wished to change the size of the array to 144 (say, sampling the temperature every 10 minutes), then we need only alter the first line to:

```
.define NUMBER = 144
```

or even, as most assemblers can do simple constant arithmetic (see also line 8):

```
.define NUMBER = 24*6
```

and then retranslate to machine code. In a program with, say, 50 references to the constant NUMBER, the alternative of altering *all* these constants from 24 to 144 is laborious and error-prone.

Of course symbolic translators demand more of the computer running them than simple hexadecimal loaders, especially in the area of memory

---

[4]The name is very old; it refers to the task of translating and *assembling* together the various modules making up a program.

and backup store. Because of this, their use in small MPU-based projects was limited until the late 1970s, when powerful personal computers appeared. Prior to this, either mainframe and minicomputers or special-purpose MPU development systems were required. Such solutions were inevitably expensive.

Translation involves two tasks:

- Conversion of the various instruction mnemonics and labels to their machine-code equivalent.
- The location of the instructions and data in the appropriate memory locations.

It is the second of these that is perhaps more difficult to understand.

Program 7.1 was designed to be processed by an **absolute assembler**. Here the programmer uses embedded directives (in this assembler distinguished by commands with leading periods) to tell the assembler to place the code in specified memory addresses. The use of the directive **.org** (for "ORiGin") means that the programmer needs to know where everything is to be placed. This *absolute assembly* is OK where a program comprises a single self-contained file.

Real projects, often consisting of more than 10,000 lines of code, require team work. With many modules[5] being written by different people, perhaps also coming in from outside sources and commercial libraries, some means must be found to *link* the appropriate modules together to give the one executable machine-code file. For example, you may have to call up one of the modules that Fred has written some time ago. You will not know exactly where in memory this module will reside until the project has been completed. What can you do? Well a module should have its entry point labelled; say, FRED: in this case. Then you should be able to jump to FRED without knowing exactly what address this label represents.

The process used to facilitate this is shown in Fig. 7.2. Central to this modular tie-up is the **linker** program which satisfies such external cross-references between the modules. Each module's **source-code** file needs to have been translated into **relocatable object code** prior to the linkage. "Relocatable" means that its final location and various addresses of external labels have yet to be determined. This translation is done by a **relocatable assembler**.

Unlike absolute assembly, it is the linker that determines where the machine code is to be located in memory, not the programmer.

In some products, the output of the linker may need some massaging to give the absolute machine-code file format that the loader program understands. The term "absolute" simply means that the machine-readable code is in its final form, and contains its fixed locations in memory.

To clarify the process we will take a single module through from the creation of its source file to the final absolute machine-code file.

---

[5]We will discuss modules in more detail in the next chapter.

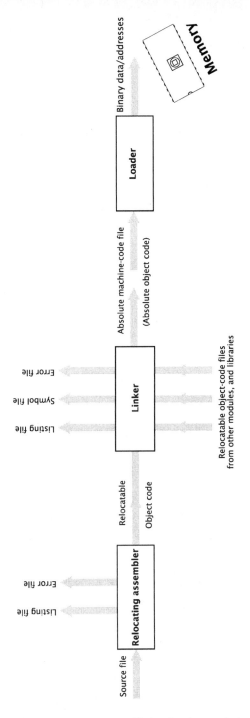

Figure 7.2 *Relocating assembly-level code translation.*

Assembling

First you have to prepare the **source file**. The source file we will use as our model is given in Program 7.2. Traditionally assembly-level source files have an extension of .s or .src.

Program 7.2 *The source file* average.s *for our averaging program.*

```
          .processor m68000      ; 1: First line of the file
          .define NUM = 24
          .psect _text           ; 3: Following is program code
AVERAGE:  movea.l #ARRAY,a0      ; 4: Point to start of array
          clr.l   d7             ; 5: Zero the sum total
LOOP:     move.b  (a0)+,d0       ; 6: Add array element n
          and.w   #0FFh,d0       ; 7: extended to word size
          add.w   d0,d7          ; 8: to grand total
          cmpa.l  #(ARRAY+NUM),a0 ; 9: Over the top yet?
          bne     LOOP           ;10: IF not THEN again
          divu    #NUM,d7        ;11: Divide total by NUM
          rts

          .psect _data           ;13: Following code is data
ARRAY:    .byte   [NUM]          ;14: Reserve 24 bytes of data
          .public AVERAGE, ARRAY ;15: Make known to linker
          .end                   ;16: The last line of the file
```

This is virtually identical to our absolute source in Program 7.1 but with the two .org directives replaced by **.psect** (for "Program SECTion"). This directive identifies data streams, which the linker will later locate in defined areas of memory. Some assemblers can support up to 16 different streams, but this assembler only recognizes two.

- •_text: This stream is normally used for program code, and is the default if no .psect directive is given. As the linker normally locates this stream in fixed ROM, then tables of *fixed* data (such as the die code look-up table of page 83) can also be placed in this stream.

- •_data: This stream is normally used to hold program variables, such as temperature readings in a data logger. The linker normally directs code in this stream to RAM memory. Space can be reserved in this area by directives such as .byte [20], which allocates twenty bytes. Although actual values can be placed in this stream, such as shown in the die look-up table, they will only be placed in their allocated position when the code is loaded in, i.e. at **load time**. Any subsequent run without a preload cannot assume that such values are still in situ at execution time (**run time**).

The source file can be created using any **text editor**. Most operating systems come with a simple text editor; for example, edit for MS-DOS and notepad for Microsoft's Windows 95. Third-party products are also available. A text editor differs from a wordprocessor in that no embedded "funny" codes are inserted, giving formatting and other information. For instance, if you want a new line then you hit the <RET> key; the text editor will not wrap around for you. However, most wordprocessors have a text mode and can be used to create program source files.[6]

The format of a line of source code in this assembler looks like:

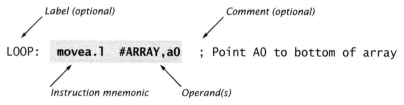

All lines, with the exception of comment-only lines, must contain an instruction (either executable by the MPU or an assembler directive) and any relevant operand or operands. If a line is labelled, then the label is delineated by a following colon.[7] A line label names the address of the first following executable instruction. This name must not start with a number and should be no more than 32 alphanumeric characters. The optional comment is delineated by a semicolon,[8] and whole-line comments are permitted (see line 2 of Program 6.1 on page 105). Comments are ignored by the assembler, and are there solely for human-readable documentation. Notes should be copious and should explain what the program is doing, and not simply repeat the instruction. For example:

```
clr.b d0 ; Clear D0.L
```

is a waste of energy:

```
clr.b d0 ; Zero the bit count
```

is rather more worthwhile. Not, or minimally, commenting source code is a frequent failing, not confined to students. A poorly documented program is difficult to debug and subsequently to alter or extend. The latter is sometimes known as program maintenance.

If there are no syntax errors, then the assembler will translate your source code into relocatable object code, which is basically machine code with additional information. For example, if a label is not found in the source code, then it is passed to the linker with the electronic equivalent of the statement "? Find this label please". Module labels that are to be passed to the linker are known as global, and are identified by the directive `.public`. If a label is not thus identified, then it is private to that module.

---

[6]For example, programs for this book were created using Wordstar 2000 in its non-document format.

[7]With assemblers that do not use a colon as a delimiter, the first character in an unlabelled line has to be a space.

[8]Many assemblers use a *.

This is necessary to help avoid clashes between modules using the same label names. Thus, what if module FRED also had the label LOOP?

Linking

The linker takes as its various inputs relocatable object-code files generated by the assembler, or other sources. Each separate stream of each of the modules is sequentially put together and external labels searched for and their value inserted. Should any unrequited labels not be found, then the linker will complain to the operator, giving appropriate error messages (see page 121), and abort the process.

Once the linker has completed its job successfully, then various documentation files may be extracted from its output absolute object file, as well as the final machine-code file.

Listing

The **listing file** of Table 7.1 reproduces the original source code together with the location in memory of each instruction and its code, all in hexadecimal. To generate this file I configured the linker to start the _text stream at 00400h (see Chapter 9 for why this address was chosen) and

```
 1                       .processor m68000        ; 1: First line of the file
 2                       .define NUM = 24
 3                       .psect  _text            ; 3: Following is program code
                         AVERAGE:
 4  000400   207C  movea.l  #ARRAY,a0            ; 4: Point to start of array
            0000E000
 5  000406   4287  clr.l    d7                   ; 5: Zero the sum total
                         LOOP:
 6  000408   1018  move.b   (a0)+,d0             ; 6: Add array element n

 7  00040A   0240  and.w    #0FFh,d0             ; 7: extended to word size
            00FF
 8  00040E   DE40  add.w    d0,d7                ; 8: to grand total
 9  000410   B1FC  cmpa.l   #(ARRAY+NUM),a0      ; 9: Over the top yet?
            0000E018
10  000416   66F0  bne      LOOP                 ;10: IF not THEN again
11  000418   8EFC  divu     #NUM,d7              ;11: Divide total by NUM
            0018
12  00041C   4E75  rts
13
14                       .psect  _data            ;13: Following code is data
                         ARRAY:
15  00E000         .byte    [NUM]                ;14: Reserve 24 bytes of data
16                       .public AVERAGE, ARRAY  ;15: Make known to linker
17                       .end                     ;16: The last line of the file


        SYMBOL  DEFIN  REFERENCES

         ARRAY    15      4      9     16
       AVERAGE     4     16
          LOOP     6     10
           NUM   -----    2      9     11    15
         _data   -----   14
         _text   -----    3
            a0   -----    4      6      9
            d0   -----    6      7      8
            d7   -----    5      8     11
        m68000   -----    1
```

Table 7.1 *The absolute listing file* average.ab.

the _data stream at 0E000*h*.

As well as the code section, a list of symbols is generated, giving which line number a label is defined (DEFIN) at and where it is referred to. This is useful when debugging a large program.

Symbols

The **symbol file** shown in Table 7.2 gives a list of global symbols[9] together with their equivalent address. In this example there are only two global labels, but in a large program there may be several hundred. Knowing the address to which a label refers is useful in setting up breakpoints when debugging programs).

```
0000e000   ARRAY
00000400   AVERAGE
```

Table 7.2 *The symbol file* average.sym.

Absolute Code

The conclusive outcome of the translation process is the **machine-code file**. As can be seen in Table 7.3, such files essentially consist of lines of hexadecimal digits representing the binary machine code, each preceded by the address of the first byte of the line. This file is ready to be loaded into memory, and subsequently run.

```
S222000400207C0000E00042871018024000FFDE40B1FC0000E01866F08EFC00184E75AD
S21C00E0000000000000000000000000000000000000000000000000000000000003
S804000400F7
```

Table 7.3 *The absolute* S2-S8 *machine-code file* average.ms2.

In the MPU world there are many different formats in common use. Although most of these de facto standards are manufacturer-specific, in the main they can be used for any brand of MPU. The format of the machine-code file shown here is known as Motorola S2-S8. Let us look at the first line, or record, which contains the code for the instructions in the program average.s in more detail:

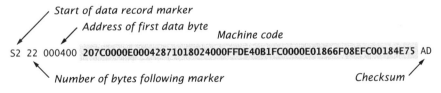

---

[9]As registered by the programmer using the .public directive, and thus known to the linker.

The loader recognizes that a code record follows when the characters S2 are received. The characters S8 signify the end-of-file line. Code records begin with the tally in hexadecimal of all characters after S2, followed by the six-digit hexadecimal address of the first code byte. The core of the record is the machine code, with typically up to 32 bytes in each line. The final byte is known as a checksum. The checksum is calculated so that a total count of all record bytes, excluding the record start characters, will always give FFh (-1). This is used by the loader program to detect download errors.

S2-S8 files are suitable for processors with addresses that can be represented as a 24-bit code (six hexadecimal digits), such as the 68000 MPU. 68020+ MPUs have 32-bit Address buses, and need eight hexadecimal representations. The S3-S7 Motorola format is similar to S2-S8 but with an eight-digit address field. In a similar manner, S1-S9 format files support processors with a four-digit address, but are sometimes used for larger MPUs that are running all their code in the first 64 Kbyte of their memory (0000 – FFFFh).

An assembler will be very particular that the syntax of the source code is correct. If there are *syntax errors*[10] then an **error file** will be generated. For example, if line 6 of Program 7.2 is mistakenly entered as:

```
A_LOOP: mov.b (a0)+,s0 ; Add array element n
```

then the error file following is generated:

```
x68030 (1):
average.s 6:        unknown op-code mov
average.s 6:        system error <> (
average.s 6:        system error <> +
average.s 6:        system error <> ,
average.s 6:        phase error s0 = 00000006H pass1 00000008H pass2
average.s 10:         invalid branch address
average.s: 6 errors detected
```

Table 7.4 *The error file* average.er.

The unknown op-code mov has been correctly picked up and also the attempt in line 10 to Branch to a non-existent line. It often happens that one syntax error causes a number of spurious alarms, as in this case.

As set up, the error in transcribing the Data register d0 as s0 was not picked up. The assembler thought that s0 was a label. As this was not

---

[10]If the assembler announces that there are no errors then there is a tendency to think that the program will work. Unfortunately a lack of syntax errors in no way guarantees that the program will do anything of the sort!

defined anywhere in the program, it was passed onto the linker for resolution — even though the programmer had not defined it with a `.external` directive. In our example, the linker also did not resolve the problem and aborted with the message:

```
missing so (average.o)
```

where the `.o` object file is the output from the assembler.

Finally, we summarize some general information specific to this assembler as an aid to reading programs in the rest of the book:

- Number representation.
  - Hexadecimal: Denoted by a following h, e.g. 41h. Some assemblers use a $ prefix, e.g. $41.
  - Binary: Denoted by a following b, e.g. 01000001b. Some assemblers use a % prefix, e.g. %01000001.
  - Decimal: The default, but optionally followed by d, e.g. 65d.
  - Character: Denoted by surrounding single quotes, e.g. 'a'. Some assemblers use only a leading single quote, e.g. 'a.
- Label arithmetic.
  - Addition: +, e.g. LOOP+6.
  - Subtraction: -, e.g. LOOP-6.
  - Multiplication: *, e.g. NUM*6.
  - Division: /, e.g. NUM/6.
- Directives
  - `.define`: Associates a value with a symbol, e.g. `.define NUM=3039`. Some assemblers use the equate directive, e.g. `NUM equ 3039`.
  - `.external`: Declares the associated symbol as being defined elsewhere, e.g. `.external NUM`.
  - `.byte, .word, .double`: Allocate, and optionally initialize, storage for one, two or four byte-sized objects respectively. For example, `.byte 1,2,4,9,25` reserves five bytes with load-time variables as shown. The directives dc (Define Constant) and ds (Define Storage) are used by some assemblers together with a size extension, e.g. `ds.w 10` to reserve ten words.
  - `.even`: Ensures that the next byte starts at an even address. This is useful where an odd-length array of bytes is followed by program code. Remember that op-codes must always lie on *even* address boundaries.
  - `.psect`: Places the following code in the named data stream for the linker. In our assembler the linker only recognizes the _text and _data streams.

Examples

Example 7.1

Write a subroutine that will evaluate the factorial of an integer n (defined as $1 \times 2 \times 3 \times \cdots \times n$) and denoted $n!$ (with 0! being given the special value of 1). The number $n!$ is to be in D7.L at the end.

Solution

The solution to the problem, shown in Program 7.3, is similar to that of Program 5.5 on page 84 except that each table entry is a four-byte long-word. The 13 data constants in the table thus are specified with a .double directive, which allocates four bytes for each entry. This can be seen more clearly in the listing file of Table 7.5. I have used the .list directive to expand out the table in the listing, which shows you the value (in hexadecimal) and location of each table element.

The program itself points A0 to the first element of the table, by moving its address 0040Eh — as symbolized by the local label F_TABLE— into the register in line 5. The value of n is then multiplied by 4, by shifting left two places, in D0.W. This accounts for the four-byte nature of the table elements. The Address Register Indirect with Index address mode then uses A0 as the base address and D0.W as the offset, to extract element n. Thus if $n = 9$ then D0 = 36 = 24h and the effective address is 0040E + 24 = 00432h. The contents of 00432:3:4:5h is 00058980h or 362,880 — which is 9!.

Program 7.3 *Source code for the factorial program.*

```
        .processor m68000
        .list      +.text
        .psect     _text
FACTORIAL:
        movea.l    #F_TABLE,a0   ; Point A0 to the bottom of table
        lsl.b      #2,d0         ; x4 as four-byte table entries
        move.l     0(a0,d0.w),d7 ; Copy nth value from table to D7.L
        rts                      ; and exit

F_TABLE:
        .double    1, 1, 2, 6, 24, 120, 720, 5040, 40320,
                   362880, 3628800, 39916800, 479001600
        .public    FACTORIAL
        .end
```

```
1                          .processor m68000
2                          .list   +.text
3                          .psect  _text
4           FACTORIAL:
5 000400 207C  movea.l #F_TABLE,a0   ; Point A0 to the bottom of table
         0000040E
6 000406 E508  lsl.b   #2,d0         ; x4 as four-byte table entries
7 000408 2E30  move.l  0(a0,d0.w),d7 ; Copy nth value from table to D7
         0000
8 00040C 4E75  rts                   ; and exit
9
10          F_TABLE:
11 00040E      .double 1, 1, 2, 6, 24, 120, 720, 5040, 40320,
         00000001
         00000001
         00000002
         00000006
         00000018
         00000078
         000002D0
         000013B0
         00009D80
12 000432 00058980       362880, 3628800, 39916800, 479001600
         00375F00
         02611500
         1C8CFC00
13               .public FACTORIAL
14               .end
```

Table 7.5 *The listing file for the factorial program.*

Self-assessment questions

7.1 Repeat the program of Example 7.1 but with the assembler/linker that you are using for your course. Try printing out the various output files. Note the effect of deliberate syntax errors.

7.2 Write a subroutine to implement the factorial function of Example 7.1 but without using a look-up table. Carefully consider the upper limit of your solution.

7.3 Show how you could initialize a table of powers of 10 from 10^0 to 10^9 in _text memory. Write a program using this table that will convert a long natural binary number in D7.L to a string of BCD digits. Reserve ten bytes in _data memory for this BCD array.

CHAPTER 8

Subroutines

Good software should be configured as a set of interacting modules rather than one large program working straight through from beginning to end. There are many advantages to modular programming, which is almost mandatory when code lengths exceed a few hundred lines or when a project is being developed by a team.

In the last chapter we referred to the need to link modules together in order to build up large programs. What form should should such modules take? In order to answer this question we will look at the use of program structures designed to facilitate this modular approach and the instructions associated with it.

After completing this chapter you will:

- *Appreciate the need for modular programming.*
- *Have an understanding of the structure of a stack and its use in the call–return subroutine mechanism.*
- *Understand the terms nested and recursive subroutine.*
- *Know how to use the* movem *instruction to push and pull data on to and out of the stack.*
- *Understand how parameters can be passed to a subroutine, by copy or reference, and altered or returned to the caller.*
- *Be able to write a subroutine having a minimal impact on its environment.*

Take a look at the inside of your personal computer. It will probably look something like the photograph in Fig. 8.1, with a motherboard hosting the MPU, assorted memory and other support circuitry, and a variable number of expansion sockets. Into this will be plugged a disk controller card and a video card. There may be others, such as a soundboard or modem. Each of these plug-in cards has a distinct and separate logical task and they interact via the services supplied by the main board — the motherboard.

There are many advantages to this **modular** construction.

- Flexibility; that is it is relatively easy to upgrade or reconfigure by adding or replacing plug-in cards.

Figure 8.1 *Modular hardware implementing a PC.*

- Can reuse from previous systems.
- Can buy in standard boards or design specialist boards in-house.
- Easy to maintain.

Of course there are a few disadvantages. A fully integrated mother-board is smaller and potentially cheaper than an equivalent mother/daughterboard configuration. It is also likely to be more reliable, as input and output signals do not have to traverse sockets/plugs. However, when they do occur, faults are often more difficult to track down and rectify.

Modular programming uses the same principle to construct "software circuits", i.e. programs. A formal definition of modular programming[1] is:

An approach to programming in which separate logical tasks are programmed separately and joined later.

Thus to write a program in a modular fashion we need to decompose the specification into a number of stand-alone routines, each implementing a well-defined task. Such a module should be relatively short, be well documented and easy for a human, not necessarily the original programmer, to understand.

---

[1] From *Chambers Science and Technology Dictionary*, Cambridge University Press, 1988.

The advantages of a modular program are similar to those for modular hardware, but even more compelling:

- Each module can be tested, debugged and maintained on a stand-alone basis. This makes for overall reliability.
- Can be reused from previous projects or bought in from outside.
- Easier to update by changing modules.

Deciding how to segment a program into individual stand-alone tasks is where the real expertise lies. The actual coding of such tasks as sub-programs is no different than the examples we have given in previous chapters, such as that shown in Program 7.3 on page 122. There are a few additional instructions associated with such sub-programs, and these are listed in Table 8.1. We will look at these and some useful techniques in contructing software in the remainder of the chapter.

Operation	Mnemonic	Description
Call		Transfer to subroutine
Jump to subroutine	jsr ea	Push PC on to stack, PC <- <ea>
Branch to subroutine	bsr[1] offset	Push PC on to stack, PC <- PC+sex|offset
Return		Transfer back to caller
from subroutine	rts	Pull original PC back from Stack
Push/Pull		Maintain a frame for local variables
regs to memory	movem[2] $\sum R_n$,ea	(-ea) <- $\sum R_n$
memory to regs	movem[2] ea,$\sum R_n$	$\sum R_n$ <- (ea+)

Note 1: Available in signed eight-bit (+127, −128) and 16-bit offset (+32,767, −32, 768) varieties. Most assemblers can chose the appropriate versions automatically. The 68020+ processors have a full 32-bit offset Branch capability.
Note 2: Only available in .w and .l sizes.

Table 8.1 *Subroutine instructions.*

Program modules at assembly level are universally known as **subroutines**, as they are in some high-level languages such as FORTRAN and BASIC.[2] Subroutines are the analog of hardware plug-in cards.

Consider the situation where a 1 second delay task is to be implemented. This may be needed to alert an aircraft pilot to look at the control panel warning lights for various scenarios (such as low fuel or overheating) by sounding a buzzer for a short time. In a modular program, this delay would be implemented by coding a 1 s subroutine which would be *called* by the main program as necessary. This is represented diagrammatically in Fig. 8.2.

---

[2]Other high-level languages use the terms function (**C** and Pascal) or procedure (Pascal).

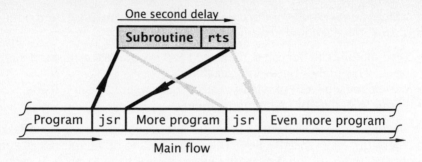

Figure 8.2 *Subroutine calling.*

In essence, calling up a subroutine involves nothing more than placing the address of the first instruction in the Program Counter (PC), that is doing a jump. Thus, if our delay subroutine were located at 00600*h*, then jmp 0600h would seem to do the trick. Of course, as we noted in the last chapter, the programmer should label the entry point, and assuming this has been done, as in Program 8.1, then we have jmp DELAY_1_S.

The problem really is how to get back again! Somehow the MPU has to remember from where in the caller program the subroutine was entered so that it can return to the *next* instruction in the caller sequence. This can be seen in the diagram, where the jumping-off point can be from *anywhere* in the main program, or indeed from another subroutine — the latter process is called **nesting**; see Fig. 8.4.

One possibility is to place this address in a designated Address register or memory location prior to jumping off. This can then be moved back into the PC at the end of the subroutine as the return mechanism. This approach breaks down whenever one subroutine wishes to call another. Then the secondary subroutine will overwrite the return address of the first, and the main program can never be regained. To get around this problem, more than one register or memory location could be used to hold a stack of return addresses. This **last-in first-out stack** structure is shown in Fig. 8.3(a).

Consider an area of memory set aside by the programmer to store subroutine return addresses. This is called the **stack**. There is nothing special about this RAM except that the programmer must ensure that nothing else is likely to overwrite these memory locations. Also, in the 68000 family of processors, the A7 Address register is set to point to *just above the top of this reserved area*. This address register is given the special name **stack pointer** and the programmer can use the mnemonic sp (see Program 8.1) interchangeably with a7 as desired. In the diagram I have arbitrarily allocated RAM from 0FFFF*h* downwards as the stack. Thus the instruction:

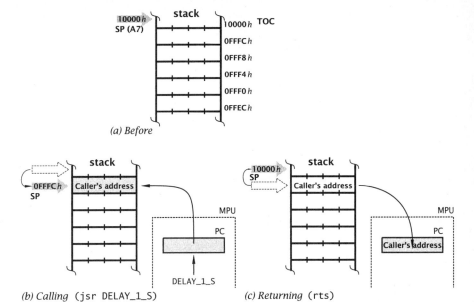

Figure 8.3 *Using a stack of memory long-words to store return addresses.*

```
movea.l   #10000h,a7    ; Point to top of stack +1
```

or

```
movea.l   #10000h,sp    ; Point to top of stack +1
```

will be placed somewhere near the beginning of the main program. *Under no circumstances should the state of the Stack Pointer be odd* or a double-bus error will occur (see page 154).

With the stack set up as shown in Fig. 8.3(a),[3] the subroutine can be called using the special Jump instruction jsr (Jump to SubRoutine).[4] This instruction automatically moves the Stack Pointer down and then copies the address of the *next* instruction in the caller program into the stack. This process is called **pushing**. Control is transferred to the subroutine in the same way as an ordinary jmp, that is by copying the destination address into the PC. As addresses are four bytes long, the RAM is shown organized as a stack of long-words for clarity, and A7 will decrement by 4 during this push.

---

[3] You would normally only set up the User Stack Pointer this way when in the User state. The Supervisor Stack Pointer is automatically initialized on reset, as described in Fig. 9.2 on page 146. However, it can subsequently be altered when in the Supervisor state in this manner. The User Stack Pointer can also be altered remotely from the Supervisor state by using the privileged instruction move #KK,usp.

[4] bsr can be used if the modules are no more than ±32 Kbyte away and in the same file.

At the end of the subroutine the last instruction should be rts (ReTurn from Subroutine). This reverses the push action of jsr and **pulls** the return address back from the stack into the PC. The Stack Pointer is moved back up to the previous position automatically.

The beauty of the stack mechanism is its handling of nested subroutines. Consider the situation in Fig. 8.4 where the main program calls the first-level subroutine SR1 which in turn calls the second-level subroutine SR2. In order eventually to get back to the main program, the outward progression sequence must be exactly matched by the inward path. This pattern is matched by the last-in first-out structure of the stack mechanism, which can handle any arbitrary nesting sequence to any depth (within reason) automatically. It can even handle the (painful) situation where a subroutine calls itself! Such a subroutine is known as **recursive**. As we shall see in the next chapter, the stack mechanism is used to handle interrupts and other exceptional circumstances. The technique is so useful that virtually all MPUs support subroutines in this manner.[5]

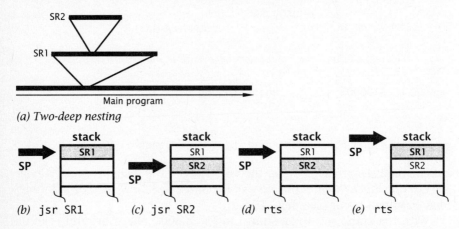

(a) Two-deep nesting

(b) jsr SR1   *(c)* jsr SR2   *(d)* rts   *(e)* rts

Figure 8.4 *Nested subroutines.*

If you are confused, then think of the stack mechanism as your diary, with the Stack Pointer as the bookmark. Every time you wish to use your diary to write down information, open it at the bookmark, which is set at your last entry, advance it one page (to the next clean page), write down your entry (the return address) and close it. Push data like this as many times as is necessary. Any time you wish to recall the entry, open the diary at the bookmark, note your posting, move the bookmark back one page and close it. Pull data out as many times as is necessary. You can intermingle pushes and pulls in any sequence. This is the last-in first-out structure.

---

[5]Some decrement the SP *after* pushing.

As we observed in Chapter 4 on page 67, the 68000 family actually has two A7s, designated A7 in the Supervisor state and A7' in the User state. This means there are two Stack Pointers, respectively designated SSP (System Stack Pointer) and USP (User Stack Pointer). Thus the programmer can keep two distinct stacks, with one allocated to each state. This helps to keep an operating system running in the Supervisor state from being corrupted by an application program running in the User state.

Once a stack has been set up, from the programmer's perspective the following points are relevant:

- The subroutine should be called using the jsr (or bsr) instruction.
- The entry point to a subroutine should be labelled, and this label is then the name of that subroutine.
- The exit point from the subroutine should be the instruction rts. As a matter of style there should only be one way out (and one way in) from a subroutine.

As an example, let us code the 1 second delay subroutine. Creating a delay in software is simply a matter of doing nothing for the appropriate duration. In Program 8.1 I have used a loop to count down from a constant n to zero. In order to calculate the value of n we need to know the processor's clock speed. Details of the number of clock cycles for each instruction/address mode combination, both for the eight-bit and 16-bit Data bus configurations (see Chapter 11) will normally be given in the processor's data sheet (see the associated Web site for this book as outlined in the Preface). If the clock is, say, 8 MHz, then each cycle takes $\frac{1}{8}\,\mu$s.

Program 8.1 *A 1 second delay subroutine.*

```
; **********************************************************************
; * FUNCTION: Delays by one second at 8 MHz                          *
; * ENTRY    : None                                                  *
; * EXIT     : D0.L = 0                                              *
; **********************************************************************
            .define N=444442
DELAY_1_S:  move.l  #N,d0       ; The start value,   12~
D_LOOP:     subq.l  #1,d0       ; Decrement,         8*N~
            bne     D_LOOP      ; to zero,           10*N~
            rts                 ; and exit,          16~
```

Each instruction in Program 8.1 is commented with the number of cycles needed (in the 16-bit Data bus mode) with K~ denoting K cycles, for a 16-bit Data bus. The majority of the time is spent executing the two instructions in the loop subq:bne, which execute a total of n times. Given that the original jsr takes 20~, then the total delay is:

Delay = (20(jsr) + 12(move) + 8N(subq) + 10N(bne) + 16(rts)) cycles

Substituting Delay for 10^6 ($10^6 \mu s$ is 1 second) and $\frac{1}{8}$ for cycles gives:

$$
\begin{aligned}
10^6 &= (20 + 12 + 16 + N \times (8 + 10))\tfrac{1}{8} \\
8 \times 10^6 &= 18N + 48 \\
18N &= 8 \times 10^6 - 48 \\
N &= 7,999,952 \div 18 \\
N &\approx 444,442
\end{aligned}
$$

Obviously instructions outside the loop contribute very little to the overall delay in this case as N is so large and they can be ignored.[6] However, for short times the sandwich instruction delays should not be omitted from the calculation (see Program 8.5).

Notice the comment box at the head of the program. It is good practice to document your subroutine by giving a short description of what data is present at entry, at exit and any working registers or other location altered by the software. Where relevant an example should be given.

Most subroutines alter their environment to some extent. By environment is meant the state of the working registers, memory locations and flags. In our example, the value of D0.L will be changed to zero on exit. Although this is documented in the header comment box, the less a subroutine disturbs its environment the easier it is to use and the scope for error is correspondingly reduced.

Program 8.2 *A transparent 1 second delay subroutine.*

```
;********************************************************************
; * FUNCTION: Delays by one second at 8 MHz                       *
; * ENTRY    : None                                               *
; * EXIT     : None                                               *
;********************************************************************
              .define N=444440
DELAY_1_S:    move.l   d0,-(sp)   ; Save the working register, 14~
              move.l   #N,d0      ; The start value,          12~
D_LOOP:       subq.l   #1,d0      ; Decrement,                12*N~
              bne      D_LOOP     ; to zero,                  10*N~
              move.l   (sp)+,d0   ; Restore the original value,12~
              rts                 ; and exit,                 16~
```

Program 8.2 is a **transparent** version of our original program where D0.L is pushed into the stack on entry and pulled back on exit. The instruction:

---

[6]The resulting factor of 6 parts in a million is rather better than the typical crystal tolerance of ±100 parts in a million!

```
move.l   d0,-(sp)   ; Push D0.L into the stack
```

or the equivalent

```
move.l   d0,-(a7)   ; Push D0.L into the stack
```

copies the original state of D0.L into memory to where the pre-decrement-ed A7 (that is the Stack Pointer) points, using the Address Register Indirect with Pre-Decrement address mode.

On exit, just *before* the `rts` pops the return address back out of the stack, the inverse pull operation:

```
move.l   (sp)+,d0   ; Pull the original value of D0.L back out
```

restores the original value of D0.L. By post-incrementing A7 (using the Address Register Indirect with Post-Increment address mode), the Stack Pointer is moved back to point to this return address. *It is critically important that the Stack Pointer should be balanced in this way so that the return address can be picked up on exit.* If the number of pushes does not equal the number of pulls, then garbage will be placed in the PC by `rts` and the system will die. This most often happens if the program is such that there are several pathways to the exit point, or even several exit points, and one of these omits a balancing pull. The same phenomenon can happen if there are several entry points. Thus good programming structure dictates that there should be only one way into and one way out of a subroutine.

Our delay program is an example of a double-void subroutine, in that no parameters (cf. signals in the hardware analog) are sent to it and nothing is returned — just the side effect of a delay.

A slightly more exciting version of our subroutine is given in Program 8.3. Here the caller determines the number of delay seconds K

Program 8.3 *Delaying for K seconds.*

```
;**********************************************************************
; * FUNCTION: Delays by K seconds at 8 MHz                          *
; * ENTRY    : K in D7.L                                            *
; * EXIT     : None                                                 *
; **********************************************************************
;
            .define N=444440
DELAY_K_S:  movem.l d0/d7,-(sp) ; Save the environment,     8+2*8~
DELAY_1_S:  move.l  #N,d0       ; The 1s start value,       12*K~
D_LOOP:     subq.l  #1,d0       ; Decrement,                12*N*K~
            bne     D_LOOP      ; to zero,                  10*N*K~
            subq.l  #1,d7       ; Decrement K,              12*K~
            bne     DELAY_1_S   ; and repeat until zero,    10*K~
            movem.l (sp)+,d0/d7 ; Restore the environment,  12+2*8~
            rts                 ; and exit,                 16~
```

by 'sending' a parameter via D7.L. Thus to call up a 1 minute delay, the caller will use the sequence:[7]

```
move.l  #60,d7   ; Sixty seconds in a minute = K
jsr     DELAY_K_S ; Go to it!
```

The actual routine itself is similar to the previous program, but each time the second is counted out, K in D7.L is decremented. Thus the total delay is $K \times 1$ s.[8]

In order to make the subroutine transparent, two Data registers have to be saved: D0.L and D7.L. It would of course be possible to use two separate pushes and two individual pulls in the manner of Program 8.2. However, if there are many registers to be saved, in the worst case all 16 of them, then this is rather inefficient.

To cope with this situation movem (MOVE Multiple registers) can push or pull any combination of Data and Address registers in a single instruction. Thus, to push D0, D3...D6, A0 and A3 we have:

```
movem.l  d0/d3-d6/a0/a3,-(sp)   ; Push them out 8+8*7~
```

In general this takes $8 + 8 \times r$ cycles, where r is the number of pushed registers. The order of pushing begins with D7 down to D0 and then A7...A0. So in this case, this would be D6, D5, D4, D3, D0, A3 and A0. The state of the stack during execution of Program 8.3 illustrated in Fig. 8.5 shows this succession, with D7 located first.

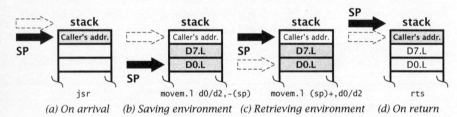

(a) On arrival   (b) Saving environment   (c) Retrieving environment   (d) On return

Figure 8.5 *The state of the stack in subroutine* DELAY_K_S.

Pulling data back to the registers also uses movem, but this time with the Address Register Post-Increment address mode.

```
movem.l  (sp)+,d0/d3-d6/a0/a3          ; Pull them back
```

In order to balance the stack, the same registers *must* be used as in the initial push. However, the assembler does not mind what order the programmer specifies, thus:

---

[7]What is the value of K that gives the longest delay (think carefully) and what is this delay?

[8]Ignoring the small fixed overheads.

```
movem.l   (sp)+,a0/d0/a3/d3-d5/d6      ; Just the same!!!
```

is perfectly legitimate as movem will enforce its own order.

movem comes only in word and long-word sizes. The former is faster by a factor of $4 \times r$ cycles, but care needs to be taken to ensure that the upper word of a register is never used in the subroutine, so it is safer always to use the .l size. Any of the Address registers can be used with movem and so "private" stacks may be set up and used to store and pass data if desired.

In all our examples we have used Data registers to **pass parameters**. Address registers can also be used to pass addresses of data structures, such as arrays (see Example 8.3). The 68000 family is blessed with a copious amount of registers, which makes this approach easy to use. However, many processors are not similarly well endowed in this area, or the quantity of data may be so large that this is not possible. In such situations, other approaches using external memory must be used.

One possibility is to use a fixed area of RAM as a passing ground (sometimes called a heap), where data can be copied for transmission. This can also be used as a working area where intermediate data generated by the subroutine can be temporarily stored. The problem here is that if all subroutines share the same block, then unintended interactions can occur. This is contrary to our stipulation that subroutines should be stand-alone with a minimal interaction with the general environment.

To avoid such interaction, each subroutine could be given its own private block of RAM, from which other software is banned. If there are many subroutines, then this technique is rather extravagant in memory usage.

A better approach is to use the stack to pass data to and fro, which can be accessed using Push and Pull operations. Furthermore, once in a subroutine, the Stack Pointer can be moved down to open a "hole" (known as a frame) in memory for local storage. On exit this frame can be closed up, and this conforms to the privacy stipulation. The 68000 family has specific instructions (link and unlk) to open and close frames. This makes this processor efficient when executing code sourced from a high-level language such as **C** which tends to use the stack for this purpose very extensively (see page 169). We will briefly return to this topic in Chapter 10, but for now we will simply use registers as our work area and to communicate with the caller.

The previous example was still void in that no data was returned to the caller on exit. For our next example we will code a subroutine that will evaluate the square root of an integer n passed to the subroutine in D0.L which is returned in D7.W.

The crudest way of doing this is to try every possible integer k from 1 upwards, generating k^2 by multiplication and checking that the outcome is no more than n. A slightly more sophisticated approach is based on the relationship:

$$k^2 = \sum_{i=0}^{k} (2 \times i) + 1$$

On this basis a possible structure for this function is:

1. Zero the loop count k
2. Set variable i to 1
3. DO forever:
   - Take i from *number*
   - IF the outcome is under zero THEN BREAK out
   - ELSE add 2 to i
   - Increment the loop count k
   - REPEAT loop
4. RETURN loop count k as $\sqrt{number}$

That is sequentially subtract the series 1,3,5,7,9,11...from *number* until underflow occurs; with the tally of successful passes being the square root. An example giving $\sqrt{65} = 8$ is given in Fig. 8.6(a) using this series approach. A flowchart visualizing the task list is also given in Fig. 8.6(b).

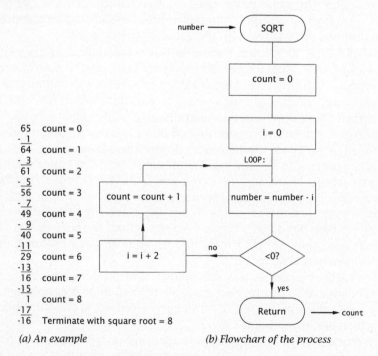

(a) An example   (b) Flowchart of the process

Figure 8.6 *Finding the square root of an integer.*

The software listed in Program 8.4 closely tracks the flowchart. D2.L is used as a working register to hold the 'magic' number i (which is incremented by 2 in line 14) and is saved together with D0.L which holds *number*, by the movem of line 9, and retrieved in line 17.

Program 8.4 *Coding the square root subroutine.*

```
        .processor m68000
;
; ****************************************************************
; * FUNCTION: Evaluates the square root of an integer number    *
; * EXAMPLE : 65 on entry returns 8                             *
; * ENTRY   : number is passed in D0.L                          *
; * EXIT    : Root is returned in D7.W                          *
; * EXIT    : No other register is altered                      *
; ****************************************************************
SQRT:   movem.l  d0/d2,-(sp) ; Protect the environment
        clr.w    d7          ; count = 0000
        moveq    #1,d2       ; i = 1
S_LOOP: subq.l   d2,d0       ; number = number - i
        blo      S_EXIT      ; Breakout if underflow
        addq.l   #2,d2       ; ELSE i = i + 2
        addq.w   #1,d7       ; count = count + 1
        bra      S_LOOP      ; and repeat
S_EXIT: movem.l  (sp)+,d0/d2 ; Retrieve the environment
        rts                  ; Return with root = count in D7.W
        .end
```

The core of the program is unexceptional. Notice how the blo instruction — which is the same as bcs — is used after the $number - i$ operation to detect underflow to below zero (which sets the Carry flag) and exit the loop.

Data register D7.W is used as a straight counter to indicate the number of successful subtractions, and as such gives the answer ready to return to the caller. The largest possible outcome is $\sqrt{4,294,967,295} = 65,535$, which can just be accommodated in a word-sized register. See also self-assessment questions 8.3 and 8.4.

Incidentally, it really is not necessary to keep a count of the number of successful subtractions as $i = (2 \times count) + 1$. Thus the square root can be deduced by keeping i in D7.L and on exit shifting right once. This divides by 2 and by throwing away the 1 that pops out into the carry, effectively predecrements by 1 (i is always odd and so its least significant bit is always 1). Try coding this alternative arrangement.

Examples

Example 8.1

Write a subroutine to give a fixed $208\,\mu s$ delay. Assume a $10\,$MHz processor clock rate.

Solution

The solution shown in Program 8.5 is similar to that in Program 8.2, but as the delay is so short, the surrounding instructions and jsr need to be accounted for. In particular the execution time of the Conditional Branch instruction is 10˜ when taken and 8˜ the one time it is not. The much shorter delay constant N means that word-sized arithmetic can be used, and this improves the subroutine's time resolution. The delay calculation is:

$$\text{Total delay is } 20 + 8 + 8 + 8 + 16 + 4N + 10(N - 1) + 8$$

$$\frac{68 + 4N + 10N - 10}{10} = 208\,\mu s$$

$$58 + 14N = 2080$$

$$14N = 2022$$

$$N \approx 144$$

Program 8.5 *A transparent 208 μs delay subroutine.*

```
;*****************************************************************
; * FUNCTION: Delays by 208 microseconds at 10 MHz             *
; * ENTRY    : None                                            *
; * EXIT     : None                                            *
; *****************************************************************
              .define N=144
DELAY_208_US: move.w  d0,-(sp)    ; Save the working register, 8˜
              move.w  #N,d0       ; The start value,            8˜
D_208_LOOP:   subq.w  #1,d0       ; Decrement,               4*N˜
              bne     D_208_LOOP  ; to zero,         (N-1)*10 + 8˜
              move.w  (sp)+,d0    ; Restore the original value,8˜
              rts                 ; and exit,                  16˜
```

Example 8.2

Many digital electronic displays are based on a selective activation of seven segments[9] in the manner shown in Fig. 8.7. Write a transparent

---

[9] Just look at your digital watch.

subroutine that will accept a four-bit binary code (BCD) $0000 - 1001b$ in D0.B and exit with the listed seven-segment code. Interface details for seven-segment displays are given in Fig. 13.5 on page 218.

11000000 11111001 10100100 10110000 10011001 10010010 10000010 11111000 10000000 10010000

Figure 8.7 *The seven-segment BCD font.*

Solution

The easiest way of implementing this task is to store the ten seven-segment codes as a look-up table, in the manner of the factorial generator of Program 7.3 on page 122. In this case, the table comprises ten bytes, so the `.byte` directive is used in Program 8.6 following the executable code. As the table has an even byte length, it is not necessary to follow the table with the `.even` directive to even out the Program Counter.

The executable core of the program follows the normal look-up table extraction technique, using the Address Register with Index address mode. The A0 register is pointed to the bottom of the table in line 9 and the data in D0.L used as the Index register to point to

Program 8.6 *The seven-segment decoder.*

```
;   *****************************************************************
;   * FUNCTION: Converts from BCD binary to BCD active-low code    *
;   * FUNCTION: Seven-segment code                                 *
;   * ENTRY    : Binary in D0.B, Table of ten 7-segments following *
;   * EXIT     : 7-segment code in D7.B; other registers unchanged *
;   *****************************************************************
SVN_SEG: movem.l   d0/a0,-(sp)     ; Save used registers in stack
         and.l     #0Fh,d0         ; Clear all upper bits in D0
         movea.l   #TABLE,a0       ; Point A0 to table below
         move.b    0(a0,d0.l),d7   ; Copy entry at TABLE+n to D7.B
         movem.l   (sp)+,d0/a0     ; Restore registers
         rts                       ; Return with the goodies in D7

; This is the table of seven-segment codes
TABLE:    .byte 11000000b, 11111001b, 10100100b, 10110000b,
                10011001b, 10010010b, 10000010b, 11111000b,
                10000000b, 10010000b
```

element n in line 10. To facilitate this, all upper bits in D0.L are cleared in line 8. Both registers are saved and retrieved using a movem in the normal way to make the subroutine transparent.

Example 8.3
One way of filtering a sequence of sampled data is to apply the relationship:

$$next\_value = 0.9 \times last\_value + 0.1 \times new\_value$$

Design a subroutine that will process an array of 50 data points generating a new word array with an equivalent precision of two decimal points.

Solution
Unlike previous examples where data were *copied* into Data registers for transmission to the subroutine, which returned a processed version, in this instance pointers to the *original* data in memory are passed. Original data in memory can be *referenced* by Address registers in this manner in order to alter or create data structures directly in memory and to save the burden of copying large quantities of data. Using these pointers, each array is walked through for a count of 50, as listed in Program 8.7.

In order to work in two-decimal-place precision, each data byte is multiplied by ten and the weighting factors of 9 and 1 are used

---

Program 8.7 *Filtering an array.*

```
; ******************************************************************
; * FUNCTION: Generates a 50-point filtered data array            *
; * ENTRY   : A0 points to raw data, A1 to filtered arrays        *
; * EXIT    : No change in registers                              *
; ******************************************************************
FILTER:  movem.l a0/a1/d0/d2/d7,-(sp) ; Save environment
         clr.w   d2                   ; Initial last_value = 00
         moveq   #50,d7               ; Use D7 as the data count
F_LOOP:  clr.w   d0                   ; Get data[n], expanded
         move.b  (a0)+,d0             ; byte to word size
         mulu    #10,d0               ; Work in x100 form
         mulu    #9,d2                ; 9 times last_value
         add.w   d0,d2                ; plus once new_value
         move.w  d2,(a1)+             ; Put this new value away
         subq.b  #1,d7                ; One more time?
         bne     F_LOOP               ; IF yes THEN go again
         movem.l (sp)+,d0/d2/d7/a0/a1 ; Retrieve environment
         rts
```

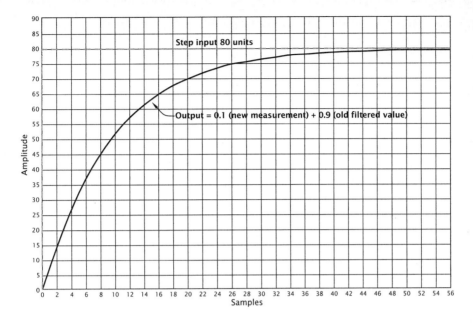

Figure 8.8 *Showing the step response of the filter.*

in place of 0.9 and 0.1. This gives a series of word-sized $\times 100$ outcomes; that is Array2[] is to a precision of two decimal places. In Line 14 again the Address register Indirect with Post Increment address mode is used to put these word-sized data away in memory. As the Move instruction is word-sized the step will be automatically in twos.

A typical response of the filter is shown in Fig. 8.8. Here a 80-unit step (all elements of Array1[] are 80 or 50h) is processed giving the output Array2[] shown. This step response looks suspiciously like the exponential response generated by a first-order capacitor–resistor network to a step input, of time constant of around 9 samples. This response can be altered by changing the proportionality of the two weighting factors.

Self-assessment questions

8.1 A frequent mistake made by students in code such as Program 8.1, is to write bne DELAY_1_S. What would happen in this situation?

8.2 Alter Program 8.2 to give a variable delay of $\frac{1}{n}$ s, where n is a parameter passed in D1.L.

8.3 One major flaw in the square root algorithm of Fig. 8.6 is that the outcome will not be to the nearest integer; for example $\sqrt{80} = 8$, whereas an outcome of 9 might be considered more accurate. One way round this would be to multiply the number by 4 (shift left twice). Taking the square root of this $\sqrt{4 \times number} = 2\sqrt{number}$ gives an outcome of twice the desired value. Subsequently dividing by 2 and adding one if the Carry bit is 1 (i.e. $\frac{1}{2}$) rounds to the nearest integer. Show how this could be coded and try it out for 80.

8.4 Modify the square root program to give a resolution of two decimal places.

8.5 Using the routine of Program 6.4 on page 108, write a subroutine to update a pseudo-random number located in RAM at a location which is pointed to by A0 on entry, with the next in the sequence.

8.6 Modify the your solution to the previous problem to return a random number in D7.B between 1 and 6, for a game of dice.

8.7 Show how you could use, say, A6 to create a private stack to save and/or pass parameters for a subroutine.

CHAPTER 9

Exceptions

Like all MPUs, the Motorola 68000 series has to be prepared to deal with a range of events that disrupt its smooth running. At the very least, on reset a processor must be able to get (vector) to the first instruction of the program. One way of tackling this is to restrict the program to beginning always at one "magic" starting address. This is rather restrictive, and in any case would not readily deal with the host of other exceptional events that can occur. The 68000 family handle such events by cordoning off the first 1024 bytes in this memory map, that is 000000 – 0003FFh to store 256 addresses which point to service routines (handlers) dealing with the various exceptional events. This address page is sacred and should normally not be used for any other purposes. Outside this 1 Kbyte **vector table**, the 68000 family allows the programmer to set up structures and locate programs anywhere. Thus in Chapter 7 programs began at 000400h, just after this vector table.

In this chapter we will be examining exception handling via the vector table for a range of events, originating both externally and internally. We will here restrict our coverage of external hardware requirements to a minimum, leaving circuit details until Chapter 14.

After reading this chapter you will:

- *Appreciate the concept of a ROM-based vector table as a jumping-off point to the various service routines.*
- *Follow the sequence of events occurring on reset.*
- *Understand the need for an interrupt handling provision and appreciate the difference in philosophy in interacting with external peripherals using a polling technique against an interrupt-driven approach.*
- *Be able to follow the sequence of events when a 68000 MPU recognizes an interrupt request.*
- *Understand how the level of a request (1–7) relates to the I2 I1 I0 bits in the Status register.*
- *Understand how the level request autovectors to the interrupt service routine.*
- *Be able to write a simple interrupt service routine.*

- *Be able to distinguish between the various hardware and software exceptions listed in the Vector table.*

What is an **exceptional** event? Generally these are happenings which butt into the normal execution of the program, frequently (but not always) in an unpredictable manner. These may arise from:

- External events, such as a reset request by the tame human operator or an interrupt request from outside hardware.
- Internal errors, for example an attempt to divide by zero or execute an undefined op-code (illegal instruction).
- Certain instructions, known as Traps.

The complete 256-vector address exception table is shown in Fig. 9.1. Rather than go through each one in turn by address, we will order our notes according to our tripart classification. In preparation for our exposition, for future reference we list here in Table 9.1 the few instructions that relate to exception processing.

Operation	Mnemonic	Description
ReTurn		Switch back to background
from Exception[1]	rte	Pulls context back from *Supervisor* stack
Synchronize		Halt until interrupt
stop[1]	stop #kk$_{16}$	(SR) <- #kk and wait for interrupt
Trap		Software-initiated interrupt-like sequence
CHecK Bounds	chk ea,dn	IF 0 > dn.w > (ea)[2] THEN exception via Vector 6
ILLEGAL Instruction	illegal	Exception via Vector 4
TRAP	trap #kk$_4$	Sixteen software interrupts via Vector 32 + #kk
TRAP on oVerflow	trapv	IF V = 1 THEN exception via Vector 7

Note 1: Privileged instructions.
Note 2: **N** flag set if dn < 0 ; cleared if dn > (ea) ELSE undefined

Table 9.1 *Exception-related instructions.*

Externally originated exceptions

The majority of vector addresses are reserved in the table for requests for exceptional service arising from hardware origins outside the processor and not under its control. The prime example of a hardware-originated exception is the chain of events that occurs when the 68000's $\overline{\text{Reset}}$ pin goes low — see also page 179. Virtually all MPUs adopt the procedure that when the reset signal is removed the processor goes to a fixed location, usually zero, and there it finds the start address of the program.[1] This is then copied into the Program Counter and away it goes.

---

[1]Variations on this theme are to use the top of the memory map or/and put a jmp <ea> instruction as the vector.

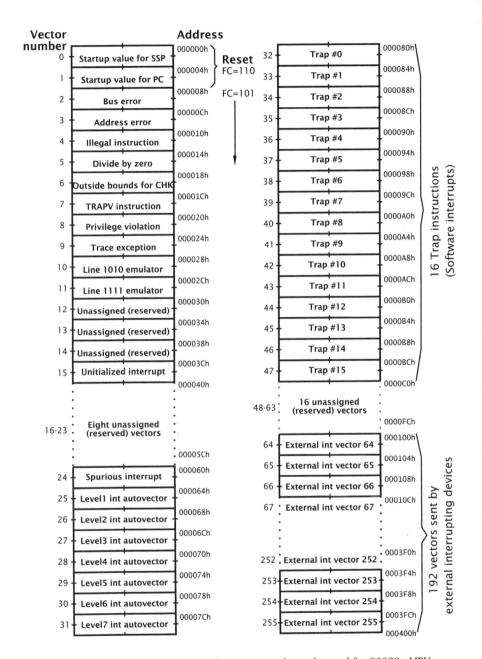

Figure 9.1 *The complete vector table. Unassigned may be used for 68020+ MPUs.*

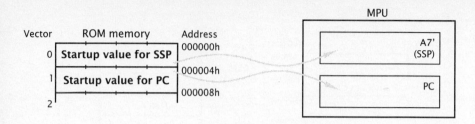

Figure 9.2 *Resetting the 68000 processor.*

The 68000 MPU has a slightly more sophisticated approach, as illustrated in Fig. 9.2. Here the lowest vector (at $000000:1:2:3h$) holds the initial value of the Supervisor Stack Pointer (SSP) and the second vector (at $000004:5:6:7h$) the address of the first instruction of the program to be executed on startup; that is the initial value of the Program Counter (PC). These Reset vectors must be in situ *before* the processor does anything and therefore at the very least this part of the vector table *must* be in ROM.[2] The State flag (**S**) in the Status register is automatically set to 1 on reset, so the MPU always begins executing in the Supervisor state with its stack set up. If the programmer desires, operations can be subsequently moved to the User state (by clearing the **S** bit, see page 99), but the response of any hardware exception is always to move the processor *back* to this Supervisor state. In a larger system this is where the operating system (OS) will be located; thus in such a setup, servicing an exceptional event is seen as being an OS's responsibility.

Consider the situation in an MPU-based monitoring system in a nuclear power plant. Many hundreds of parameters will be monitored (polled) in a repetitive and systematic manner. Supposing there is a sudden loss of coolant pressure in Reactor 3. It may well be that this pressure has just been checked and the next reading is not due for 5 minutes. A lot can happen in 5 minutes! In the situation where external processes happen in their own good time and are in no way synchronized to the MPU's internal processes, there has to be some way for certain events to **interrupt** the process and direct it to attend to their immediate need.

Polling a series of outside events is adequate where nothing much happens quickly outside and/or there are few parameters to monitor and little processing to do. The possibility of missing anything important can be reduced by increasing the polling rate, but there comes a time when the MPU does little else but read peripheral data. This resource burnout is especially a problem when there are many signals to poll.

---

[2]Generally the whole of the vector table is in ROM, and thus a 68000-based system usually has a ROM at the bottom of its memory map. It is possible to shadow all vectors above 1 in RAM by using appropriate address decoding circuitry, although this is rarely done.

The downside of interrupt-driven real-time monitoring is the need to use external hardware (see Chapter 14) and the greater complexity of the hardware–software interface. If you are confused, consider the telephone system. It would be possible to have a telephone network where the subscriber would pick up the phone every, say, 5 minutes and ask "Is there anyone there?". Apart from the bother (processing overhead) of doing this,[3] the caller may have got fed up and hung up. You could reduce the chance of this happening by increasing the polling rate to, say, once per minute. But you could then end up spending all your time on the phone and, depending on how popular you are, getting only a few hits a day. That is, 99% of your effort is wasted.

This is obviously ridiculous, and in practice an interrupt-driven technique is used so that you only respond when the bell/buzzer sounds. Highly efficient, but at the cost of a lot more complexity for the phone company, as the signalling side of the system can be more complex than the speech side. There is another problem too, in that you (cf. the processor) have no idea when the phone will ring. And it surely will be at the most inconvenient time. Thus you have to (unless you have an iron will) break off what you are doing at the drop of a hat. For example, if you happen to be in the middle of solving an equation in your head you should save your partial results before responding, so, when finished, you can return to where you left off.

Keeping this apparent randomness (at least as seen by the MPU) in mind, although the minutiae of the response to an interrupt request vary considerably from processor to processor, the following phases can usually be identified.

1. Finishing the current instruction.

2. Ignoring the request if the appropriate interrupt mask bits (if any) are set.

3. Saving at least the MPU's context; that is the state of the Program Counter (which is needed to get back) and the Status register — which is bound to be altered by the interrupt service routine.

4. Entering the appropriate interrupt service routine.

5. Implementing the defined task.

6. Restoring the processor state and returning to the point in the background program from where control was first transferred.

Thus essentially, signalling an interrupt causes the MPU to drop whatever it is doing, push out its internal *state* into the Supervisor stack and go to a special subroutine known as an **interrupt service routine (ISR)**. This

---

[3]It would of course make it easier just to ignore the phone...!

is just a subroutine entered at the behest of an external (i.e. hardware) signal.

Requests for service by outside agencies are by definition not linked in any way to the MPU's clock cycle. The apparent randomness of such interrupt requests means that the MPU's response to such events must ensure that the interrupted program (the **background program**) is oblivious to the fact that the processor has 'gone away' for a while to service an external request. This means that the interrupt service routine, or **foreground program**, must not affect the state of the internal processor registers in any way, i.e. the environment must be preserved. This is akin to transparency in regular subroutines (see page 134) but even more so, as the settings of the various bits in the Status register must also be preserved. If this were not the case and an interrupt struck between testing an object and the following Branch instruction, then any alteration in a Code Condition flag might give an erroneous outcome. With this in mind, just about all MPUs will automatically save the Code Condition/Status register, in addition to the Program Counter which is normally put away for an ordinary subroutine.[4] Saving the additional 16 internal registers would increase the response time to the interrupt, known as the **latency**. The 68000 MPU has a latency of 44 clock cycles ($5.5\,\mu$s at 8 MHz) in the autovector 16-bit Data bus mode. ISRs are terminated by a ReTurn from Interrupt (`rti`) instruction (`rte` with the 68000), which is similar to `rts` but restoring any additional registers automatically stacked as the MPU's response to the interrupt request.

To illustrate how the 68000 MPU handles an interrupt request, let us take as an example the problem of keeping a clock so that accurate time markers can be attached to events occurring in real time. One approach would be to use a delay loop, as described in Chapter 8, to sound out the seconds — or whatever is the desired resolution. In practice this would be rather useless, as keeping such a clock would be a full-time occupation, with no time left over to do anything else of consequence. This is an ideal application for interrupts, as all that is necessary is to use an external precision oscillator to 'kick' the MPU on each tick. The MPU then updates its time count and goes back to its background task. If the oscillator ticks at 1000 times a second and the update ISR takes, say, $30\,\mu$s, then only 3% of the background processing time is lost.

All MPUs supporting interrupts will have at least one pin through which an external process can request its wish for service. The 68000 MPU has three, labelled $\overline{\text{IPL2}}$ $\overline{\text{IPL1}}$ $\overline{\text{IPL0}}$ (for Interrupt Priority Level). The interrupting device simply places a three-bit active-low code on these pins, signifying the desired level of service, e.g. 010 for 5 (active-low 101). We will look

---

[4]Some MPUs, like the 6800/11, also automatically save all their internal registers on the stack, but this is unusual with newer devices, which have a large complement of registers.

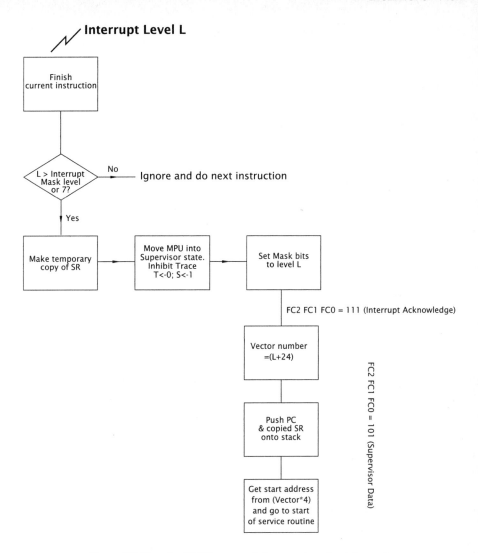

Figure 9.3 *How the 68000 responds to an autovector interrupt.*

at the hardware aspects of all this later in Chapter 14; here we will just observe that it is the responsibility of this external hardware to remove its request before the system returns from the interrupt service routine.

Taking again our example of a 1 ms resolution real-time clock, we assume that the oscillator is connected to $\overline{IPL2}$ $\overline{IPL1}$ $\overline{IPL0}$ in such a way as to request a Level-5 service 1000 times a second (see Fig. 14.2 on page 239). How will the MPU respond?

The 68000 MPU has two ways of dealing with interrupts. The simplest of these, shown in Fig. 9.3, is known as **autovectoring**. Here the MPU goes to a fixed location in the Vector table (000074:5:6:7h is the Level-5 interrupt autovector from Fig. 9.3) to pick up the start address of the appropriate ISR. To force the MPU to follow this procedure, its $\overline{\text{AVEC}}$ pin[5] must be brought low, as shown in Fig. 14.2 on page 239.

Assuming all this hardware is in situ, then this is how the 68000 MPU handles an interrupt request at level n.

1. Check for an interrupt request *between* each instruction's execution.

2. If n is *above* the setting of the three Interrupt mask bits I2 I1 I0 in the Status register (see Fig. 4.4 on page 66) or is Level 7, then commence the sequence of events leading to entry to the ISR itemized:

   • Make a interim copy of the Status register *before* fiddling with any bits.

   • Set the **T** bit to 0 (Trace off) and **S** bit to 1 — move into Supervisor state.

   • Set the mask bits I2 I1 I0 in the Status register to Level n to avoid further interrupts at this or a lower level until return. However, a subsequent request at a higher level can interrupt the ISR.

   • Push the Program Counter (i.e. the return address) and the *copy* of the original Status register on to the Supervisor stack.

   • Go to the address stored in the Vector table as appropriate to the Level n being serviced (at table entry $24 + n$; for example 29 for Level 5). This address is the start point for the ISR.

   • Execute the ISR foreground program.

   • The ISR terminates with an `rte` (ReTurn from Exception) instruction which restores the state of the Status register and Program Counter (the MPU's **context**) to their pre-interrupt values.

3. Proceed to the next instruction in the background software.

If all this seems rather complicated, remember that most of it happens automatically, and from the software point of view an ISR is very like a transparent subroutine but keeping the following points in mind.

• The ISR should be terminated by `rte` instead of `rts`.

• Any Data or Address registers that that are used should be saved at the beginning and restored at the end using the `movem` instruction.

• Parameters cannot be passed to and fro to an ISR, as in a subroutine. Instead global variables (variables in known memory locations) should be used as required.

• ISRs should be as short as possible, to ensure that another external event of the same or lower priority (that is of a masked-out level) will

---

[5] Older versions of the 68000 call this pin $\overline{\text{VPA}}$ (see page 182).

not be missed. This is a problem in a system with many sources of interrupt.

Before writing the ISR for our real-time clock, the interaction between the **Interrupt mask** bits (I2 I1 I0) in the Status register and the interrupt system needs some clarification. When the MPU is reset, the three mask bits (see Fig. 4.4 on page 66) I2 I1 I0 are set to 111. In this state only a Level-7 interrupt request[6] will be serviced. If we wanted to set up the MPU so that, say, a Level-5 request could be acted upon, then these bits need to be changed to 100 (4) or lower. The instruction:

```
andi #11111 100 11111111b,sr
```

will clear I1 I0 and leave I2 unaltered (see pages 89 and 99). The instructions that alter the Status register (move, andi, ori, eori to sr) are privileged, that is are only legal if executed when in the Supervisor state (**S** bit is 1) — see page 67. However, the processor always resets to this state. If the programmer subsequently moves the MPU to the User state (the **S** bit to 0), then the processor will automatically move into the Supervisor state (**S** → 1) when responding to an interrupt. As the Status register is restored at the ISR's terminating rte, then the processor will return automatically to whatever state the background program was in.

Another way of changing the Mask bits is to use the stop instruction. This instruction, which is also privileged, moves its immediate operand into the Status register and advances its Program Counter to point to the next instruction. The processor then halts. For example:

```
stop #00100 011 00000000b ; Trace off, Supervisor state, Mask 3
```

will halt the processor until an interrupt occurs *above* Level 3. The MPU then vectors to the appropriate ISR. Interrupts at or below this level are ignored.

Now to our example. We wish to keep a tally of 1 ms "ticks" since reset. Using a 1 kHz oscillator to interrupt the MPU periodically at Level 5 means that the Level-5 ISR only has to increment the memory location holding the count. Anytime the main background program wishes to know the time, all it has to do is read the value from this location. In Program 9.1, four bytes are set aside in line 3 in RAM memory (program section _data — see page 116) for this purpose and labelled JIFFY. This long-word is globally known within the file, that is it can be accessed by both foreground and background routines. If it is declared .public (see page 117), then it can be accessed from any file.

Program 9.1 is logically divided into three zones.

---

[6]Sometimes known as a non-maskable interrupt, as it cannot be locked out.

Program 9.1 *Handling the interrupt-driven real-time clock.*

```
        .processor m68000
; This is the global variable holding the count
        .psect  _data
JIFFY:  .double [1]      ; Reserve 1 long-word in RAM called JIFFY

; This is the Vector table
        .psect  _text
VECTOR: .double 10000h ; The initial value of the Supervisor SP
        .double MAIN    ; Start address of the background program
        .double [27]    ; Omit the next 27 vectors
LEV_5:  .double CLOCK   ; Put Level_5 ISR start in here
        .org    VECTOR+0400h
; Now up the first location after the Vector table

; the background program
MAIN:   andi    #0FCFFh,sr  ; Set I2I1I0 to 100 (level 4)
        clr.l   JIFFY       ; Zero time count
M_LOOP: .....   .....       ; Rest of background program
        .....   .....
        bra     M_LOOP      ; is an endless loop

; This is the foreground program
CLOCK:  addq.l  #1,JIFFY    ; One more tick
        rte                 ; Return
        .end
```

The Vector table
The vector table is located in the _text data stream, which we assume will be linked to begin at 00000h. There are only three entries in this table.

- •The initial value of the Supervisor Stack Pointer, which here is set to 10000h[7] using a .double directive at the beginning of the _text section, that is 000000 – 000003h.
- •The start value of the Program Counter, which is the address labelled MAIN, follows at 000004 – 7h.
- •After a gap of 27 long-word addresses (6Ch bytes), the starting address of the Level-5 ISR CLOCK is placed in 000074–7h.

The final line of this phase moves the _text stream on to the first location above the Vector table. Thus the background code begins at 000400h.

Background code
The background program, labelled MAIN, sets the Interrupt mask in the

---

[7]Assuming that there is RAM available from 0FFFFh downwards for use as a stack; see Fig. 15.6 on page 258.

Status register to Level 4, as described, and clears the count. The rest of the program can be anything, provided that these two lines are not executed again. Optionally the background program can now switch to the User state by replacing the first line by:

```
andi    #1101110011111111b,sr   ; Clear S bit & set mask level to 4
```

which also clears the **S** bit.

Foreground program

This routine, labelled CLOCK, is a model of simplicity; all it does is add 1 to the long-word variable JIFFY. As the ISR is only entered once per millisecond, then JIFFY records 1 ms ticks, with an upper limit of $(2^{32} - 1)/1000 \approx 4,294,967$ s. As no internal registers are used in this ISR, then nothing needs to be saved at the beginning and retrieved at the end.

In practice the ISR usually needs to activate external hardware to deactivate the Level-5 request before the final rte exit. Program 14.1 on page 240 shows this addition.

Looking at the exception table of Fig. 9.1 we see that Vectors 15, 24 and 64–255 are also used for interrupts. To illustrate their function we must briefly explain the 68000's alternative to autovectoring, known as **external vectoring**. After the MPU sets its Mask bits to L (see Fig. 9.3) it checks its $\overline{\text{AVEC}}$ pin. If this is low then it continues with its autovector service as recounted. If not, it then checks its $\overline{\text{DTACK}}$ pin (see page 179). If this is low then the external vector process is initiated. Here the MPU goes out to the device that sent the interrupt request in the first place and politely asks it to send a vector number. This external vector number will normally point to somewhere between Vector 64 and 255, the **External Interrupt vectors**. Although flexible, this is a relatively complex hardware process, and usually confined to 68000-family peripheral devices, such as the 68230 Peripheral Interface/Timer (PI/T). This has an internal register that can be set up by software to the appropriate vector number. If this has not been done, then this register points to the **Uninitialized Interrupt vector** when the peripheral chip is reset. The ISR accessed from here can then take the appropriate action.

Besides the three $\overline{\text{IPL2}}$ $\overline{\text{IPL1}}$ $\overline{\text{IPL0}}$ pins, the 68000 has an additional interrupt pin labelled **Bus Error** ($\overline{\textbf{BE}}$). If $\overline{\text{BE}}$ is pulled low the processor will go immediately[8] to the appropriate ISR vector after pushing information on to the Supervisor stack. This **Bus Error vector** is at 0000008-Bh. The Bus Error interrupt is normally used by external circuitry to detect that a malfunction has occurred in the connection between the MPU's buses and its external hardware resources, such as memory, or that the MPU has run 'off the rails' due to noise or a software error — see page 179.

---

[8]Without even waiting for the end of the instruction.

If the $\overline{\text{BE}}$ signal persists when the processor tries to push its state on to the Supervisor state, then this catastrophic failure situation is sensed as a **Double Bus error**. The MPU then halts and brings both its $\overline{\text{Reset}}$ and $\overline{\text{Halt}}$ pins low. A Double Bus error also occurs on reset when the Supervisor Stack Pointer has been set to an odd number[9] in the vector table.

In the situation where a regular interrupt is being processed, if neither $\overline{\text{AVEC}}$ nor $\overline{\text{DTACK}}$ is low, then the MPU tries the $\overline{\text{BE}}$ pin. If this is low then the processor vectors to the ISR pointed to by the **Spurious Interrupt vector** at 00006C–Fh.

Internal errors

Certain dubious events, such as attempting to divide by zero, can initiate a response similar to a hardware interrupt, i.e. is a change to the Supervisor state, pushing the PC and SR (the context) on to the Supervisor stack, and vectoring to an ISR. The **I2 I1 I0** mask bits have no effect. Software-initiated interrupts are sometimes called **traps**, and a list of implicit traps triggered by some internal event supported by the 68000 MPU is:

Address Error, 00000C–Fh
Entered when a word or long-word access to an odd address is attempted.

Illegal Instruction, 000010–3h
Entered if an illegal op-code is encountered, but see Line A and Line F exceptions below.[10]

Divide by Zero, 000014–7h
Entered when the divisor for divu/divs is zero.

Privilege Violation, 000020–3h
Entered when there is an attempt to execute a privileged instruction (e.g. stop) when in the User state.

Trace, 000024–7h
Entered after *each* instruction if the **T** bit is set in the Status register. Used during debugging to monitor the state of the processor if the appropriate Trace ISR is in situ.

Line A Op-Code, 000028–Bh
Entered when the upper four bits of the op-code are 1010b. These op-codes are unused, but this facility provides the means for emulating unimplemented instructions in software.

Line F Op-Code, 00002C–Fh
This trap is entered when the top four bits of the op-code are 1111b. The 68020+ MPUs use these codes for their mathematical co-processor

---

[9]Remember that addresses to word/long-word objects should *never* be odd; thus *no* entry in the vector table should be odd.

[10]There is an instruction illegal which Motorola guarantee will always trigger this trap for *all* 68000+ family members.

instructions, and therefore service routines here can be used to simulate these missing instructions in software.

Traps

The remaining vectors are reserved for instructions that generate an interrupt-like response; that is they move to the Supervisor state, save the PC and SR on the Supervisor stack and vector to a ISR. The 68000 has 17 of these so called **Trap instructions**.

Explaining what these software interrupts do is easier than what use they are. As an example, consider an environment where an application is being written for a specific computer system. This system will have various means of communicating to the world, using typically a keyboard, VDU, serial and parallel ports, interrupts and assorted disk drives. Knowing the characteristics of all these input/output (I/O) devices, the programmer can write a suite of subroutines known as device handlers. Once this has been done, data can be transferred by calling up the appropriate handler. However, a change of environment to a different computer is likely to require a complete rewrite of these handlers.

This approach is often adopted by the designers of special-purpose microprocessor systems, where the hardware structure is usually highly individualistic. Some standardization is possible for mass-produced computing machines, such as engineering workstations and personal computers. These normally come with an **operating system**, which can be thought of as a shell around the applications software shielding the programmer from the realities of the hardware. Typical operating systems are UNIX, MS-DOS and Windows NT. These systems are mainly disk-based, loaded into RAM, but work in tandem with a Basic Input/Output System (BIOS), usually located in ROM. The applications programmer can then call up the appropriate subroutine in the BIOS, to communicate with a peripheral. The BIOS ROM will vary with different machines, but in such a way as to hide the hardware details from the OS. The use of an OS leads to the concept of system-independent (portable) software.

Using a Trap call to communicate with the OS, rather than a subroutine, has the advantage that the address of the procedure need not be explicitly known, as the vector table will be in the BIOS. Hiding explicit details of the BIOS is important for portability. As an example, INT #25 in an MS-DOS environment will enable a Read from a magnetic disk (INT is the 8086 family mnemonic for TRAP). Parameters such as track, sector and drive are placed in registers prior to the Trap. In 68000-family based systems, the OS normally resides in the Supervisor state, completely separated from the application program in the User state memory space.

Sixteen of these instructions — trap #0 to trap #15 — are unconditional and trapv is only implemented if the **V** flag is set at execution time. However, two other instructions function as software interrupts.

The `illegal` instruction will vector via 000010-3 h and the `chk` (CHecK register) instruction vectors via 000018-1Bh if the designated Data register is below zero or above the designated limit.

Examples

Example 9.1
Code an ISR to update a word in RAM with the next in the 16-bit Pseudo-Random Number (PRN) sequence of Fig. 6.5 on page 107 on each interrupt.

Solution
The core of the interrupt handler of Program 9.2 is based on the algorithm coded in Program 6.4 on page 108 and will not be discussed here. This core is sandwiched by pushing and pulling Data registers 7-4 to ensure transparency, and terminated by `rte` which returns the Status register and Program Counter automatically saved prior to entry. The 16-bit word RANDOM is moved in from memory and

Program 9.2 *Updating a PRN on interrupt.*

```
;   ****************************************************************
; * FUNCTION: Generates the next in the 16-bit PRNG sequence    *
; * ENTRY    : A0 points to the PRN in RAM                       *
; * EXIT     : PRN updated, no register altered                 *
;   ****************************************************************
PRNG:    movem.w  d4-d7,-(sp)  ; Save the environment
         move.w   (a0),d7      ; Get existing PRN
         bne      P_CONT       ; IF non-zero THEN continue
         subq.w   #1,d7        ; ELSE make legal PRN
P_CONT:  move.w   d7,d6        ; Copy 1 of PRN
         move.w   d7,d5        ; Copy 2 of PRN
         move.w   d7,d4        ; Copy 3 of PRN
         lsr.w    #2,d6        ; Align bit 2 with bit 0
         rol.w    #1,d5        ; Align bit 15 with bit 0
         rol.w    #5,d5        ; Align bit 11 with bit 0
         eor.w    d7,d6        ; 0 EOR 2
         eor.w    d6,d5        ; (0 EOR 2) EOR 15
         eor.w    d5,d4        ; ((0 EOR 2) EOR 15) EOR 11
         lsr.w    #1,d4        ; Move above into X flag
         roxl.w   #1,d7        ; and into the new PRN
         move.w   d7,(a0)      ; Update PRN
         movem.w  (sp)+,d4-d7  ; Retrieve the environment
         rte                   ; and return
```

checked for zero, the only illegal sequence value. The value zero causes the sequence to lock up, and if so subtracting 1 gives the legitimate value FFFFh. Once in a non-zero state, RANDOM should never return to zero, so this check could be done more efficiently once only at the beginning of the main background routine, which might look something like:

```
           .psect  _data
RANDOM:     .word   [1]        ; Reserve 1 word in the _data stream
           .psect  _text
MAIN:       tst.w   RANDOM     ; Check that RANDOM is non-zero
            bne     MAIN_NEXT  ; IF not THEN OK
            subq.w  #1,RANDOM  ; ELSE set to FFFFh
MAIN_NEXT:  andi    #FCFFh,sr  ; Set to Level 4
            .....   .....
```

Efficiency is improved as the test is not done on each entry to the ISR. However, encapsulating the test within the ISR is more robust in that if, say, due to a software error the variable should ever become zero, then lockup will be avoided.

Example 9.2
A MPU-based system is to be designed to act as a depth sounder for a boat. The MPU is to activate an ultra-sonic sounder as part of the main background routine. When the echo arrives back, the receiver is to interrupt the MPU, which can then determine the time taken.

You can assume that the 1 kHz clock of Program 9.1 is in situ and that the variable JIFFY is zeroed in the main routine when it activates the sounder. The speed of sound in water is 366 meters/second and the distance in meters is to be placed in a global byte variable called DISTANCE.

Solution
Remembering that the total time actually measured is due to the propagation delay between the ship's hull, river bottom and back again (assuming the ship is stationary) the relationship between depth and time in milliseconds is 0.183 meters per milliseconds. On that basis and assuming that the range of the sounder is such that only the lower word of the JIFFY variable need be read, a possible ISR might be that shown in Program 9.3 (see also Program 14.2 on page 242).

There are of course two ISRs in this system. These will be at different levels, and assuming that the 1 ms real-time clock ISR is at Level 5 and Program 9.3 is at Level 4, then the Vector table could be set up something like this:

```
                .psect  _data      ; RAM
JIFFY:  .double [1]        ; Reserve 1 long word for 1ms time count
DEPTH:  .word   [1]        ; and one word for the depth


                .psect  _text
VECTOR: .double 10000h     ; The initial value of the Supervisor SP
        .double MAIN       ; Start address of the background prog
        .double [26]       ; Omit the next 26 vectors
LEV_4:  .double DEPTH_SOUND ; Put Level 4 ISR start address here
LEV_5:  .double CLOCK      ; Put Level 5 ISR start address in here
        .org    VECTOR+0400h ; Now up to 1st byte after table

; This is the background program
; First set I2I1I0 to 011 (Mask 3)
MAIN:   andi    #1111101111111111b,sr
        clr.w   DEPTH      ; Initial value for the depth
        .....   .....      ; Lots of useful things in background
```

Hardware to generate the two distinct interrupts is shown in Fig. 14.3 on page 241.

Program 9.3 *Evaluating the hull–river bottom distance.*

```
;  ****************************************************************
;  * ISR updates distance to river bottom on sounder's return    *
;  * ENTRY: Global word JIFFY is time in ms since pulse is sent  *
;  * EXIT : Global byte DISTANCE in meters                       *
;  ****************************************************************
DEPTH_SOUND: movem.l d0,-(sp)     ; Save the environment
             move.w  JIFFY,d0     ; Read current time
             mulu    #183,d0      ; Multiply by 0.183
             divu    #1000,d0     ; To give meters
             move.b  d0,DISTANCE  ; Update the distance
             movem.l (sp)+,d0     ; Retrieve the environment
             rte
```

The main background program will of course be doing lots of useful things, such as controlling the sounder, showing the depth on seven-segment displays and sounding an alarm if too shallow, say under 5 meters. It may also attempt to correct for the boat's horizontal speed and change of the speed of sound with temperature.

Self-assessment questions

9.1 A certain 68000-based system requires a reference to the time of day in the 24-hour format (HR:MIN:SEC:JIFFY), where each sector is stored as a single byte in memory and JIFFY is the placeholder for tenths of a second. Assuming a 10 Hz oscillator is available as a time base, interrupting at Level 6, write a suitable ISR to code this task, showing the setting up of the Vector table and the reservation of the four time bytes in the _data stream.

9.2 The real-time clock of the previous example is to be used as part of a central heating controller. At 09:00:00:0 hours the pump is to be toggled (hopefully from on to off). One day this has been done, the heating is off and the time is now 09:59:59:9. The main background program reads the hours as 9. Getting interested, it is just going to read the minutes when the Jiffy oscillator 'ticks'. What will happen and how could you avoid this problem?

9.3 The ISR for the 24-hour real-time clock has been modified to use a 250 Hz Jiffy timebase and print out the time once a second, via the system's serial port (see Fig. 13.13 on page 231). The message is 11 characters long and the transmission rate to the printer's buffer is 960 characters per second.

On test the system runs slow by $\approx$ 1%. Why, and what could be done about it?

9.4 A certain data logger measures the current temperature each time it is interrupted. The ISR is to update a byte array of the seven previous readings plus the current one, and to compute their average as a global variable. Assuming the eight readings are also global variables, code a suitable ISR.

You can assume that the current value can be read from an analog to digital converter at 09000h.

CHAPTER 10

High-level language

All the programs we have written in the last seven chapters have been in symbolic assembly language. Whilst assembly-level software is a quantum step up from pure machine-level code (see page 112) nevertheless there is still a one-to-one relationship between machine and assembly-level instructions. This means that the programmer is forced to think in terms of the MPU's internal structure — that is of registers and memory — rather than in terms of the problem algorithm. Although most assemblers have a macro facility, whereby several machine-level instructions can be grouped to form pseudo high-level instructions, this is only tinkering with the difficulty. What is this difficulty with machine-oriented language? In order to improve the effectiveness, quality and reusability of a program, the coding language should be independent of the underlying processor's architecture and should have a syntax more oriented to problem-solving.

We are not going to attempt to teach a high-level language in a single short chapter. However, after completing this chapter you will:

- *Understand the need for a high-level language.*
- *Appreciate the advantages of using a high-level language.*
- *Understand the problems of using a high-level language for embedded MPU and microcontroller applications.*
- *Be able to write a short program in* **C**.

The difficulty in coding large programs in a computer's native language was clearly appreciated within a few years of the introduction of commercial systems. Apart from anything else, computers quickly became obsolete with monotonous regularity, and programs needed to be rewritten for each model introduction. Large applications programs, even at that time, required many thousands of lines of code. Programmers were as rare as hen's teeth and worth their weight in gold. It was quickly appreciated that for computers to be a commercial success, a means had to be found to preserve the investment in scarce programmers' time. In developing a universal language, independent of the host hardware, the opportunity would be taken to allow the programmer to express the code in a more natural syntax related to problem-solving rather than in terms of memory, registers and flags.

Of course there are many different types of problem tasks which have to be coded, so a large number of languages have been developed since.[1] Amongst the first were Fortran (FORmula TRANslation) and COBOL (COmmon Business Oriented Language) in the early 1950s. The former has a syntax that is oriented to scientific problems and the latter to business applications. Despite being around for over 40 years, the inertia of the many millions of lines of code written has made sure that many applications are still written in these antique languages. Other popular languages include Algol (ALGOrithmic Language), BASIC, Pascal, Modula, Ada, **C** and **C++**.

Although writing programs in a high-level language may be easier and more productive for the programmer, the process of translation from the high-level source code to the target machine code is much more complex than the assembly process described in Chapter 7. The translation package for this purpose is called a **compiler** and the process **compilation**.

The complexity and cost of a compiler was acceptable on the relatively powerful and extremely expensive mainframe computers of that time. However, until the mid-1980s the use of high-level languages as source code was virtually unknown for MPU-controlled circuitry. In the last decade the easy availability of relatively powerful and cheap personal computers and workstations, capable of running compilers, together with the growing power of MPU targets and financial importance of this market, is such that the majority of software written for such targets is now in a high-level language.

If you are going to code a task in a high-level language to run in a system with an **embedded** MPU, for example, a washing-machine controller, then the process is roughly as follows.

1. Take the problem specification and break it up into a series of modules, each with a well-defined task and set of input and output data.
2. Devise a coding to implement the task for each module.
3. Create a source file using an editor in the appropriate high-level syntax.
4. Compile the source file to its assembly-level equivalent.
5. Assemble and link to the machine-code file.
6. Download the machine code to the target's program memory.
7. Execute, test and debug.

This is virtually identical to the process outlined in Fig. 7.2 on page 115, but with the extra step of compilation. Some compilers go directly from the source file to the machine-code file; however, the extra flexibility of going through the assembly-level phase, as shown in Fig. 10.1, is nearly universal when embedded MPU circuitry is targeted.

---

[1] A definition of a computer scientist is one who, when presented with a problem to solve, invents a new language instead!

```
while(n>0)
{
    sum = sum + n;
    n--;
}
```

Compile

```
L1:    move.w   d1,d7
       ble      L11
       ext.l    d7
       add.l    d7,d2
       subq.w   #1,d2
       bra      L1
L11:
```

(a) First, compile to assembly-level code.

```
L1:    move.w   d1,d7
       ble      L11
       ext.l    d7
       add.l    d7,d2
       subq.w   #1,d2
       bra      L1
L11:
```

Assemble

```
0011111000000001
0110111100001000
0100100011000111
1101010010000111
0101001101000001
0110000011110100
```

(b) Second, assemble-link to machine code.

Figure 10.1 *Conversion from high-level source code to machine code.*

The choice of a high-level language for embedded targets is crucial. Of major importance is the size of the machine code generated by a high-level language task implementation as compared with the equivalent assembly-level solution. Most embedded MPU circuitry is lean and mean, such as the remote controller for your television. Lean translates to physically small and mean maps to low processing power and memory capacity — and cost! Actually, a **microcontroller** (MCU)[2] is usually at the heart of such products rather than a plain MPU. An MCU is an MPU plus memory and input/output peripherals all on the one chip. Most low-cost MCUs have a low-capability processor with a few hundred bytes of RAM and a few kilobytes of ROM at best. Thus to be of any use the high-level language and the compiler must generate code, that if not as efficient as assembly-level (low-level), at least is in the same ball park.[3]

By far the most common high-level language used to source code for embedded MPU circuitry is **C**. Historically **C** was developed as a language for writing operating systems. At its simplest level, an operating system (OS) is a program which makes the detailed hardware operation of the computer's terminals, such as keyboard and disk organization, invisible to the operator. As such, the writer of an OS must be able to poke about the various registers and memory of the computer's peripherals and easily integrate with assembly-level driver routines. As conventional high-level languages and their compilers were profligate with resources, depending on a rich and fast environment, assembly language was mandatory up to

---

[2]The 68300 family is the microcontroller equivalent of the 68000 family MPU.
[3]In the author's experience a code size increase factor of $\times 1.5 \ldots \times 2.5$ is typical.

the early 1970s, giving intimate machine contact and tight fast code. However, the sheer size of such a project means that it is likely to be a team effort, with all the difficulties in integrating the code and foibles of several people. A great deal of self-discipline and skill is demanded of such personnel, as is attention to documentation. Even with all this, the final result cannot be easily transplanted to machines with other processors, needing a nearly complete rewrite.

In the early 1970s, Ken Thompson — an employee at Bell Laboratories — developed the first version of the UNIX operating system. This was written in assembler language for a DEC PDP7 minicomputer. In an attempt to promote the use of this operating system (OS) within the company, some work was done in rewriting UNIX in a high-level language. The language CPL (Combined Programming Language) had been developed jointly by Cambridge and London universities in the mid-1960s, and has some useful attributes for this area of work. BCPL (Basic CPL) was a somewhat less complex but more efficient variant designed as a compiler-writing tool in the late 1960s. The language B (after the first letter in BCPL) was developed for the task of rewriting UNIX for the DEC PDP11 and was essentially BCPL with a different syntax.

Both BCPL and B only used one type of object, the natural size machine word (16 bits for the PDP-11). This typeless structure led to difficulties in dealing with individual bytes and floating-point computation. C (the second letter of BCPL) was developed in 1972 to address this problem, by creating a range of objects of both integer and floating-point types. This enhanced its portability and flexibility. UNIX was reworked in C during the summer of 1973, comprizing around 10,000 lines of high-level code and 1000 lines at assembly level. It occupied some 30% more storage than the original version.

Although C has been closely associated with UNIX, over the intervening years it has escaped to appear in compilers running under virtually every known OS, from mainframe CPUs down to single-chip MCUs. Furthermore, although originally a systems programming language, it is now used to write applications programs ranging from Computer Aided Design (CAD) packages down to the intelligence behind smart egg-timers!

For over 10 years, the official definition was the first edition of *The C Programming Language*, written by the language's originators, Brian W. Kernighan and Dennis M. Ritchie. It is a tribute to the power and simplicity of the language that over the years it has survived virtually intact, resisting the tendency to split into dialects and new versions. In 1983 the American National Standards Institute (ANSI) established the X3J11 committee to provide a modern and comprehensive definition of C to reflect the enhanced role of this language. The resulting definition, known as Standard or ANSII C, was finally approved during 1990.

Apart from its use as the language of choice for embedded MPU circuits, **C** (together with its **C++** object-oriented offspring) is without doubt the most popular general-purpose programming language at the time of writing. It has been called by its detractors a high-level assembler. However, this closeness of **C** to assembly-level code, together with the ability to mix code based on both levels in the one program, is of particular benefit for embedded targets.

The main advantages of the use of high-level language as source code for embedded targets are:

- It is more productive, in the sense that it takes around the same time to write, test and debug a line of code irrespective of language. By definition, a line of high-level code is equivalent to several lines of assembly code.
- Syntax is more oriented to human problem-solving. This improves productivity and accuracy, and makes the code easier to document, debug, maintain and adapt to changing circumstances.
- Programs are easier to port to different hardware platforms, although they are rarely 100% portable. Thus they are likely to have a longer productive life, being relatively immune to hardware developments.
- As such code is relatively hardware-independent, the customer base is considerably larger. This gives an economic impetus to produce extensive support libraries of standard functions, such as mathematical modules, which can be reused in many projects.

Of course there are disadvantages as well, specifically when code is being produced to run in poorly resourced MPU/MCU-based circuitry.

- The code produced is less space-efficient and often runs more slowly than native assembly code.
- The compiler is much more expensive than an assembler. A professional product will often cost several thousand pounds/dollars.
- Debugging can be difficult, as the actual code executed by the target processor is the generated assembler code. The processor does not execute high-level code directly. Products that facilitate high-level debugging are, again, very expensive.

Program 10.1 is an example of a **C** function (a function is the counterpart to a subroutine) that evaluates the relationship

$$sum = \sum_{k=1}^{n} k$$

for example, if $n = 5$ then we have:

$$sum = 5 + 4 + 3 + 2 + 1$$

In the implementation n is the integer passed to the function, which computes and returns the integer sum as defined. The program implements this task by continually adding n to the pre-cleared sum, as n is decremented to zero.

Program 10.1 *A simple function coded in* **C**.

```
1:   unsigned long summation(unsigned short register n)
2:       {
3:       unsigned long register sum = 0;
4:       while(n>0)
5:          {
6:          sum = sum + n;
7:          n--;
8:          }
9:       return sum;
10:      }
```

Let us dissect it line by line. Each line is labelled with its number. This is for clarity in our discussion and is not part of the program.

Line 1: This line names the function (subroutine) summation, declares that it returns an unsigned long integer (a 32-bit unsigned object) and expects an unsigned short integer (a 16-bit unsigned object) to be passed to it called n. The qualifier register is a *suggestion* by the programmer to the compiler that the variable n might usefully be kept in a data register rather than being swapped in and out of external data memory.

Line 2: A left brace { means begin. All begins must be matched by an end, which is designated by a right brace }. It is good practice to indent each begin from the immediately preceding line(s). This makes it easier to ensure each begin is paired with an end. In this case line 10 is the corresponding end brace. Between lines 2 and 10 is the body of the function summation().

Line 3: There is only one variable that is local to our function. Its name and type are defined here. Thus sum is of type unsigned long register. In **C** all objects have to be defined before they are used. This tells the compiler what properties the named variable has, for example its size (32 bits), to allocate storage and its arithmetic properties (unsigned). Again it is suggested that sum be located in a data register rather than out in memory. At the same time sum is given an *initial* value of zero. The complete statement is terminated by a semicolon, as are all statements in **C**.

Line 4: In evaluating sum we need to repeat the same process as long

as n is greater than zero. This is the purpose of the `while` construction introduced in this line. The general form of this loop
construct is:

```
while(true)
    {
    do this;
    do that;
    do the other;
    }
```

The body of the loop, i.e. is the set of statements that appears
between the following left and right braces of lines 5 and 8, is
continually executed as long as the expression in the brackets
evaluates as non-zero (anything non-zero is considered true by
C). This test is done before each pass through the body. In our
case the expression n>0 is evaluated. If true, then n is added to
sum. n is then decremented and the loop test repeated. Eventually n>0 computes to false (zero) and the statement following
the closing brace is entered (line 9).

Line 5: The opening brace defining the `while` body. Notice that for style
it is indented.

Line 6: The expression to the right of the assignment = is evaluated to
sum + n and the resulting value given to the left variable sum. In
adding a 16-bit to a 32-bit variable, **C** will automatically extend
to 32-bits (see Program 10.2, lines 18 and 19).

Line 7: The value of n is decremented, as commanded by the -- Decrement operator.[4] This is equivalent to the statement n = n - 1;
As an alternative, most **C** programmers would incorporate this
into the `while` test expression thus: `while(n-- > 0)`.

Line 8: The end brace for the `while` body. Again note how the opening
(line 5) and closing braces line up. The compiler does not give
a hoot about style; this is solely for human readability and to
reduce the possibility of errors.

Line 9: The `return` instruction passes one parameter back to the caller,
in this case the completed value of sum. The compiler will check
that the size of this parameter matches the prefix of the function
header in line 1, that is unsigned long. This returned parameter is the value of the function, i.e. the function can be used
as a variable in the same way as any other. Thus, if we had
a function called sqr_root that returned the square root of a
constant passed to it (see self-assessment question 10.1), then
the statement in the calling program:

---

[4]The analogous Increment operator ++ has given the name **C++** to the next development
of the **C** language.

```
x = sqr_root(y);
```

would assign the returned value of `sqr_root(y)` to x.

Line 10: The closing brace for function `summation()`.

We see from Fig. 10.1 that the output from the compiler is assembly-level code, which can then be assembled and linked with other modules[5] in the normal way. To illustrate this process, Program 10.2(a) shows the assembly-level code generated when the **C** code of Program 10.1 is passed through the COSMIC 68K Cross-C compiler. This is not the place to go through the listing in any detail, but it is instructive to look at the high-lights. The assembler used to process the compiler output is a little different than that used in this text. As far as we are concerned here, the differences are:

- Comments are prefixed by a * rather than ;. Notice how the original lines of **C** source code are embedded as comments in the assembly-level listing.
- `.text` is the same as `psect _text`.
- `.globl` is the same as `.public`.

The parameter n is pushed out into the stack by the caller and the `link` instruction of line 8 simply points Address register A6 to the value of the Stack Pointer on entry to the subroutine to act as a reference, the Frame Pointer. In line 9, n is moved out of the stack (at 10 bytes above the Frame Pointer) into Data register D1.W. As suggested by the `register` prefix, it remains there for the duration of the subroutine. In the same way, the local variable sum is located in D2.L for the duration. If the `register` prefix had not been used for this variable, line 8 would have been `link a6,#4`, which would have reserved four bytes in the stack as a frame (see page 135) and sum would have been swapped in and out of memory as required at `-4(a6)`.

Lines 14 and 15 implement the `while(n>0)` loop as a test and branch pair. The body of the loop, lines 18–24, simply extends the 16-bit n to 32 bits[6] in D7.L and adds this to the 32-bit sum. n-- is implemented as a Quick Subtract.

The final machine-code file is shown in Program 10.2(b) and gives a total length of only 30 bytes. Example 10.1 compares this outcome with a hand-crafted equivalent.

---

[5]Some of which can be functions hand-coded in native assembly-level language for efficiency, and from libraries supplied with the compiler or bought in.

[6]It would have been more efficient to do this once only outside the loop!

Program 10.2 *Resulting assembly-level compiler output after linking.*

```
¨¨1COSMIC 3.32 as68k
  1                    * Compilateur C pour MC68000 (COSMIC-France)
  2                    * Version 3.50.2 - Sep 27 1994
  3                    * 1   unsigned long summation(unsigned short register n)
  4                    * 2       {
  5                              .text
  6                              .even
  7 00400 T                 _summation:
  8 00400 T 4e56 0000       link    a6,#0
  9 00404 T 322e 000a       move.w  10(a6),d1
 10                    * 3       unsigned long register sum = 0;
 11 00408 T 7400           moveq.l #0,d2
 12 0040a T           L1:  *line 4, words 8
 13                    * 4      while(n>0)
 14 0040a T 4a41           tst.w   d1
 15 0040c T 67 0a          beq.s   L11
 16                    * 5      {
 17                    * 6        sum = sum + n;
 18 0040e T 7e00           moveq.l #0,d7
 19 00410 T 3e01           move.w  d1,d7
 20 00412 T d487           add.l   d7,d2
 21                    * 7        n--;
 22 00414 T 5341           subq.w  #1,d1
 23                    * 8      }
 24 00416 T 60 f2          bra.s   L1
 25 00418 T           L11: *line 8, words 15
 26                    * 9      return sum;
 27 00418 T 2e02           move.l  d2,d7
 28 0041a T 4e5e           unlk    a6
 29 0041c T 4e75           rts
 30                               *fnsize=21
 31                              .globl  _summation
 32                    * 10     }

no assembler errors
code segment size = 30    data segment size = 0
```

(a): Assembly-level code listing file after linking.

```
S2220004004E560000322E000A74004A41670A7E003E01D487534160F22E024E5E4E75BE
S804000400F7
```

(b): Executable S2-S8 machine-code file.

Examples

Example 10.1
Code an equivalent to Program 10.1 using native assembly-level language. Comment on your outcome.

Solution
The listing shown in Program 10.3 comprizes only seven instructions and assembles to 18 bytes, as compared to 30 bytes generated by

the **C** source. To reduce its size, n has been passed in D1.L and the computation of sum done in D7.L, which is the return register. By extending n to 32 bits (line 10) *outside* the loop (lines 11–14), the time efficiency of the coding is improved.

Although at face value the **C** coding has a total length some two-thirds greater than its native assembly-level equivalent, most of this overhead is accounted for by opening and closing the frame (Program 10.2, lines 8, 9 and 28). Omitting these gives a length of only 20 bytes. Apart from the advantages of passing parameters through the stack (see page 135), this opening/closing overhead is less significant for the more typical longer functions/subroutines.

An analysis of execution time shows that the **C**-sourced program takes (66 + 40n) clock cycles whilst the assembly-level equivalent executes in (40 + 32n) cycles. For larger values of n this gives a ≈ 25% overhead.

Whilst not exhaustive, the outcome of this analysis shows that using **C** source code is a viable alternative to assembly-level code for all but the most critical applications.

Program 10.3 *Listing file for the hand-assembled sum-of-n-integers problem.*

```
 1                              .processor   m68000
 2                      ; ***********************************************
 3                      ; * FUNCTION: Sums all integers up to n         *
 4                      ; * EXAMPLE : n = 5, sum = 5+4+3+2+1 = 15        *
 5                      ; * ENTRY   : n in D1.W                          *
 6                      ; * EXIT    : sum in D7.L                        *
 7                      ; * EXIT    : D1.L = 0                           *
 8                      ; ***********************************************
 9 000400   4287     SUMMATION: clr.l    d7           ; sum = 0;
10 000402   0281 0000FFFF      and.l    #0FFFFh,d1   ; n extended to long
11 000408   6706     LOOP:      beq      SUM_EXIT     ; while n > 0 do
12 00040A   DE81                add.l    d1,d7        ; sum = sum + n;
13 00040C   5381                subq.l   #1,d1        ; n--;
14 00040E   60F8                bra      LOOP         ; end while
15 000410   4E75     SUM_EXIT:  rts                   ; return sum;
16                              .end
```

Example 10.2

A K-type thermocouple is characterized by the equation:

$$t = 7.550162 + 0.0738326 \times v + 2.8121386 \times 10^{-7} v^2$$

where t is the temperature difference across the thermocouple in degrees Celsius and v is the generated emf spanning the range 0–52,398 μV, represented by a 14-bit unsigned binary number, for a temperature range of 0–1300°C. Write a **C** function which will take as its input parameter a 14-bit output from an analog to digital converter and return the integer temperature in Celsius measured by the thermocouple.

Solution

Like Program 10.1 this function, named `thermocouple` in line 1 of Program 10.4, takes one unsigned short integer (16-bit) parameter, named `emf` and returns a similar 16-bit value. The internal variable `temperature` is defined in line 3 to be a floating-point object[7] to cope with the complex fractional mathematics of line 5.

As we are told that only the 14 lower bits of `emf` have any meaning, line 4 ANDs the 16-bit object with 3FFF*h* (0x3FFF) to clear the upper two bits. The 0x prefix is **C**'s way of denoting hexadecimal.

Finally, the resulting `temperature` from line 5 is returned. The (unsigned short) prefix to the floating-point `temperature` casts this complex representation to the nearest 16-bit integer equivalent.

Program 10.4 *Linearizing a K-type thermocouple.*

```
unsigned short thermocouple(unsigned short emf)
  {
  float temperature;
  emf = emf & 0x3FFF;            /* Clear upper two bits */
  temperature = 7.550162+0.073832605*emf+2.8121386e-7*emf*emf;
  return (unsigned short)temperature;
  }
```

Self-assessment questions

10.1 Write a **C** function to evaluate $\sqrt{n}$, where n is passed as a long integer and the returned value is an unsigned short integer. Use the algorithm shown in Fig. 8.6.

10.2 Write a **C** function to convert from °C to °F. The Celsius temperature is to be passed to the function as a short unsigned integer (range 0–65,535) and the Fahrenheit equivalent returned as a long unsigned integer.

---

[7]Having a mantissa and exponent of the form $m \times 10^e$.

10.3 A cold-weather indicator in an automobile dashboard display comprizes three LEDs, which are located in memory at 9006*h* (see Fig. 13.5 on page 218). Bit 2 of this location is connected to the red LED, which is to light if the Fahrenheit temperature is less than 30. Bit 1 is the yellow LED for temperatures below 40°F, and bit 0 is the green LED. Write a function, whose input is °C, that activates the appropriate LED and also returns the °F equivalent.

Access to the fixed memory location 9006*h* in **C** can be accomplished by placing the following line of code at the head of the program:

```
#define  LED  *(char *)0x9006
```

whereupon the variable LED can be altered like any other variable.

You will also need to use the if-else conditional construction:

```
if(something is true)
    {do this;}
else if(whatever is true)
    {do that;}
else
    {do the other;}
```

10.4 Write a function to return the unsigned long factorial of an unsigned integer in the range 0–12. To do this, specify the look-up table (see Program 7.3 on page 122) as an array thus:

```
unsigned long table[13] =
{1,1,2,6,24,120,720,5040,43320,362880,3628800,39916800,479001600};
```

PART III

Interacting with the outside world

Apart from our brief discussion of the von Neumann computer structure in Chapter 3, we have confined our discussions to the internal structure of the microprocessor and its software. This final part looks at how the processor monitors and controls the environment physically beyond the confines of its pins. This process involves consideration of the interaction of the software and hardware, ending up with a case study which builds a complete stand-alone embedded controller. On the way you will:

- *Look at the timing involved during a Read and a Write bus cycle.*
- *Consider the ebb and flow of data between the various interfaces communicating through the Data bus.*
- *Analyze the function and design of some typical address decoders.*
- *See what is involved in designing ports which allow ingress between external peripherals and the Data bus.*
- *Examine the hardware interface between peripherals requesting real-time service via interrupts and the processor.*
- *Design an embedded microprocessor-based viva timer.*
- *Consider how a system may be tested and debugged.*

CHAPTER 11

The real world

Up to this point we have concentrated on how the various instructions and address modes have interacted with the processor's internal registers and data objects located externally in memory space. In particular we have characterized an external object, be it instruction code or data, in terms of its location in memory, and the contents of that address. Now, as a prelude to how the MPU monitors and controls its external environment, i.e. the *real world* outside its pins, we need to look in more detail at the interplay between the data and address signals and the various controls and protocols involved in the ebb and flow of information between the MPU and the various devices attached to its buses.

After reading this chapter you will:

- *Recognize the pivotal role of the Data bus in carrying information to (reading to) and from (writing from) the MPU. In particular, this bus is a common resource, which is time-shared between all devices — memory and interface ports — which communicate with the processor.*
- *Know that the Address bus facilitates a selection mechanism between the various things which share the common data highway, so that only one communication link is set up at any time.*
- *Understand that the control signals, collectively known as the Control bus, provide information on the status of the MPU, synchronize and monitor the interchange of data between the MPU and devices hung on the bus, and select its mode of operation. The key signals discussed in this chapter are R/$\overline{\text{W}}$, $\overline{\text{AS}}$, $\overline{\text{UDS}}$, $\overline{\text{LDS}}$, $\overline{\text{DTACK}}$, Clock, Mode and FC.*
- *Understand that all fetch and execute operations comprise a series of Read and Write bus cycles, and be able to describe the sequence of interactions between the various bus signals during both types of cycle.*
- *Appreciate the advantage of regulating the bus cycle duration by inserting wait states according to the response time of the addressed memory or port, and how $\overline{\text{DTACK}}$ is used to implement this asynchronous strategy.*
- *Comprehend how $\overline{\text{UDS}}$ and $\overline{\text{LDS}}$ are used to access a single eight-bit byte via a 16-bit word Data bus.*
- *Understand the difference between the 8- and 16-bit Data bus modes.*

Let us begin by looking at the architecture of a complete MPU-based circuit. The structure of Fig. 11.1 is really just a more detailed version of Fig. 3.1 on page 34, with the CPU (MPU in this case) controlling data flow to and from memory, monitoring events via an input port and controlling events using an output port.

Central to all this ebb and flow of information is the **Data bus**. This snakes between the MPU and *all* devices, memory or interface ports, with which it must communicate. The key features of this bus are that:

- It is a *common* highway shared between *all* sources of information which must communicate with the master controller — the MPU.
- Normally the MPU can only communicate with *one* device at a time through the bus.
- It is bidirectional (sometimes termed duplex) in that it can support a flow between MPU and device (write action) or an inflow (read action). Only *one* direction (half duplex) is supported at any time.

Taking a loose analogy with the public telephone system, the Data high-way is the communications link which is set up to enable two subscribers to talk to each other; although in this case it is possible for both parties to converse at the same time — if rather unproductively. This full duplex communications link contrasts with the half duplex mode of operation of the Data bus.

For simplicity I have drawn the Data bus in Fig. 11.1 with eight lines only, $d_7 \ldots d_0$. While this is applicable to the 68HC001/EC000 in their eight-bit mode of operation, the 16-bit mode uses 16 data lines, $d_{15} \ldots d_0$, whilst the 68020+ has 32 data lines, $d_{31} \ldots d_0$.

If we pursue the telephone analogy a little further; before the conversation can begin, a link must be established between subscriber 1 and subscriber 2. This is a complex business, but in essence involves sending sequences of pulses or tones to the exchange, representing the distant subscriber number. In a similar manner, to a MPU all objects that it will communicate with are characterized by an **address**. This location code is placed on the **Address bus**, where it can be picked up by decoding circuitry and used to enable the intended device. The **address decoder** is then analogous to the telephone exchange. We will examine the decoding circuitry in detail in the next chapter.

The Address bus:

- Carries the location code or address of the object in memory space that the MPU wishes to communicate with.
- Is unidirectional (simplex), in that an address is always output from the MPU and never received from an external device.

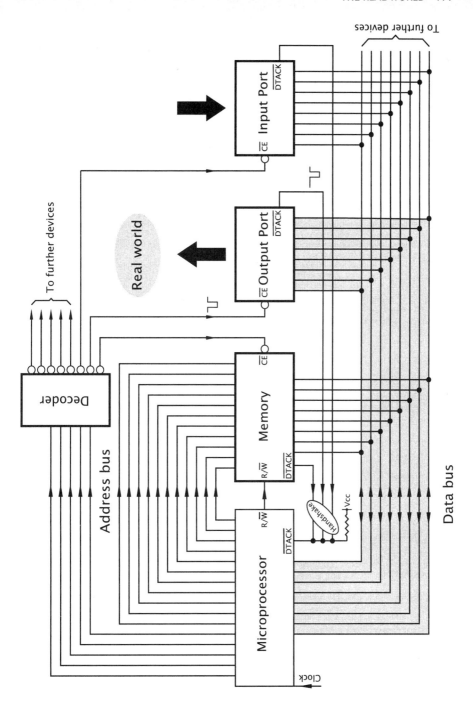

Figure 11.1 *Simplified structure of a 68000-based system; showing a 'write to output port'
in action.*

I have only shown 16 Address lines in the diagram, again for simplicity. The 68000 MPU effectively has 24 lines, giving an address space of $2^{24} = 16$ Mbytes $= 16,777,216$ bytes, whilst the 68020+ MPUs have a 32-line Address bus, giving $2^{32} = 4$ Gbytes $= 4,294,967,296$ byte address space.

Once the address has been sent out and communication has been made with the target, that device must signal that it is ready to proceed with the transaction, by activating its Data Transfer ACKnowledge ($\overline{\text{DTACK}}$) status line. When the MPU senses that its $\overline{\text{DTACK}}$ pin has gone low, it completes the cycle by either *reading in* the packet on the Data bus (incoming data) or alternatively *writing out* data to the addressed device. In the former case the R/$\overline{\text{W}}$ pin is high for a read, otherwise a low signals a Write cycle. The shaded region of Fig. 11.1 shows a Write cycle in progress, with the output port being enabled by the address decoder and using its $\overline{\text{DTACK}}$ line to give the MPU the message "I am ready to accept data, please go ahead". As all devices hung on the bus must generate their own $\overline{\text{DTACK}}$, these are usually wire-ORed together, as described on page 17, to the one MPU pin.

The miscellany of control, status, clock and power supply signals supporting the MPU are conventionally described as a **Control bus**. Unlike the Data and Address buses, the Control bus is very particular to the actual MPU family. R/$\overline{\text{W}}$ and $\overline{\text{DTACK}}$ are examples of Control lines. Despite the considerable variation in function and action, in general the Control bus can be described as a collection of signals that:

- Select the operating mode of the MPU.
- Synchronize the interchange of data between the addressed device and the processor.
- Provide status information on actions carried out by the MPU.

Many of these functions will not be described until later chapters, but we will summarize these signals here for reference.

Address Strobe ($\overline{\text{AS}}$)
This status signal is asserted whenever the state of the Address bus is valid; see Figs 11.2 and 11.3.

Upper Data Strobe ($\overline{\text{UDS}}$) and Lower Data Strobe ($\overline{\text{LDS}}$)
These strobes lines have two functions.

- They indicate that the state of the Data bus is stable during a Write cycle. During a read cycle $\overline{\text{UDS}}$ and $\overline{\text{LDS}}$ are indistinguishable from $\overline{\text{AS}}$.
- When the processor is in 16-bit mode they are used to enable either the upper or lower eight-bit byte of an addressed peripheral connected to the appropriate part of the 16-bit Data bus. Figure 11.6 shows how these signals are used in this role.

Processors configured in the eight-bit mode only use $\overline{\text{LDS}}$, with $\overline{\text{UDS}}$ permanently high. In the obsolete 68008 MPU this was simply labelled $\overline{\text{DS}}$.

Read/Write (R/$\overline{\text{W}}$)
This status signal is low during a Write cycle and high during a read cycle.

Reset
Asserting both $\overline{\text{Reset}}$ and $\overline{\text{Halt}}$ together initiates a total reset of the processor. This must be held for at least 100 ms when the power is initially applied, to ensure stabilization of the internal bias voltage and external clock generator. Otherwise a duration of ten clock cycles is sufficient.

An external reset causes the contents of the long-word at 00000000–3h to be moved into the Supervisor Stack Pointer (A7) (its initial value) and the contents of 00000004-7h into the Program Counter (the start of the executable program), as described in Fig. 9.2 on page 146. The Status register's **S** bit is set to configure the MPU to the Supervisor state and Trace is turned off by clearing **T**. No other registers are affected.

$\overline{\text{Reset}}$ can also act as an output signal, activated by the privileged instruction reset. This drives this pin low for 124 clock periods, which can be used to reset peripheral devices. Because of this bidirectional action, external restart circuitry must be more complex than a simple switch. An example of a typical circuit is shown in Fig. 15.3 on page 254.

Halt
Like $\overline{\text{Reset}}$, this is also a bidirectional line. As an input it can be used in conjunction with $\overline{\text{Reset}}$ or alone. When asserted alone, it will stop the processor after the current bus cycle (see page 182) is finished. The Address and Data buses will then go open circuit (floated), and other control outputs deactivated. If $\overline{\text{Halt}}$ is then released for one clock cycle, the processor will execute the next instruction and then stop. Thus $\overline{\text{Halt}}$ can be used to single-step the processor for debug purposes.

As an output, $\overline{\text{Halt}}$ is driven low when the initial Supervisor Stack Pointer or Program Counter setting obtained from the Vector table on Reset is odd or the Bus Error pin is active during an exceptional event (see Chapter 9). This is known as a **Double-Bus fault**. Halting the MPU is the obvious thing to do in these cases, as such events are unrecoverable.

Mode
The 68EC000 and 68HC001 processors can be configured to use either an eight-bit or 16-bit Data bus; the original 68000 is always in 16-bit mode. If Mode is grounded at reset, the MPU will be in eight-bit mode, which uses only the lower eight Data lines $d_7 \ldots d_0$ as its Data bus. Conversely all 16 Data lines $d_{15} \ldots d_0$ are utilized for the 16-bit Data bus. This input should not be altered during normal running.

Data Transfer ACKnowledge ($\overline{\text{DTACK}}$)
This is a signal sent back by the addressed device to indicate that the peripheral's data is valid during a read cycle or that it is ready to accept the data during a Write cycle. This asynchronous protocol is illustrated later in this chapter.

Interrupt Priority Level (IPL2 IPL1 IPL0)

These input pins are driven from external devices requesting an interrupt. The three-bit *active-low* code thus placed is its requested priority level, ranging from zero (111) for no interrupt request to seven (000) for a top-priority request. The IPL pins are constantly monitored, and any change lasting a minimum of two clock periods is internally latched. At the end of each instruction, the latched requested level is compared with the Interrupt mask bits setting in the Status register and acted upon if *higher*. If masked to Level-7, a *change* up from a lower level to a Level-7 request will trigger an edge-triggered non-maskable interrupt response. More details are given in Chapters 9 and 14.

Bus ERRor (BERR)

This input acts as a special type of interrupt, used to inform the processor that something has gone wrong outside. As an example of what can go awry, the addressed peripheral may not send back its DTACK acknowledge signal. If this continues indefinitely, the processor will hang up forever waiting for the go-ahead command that never comes. Using a counter reset by DTACK to drive BERR would ensure that in the absence of a correct response, say within 80 clock cycles, the counter will overflow and alarm the MPU. The use of a **watchdog timer** like this can be extended to ensure the veracity of the program in high-noise situations, which can corrupt data and address lines, causing the processor to go off to some illegal memory space and thus run amok. By using a few lines of the legitimate program to trigger a watchdog at some regular interval, a Bus Error can be signalled if this area of program is not entered. If a Bus Error occurs during the restart process, signalling that the Reset vectors cannot be accessed, the the MPU stops with the Halt pin low.

When a Bus Error occurs, the processor pushes data on to the Supervisor stack, which can then be used by the operating system for diagnostic purposes. If a Bus Error continues to be signalled, then a Double-Bus fault is said to have occurred. The processor signals this catastrophe by bringing Halt low and stopping.

Function Code (FC2 FC1 FC0)

These three outputs inform the outside world which state the processor is operating in according to the codes:

FC2	FC1	FC0	
0	0	1	Accessing data from memory when in the User state
0	1	0	Accessing program code when in the User state
1	0	1	Accessing data from memory when in the Supervisor state
1	1	0	Accessing program code when in the Supervisor state
1	1	1	Responding to an interrupt request

Essentially, if pin FC2 is high the processor is in the Supervisor state. If desired this can be utilized to switch address decoders so that the Supervisor mode can have a completely separate address space from the User state (see Fig. 12.5 on page 204). In effect parallel universes. Thus a computer operating system could run in the Supervisor mode on switch-on (boot-up) and then change over to the User mode to run the application program. If something goes wrong with this, then the OS's memory should then not be compromised.

As well as distinguishing between states, the FC pins can let external circuitry know if the processor is fetching down instruction words, i.e. implementing the fetch portion of the fetch and execute cycle, or accessing data during the execute phase. Typically program data is stored in ROM memory (program space) and variables in RAM memory (Data space). This status, available from the FC pins, can be valuable in debugging system hardware.

Finally FC2 FC1 FC0 = 111 signals that an interrupt situation is being serviced. This can be used to generate an Interrupt ACKnowledge status signal, which is useful in telling the sender that its request has been acted upon (see Fig. 14.2 on page 239).

Bus Request ($\overline{\text{BR}}$)
External devices that wish to take over the buses for direct memory access (DMA) can do so by asserting the $\overline{\text{BR}}$ line for as long as necessary.

Bus Grant ($\overline{\text{BG}}$)
The 68000 MPU asserts $\overline{\text{BG}}$ in response to a Bus Request. Once the $\overline{\text{AS}}$ is negated, the DMA can take over the buses.

Bus Grant ACKnowledge ($\overline{\text{BGACK}}$)
Before taking over the buses, the DMA device checks that no other DMA device is asserting $\overline{\text{BGACK}}$. If it is, the new device waits until $\overline{\text{BGACK}}$ is negated before asserting its own $\overline{\text{BGACK}}$ and proceeding. All DMA devices have their $\overline{\text{BGACK}}$ outputs wire-ORed together to facilitate this. The 68EC000 does not have this output status line.

CLocK (CLK)
This input must be driven by an external TTL-compatible oscillator. Small crystal-controlled circuits are readily obtainable for this purpose. NMOS 68000 MPUs are available with maximum ratings up to 16 MHz, and CMOS versions to 20 MHz. 68020+ processors can have clock rates up to 50 MHz. These processors have internal dynamic circuitry, and so have a lower frequency bound, typically 4–8 MHz.

E
This output is the CLK frequency divided by 10. It is equivalent to the same-named signal in the older 6800-series MPUs and is used when interfacing to specialized 6800-oriented peripheral interface devices. The provision of 6800-style control signals meant that existing eight-bit peripheral devices could be used when the 68000 MPU was first introduced. The 68EC000 does not support 6800-type transfers, so does not have this output signal.

Valid Memory Access (VMA)

This is also an "old-style" 6800-type signal. It indicates that the Address bus signal is valid, and is synchronized to the E clock. It is only generated when external circuitry asserts the MPU's $\overline{\text{VPA}}$ pin, and then will take some time to lock into the E signal. Again the 68EC000 does not have this output.

Valid Peripheral Address (VPA)

This input tells the MPU that the location it wishes to access is populated with a 6800-style peripheral interface circuit, and that a special 6800-type data transfer cycle (using E and $\overline{\text{VMA}}$) should be used. $\overline{\text{VPA}}$ is also used to indicate to the processor that it should use automatic vectoring to respond to an interrupt, as described in Chapter 14. Although the 68EC000 does not have this input, it uses $\overline{\text{AVEC}}$ to force automatic interrupt vectoring.

Automatic VECtoring (AVEC)

The 68EC000 employs this input to tell the processor that it should use automatic vectoring to respond to an interrupt, in the same manner as $\overline{\text{VPA}}$ in the other 68000 family members.

Power (VCC and GND)

The HMOS 68000 MPU dissipates 1.5 W maximum at a V_{CC} of 5 ± 0.25 V and a mean current of 300 mA. The CMOS 68HC000/1 and 68EC000 use a maximum average current of 25 mA at 8 MHz (70 mA at 20 MHz). These values do not include any current taken by loads on the buses.

Except when an internal process is occurring, the MPU is continually passing data to and from its memory circuits and input/output ports along its various *external* bus wires. Even when the operands of an instruction target internal Data or Address registers, the operation code itself must be fetched along the Data bus. This activity is organized as "packets" of four clock cycles or **bus cycles**. Each bus cycle can be classified as Read or Write, depending on the direction of data flow — inwards or outwards respectively. The **Read cycle** shown in Fig. 11.2 shows the following sequence of events, which corresponds to the numbers on the diagram.

1. The address stabilizes near the beginning of the bus cycle.
2. Shortly afterwards, the $\overline{\text{AS}}$ strobe is activated to show that this address is stable.
3. The addressed device eventually responds, activating $\overline{\text{DTACK}}$ to say that it is ready to provide data.
4. The device then outputs data on to the Data bus.
5. The MPU reads this data into an internal register and negates the $\overline{\text{AS}}$ strobe, and then its address.
6. The addressed device is now free to negate its $\overline{\text{DTACK}}$ and remove its data; thus completing the bus cycle.

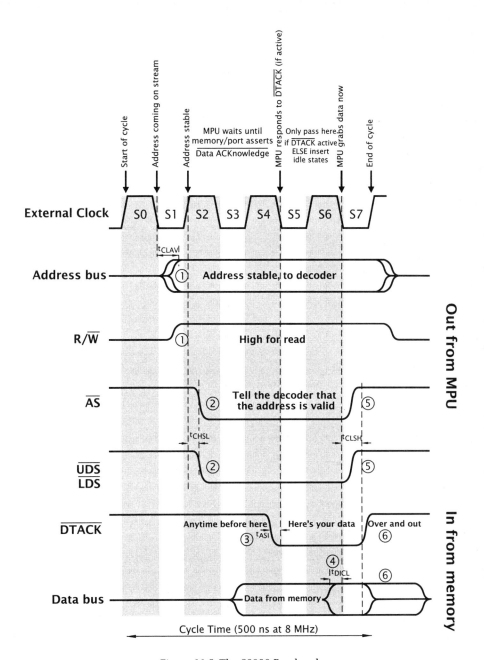

Figure 11.2 *The 68000 Read cycle.*

Buses, which are really collections of related signals, some going high and some low, are depicted in Fig. 11.2 by a double trace. Dual rise and fall transitions are used to indicate likely time jitter or permissible spreads of changeover levels.

With this general picture in mind we can look at the timing in a little more detail. The sequence of events is synchronized by the external processor clock, which is shown in Fig. 11.2 split into eight states or phases, making up four clock periods. At a clock frequency of 8 MHz this gives a minimum bus cycle duration of 500 ns. The times given are for 8 MHz devices (68EC000 times differ and are indicated in parentheses).[1] We then have:

1. The Address bus's data will be stable within t_{CLAV} (Clock Low to Address Valid) following the end of State 0. The same timings apply to the R/$\overline{W}$ and Function Code signals. This is no more than 62 ns (35 ns).
2. The $\overline{AS}$ strobe is asserted no more than 60 ns (35 ns) (t_{CHSL} — Clock High to Strobe Low) after the end of State 1. In a Read cycle the $\overline{DS}$ strobes have the same timings as $\overline{AS}$.
3. The memory/port must now respond by asserting its $\overline{DTACK}$ line. If it can do this by no later than 10 ns (5 ns) (t_{ASI} — Asychronous Setup Input) *before* the end of State 4, then the bus cycle will complete without delay. Otherwise the processor will insert wait states, as shown in Fig. 11.4.
4. The memory/port must then output its data no later than 10 ns (5 ns) (t_{DICL} — Data Input to Clock Low) before the end of State 6. At the ⌐_ of State 6 the MPU will grab whatever data is on the bus and place it in an internal register.
5. The $\overline{AS}$ and $\overline{DS}$ strobes are then negated by no more than 62 ns (35 ns) (t_{CLSH} — Clock Low to Strobe High) into the final Clock State 7.
6. The memory/port has up to 240 ns (110 ns) after the Strobes are negated to remove its data and negate $\overline{DTACK}$ in order not to clash with the next bus cycle.

The actual values of these setup and hold times are not significant here, and anyway will vary according to the processor type and speed rating. They can always be found in the appropriate data sheet. They are important in calculating the speed ratings of the memory devices which can respond to these signals. An example of this is given on page 225 in Chapter 13.

The **Write cycle** waveforms shown in Fig. 11.3 are very similar to the Read cycle. The essential difference is of course that this time it is the MPU originating the data. As a consequence the $\overline{DS}$ strobes are used to

---

[1] HMOS 68000 devices manufactured before week 27 in 1988 — date code 8827 — had slightly less favorable timings.

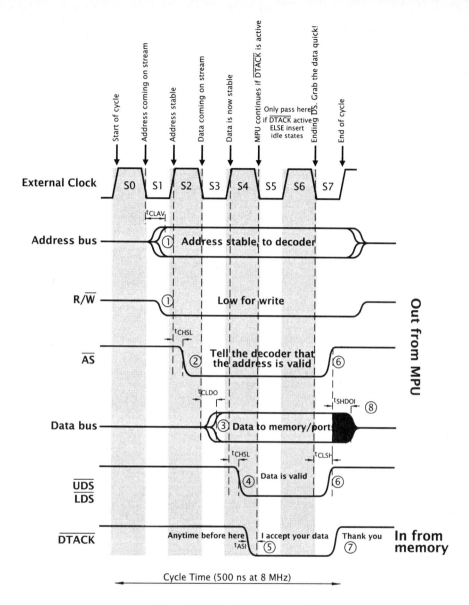

Figure 11.3 *The 68000 Write cycle.*

tell the outside world that this data is valid, rather than simply copying
$\overline{\text{AS}}$.

Briefly the following sequence of events occurs during the eight clock
states making up the bus cycle.

1. The address stabilizes near the beginning of the cycle.

2. Shortly afterwards, the $\overline{\text{AS}}$ strobe is activated to show that this address is stable.
3. The MPU then puts its data on the bus,
4. and asserts its $\overline{\text{DS}}$ strobes to tell the outside world that this data is valid.
5. The addressed device then responds to say that it is ready to accept the data by activating its $\overline{\text{DTACK}}$.
6. All strobes are then negated.
7. Anytime after this the addressed device can lift its $\overline{\text{DTACK}}$ handshake.
8. The data is then removed from the Data bus to finish off the cycle.

We can now look at the timing in more detail. As for the Read cycle, we will give times for the 8 MHz 68000 devices, with the 68EC000's values in parentheses.

1. The Address bus's data will be stable within a minimum of 62 ns (35 ns) (t_{CLAV} — Clock Low to Address Valid) following the end of State 0. Similarly R/$\overline{\text{W}}$ goes low to signal a write action.
2. $\overline{\text{AS}}$ is asserted no more than 60 ns (35 ns) (t_{CHSL} — Clock High to Strobe Low) after the end of State 1.
3. The MPU sends out data on the bus no later than 62 ns (35 ns) (t_{CLDO} — Clock Low to Data Out) after the end of State 2.
4. $\overline{\text{UDS}}$ and $\overline{\text{LDS}}$ are asserted by no later than 60 ns (35 ns) (t_{CHSL} — Clock High to Strobe Low) following State 3.
5. The memory/port must now respond when ready to accept this data by asserting its $\overline{\text{DTACK}}$ line. If it can do this by no later than 10 ns (5 ns) (t_{ASI} — Asynchronous Setup Input) *before* the end of State 4, then the bus cycle will complete without delay. Otherwise wait states will be inserted.
6. Once $\overline{\text{DTACK}}$ has been asserted then the processor negates its strobe signals by no more than 62 ns (35 ns) (t_{CLSH} — Clock Low to Strobe High) after State 6.
7. The memory/port can now remove its $\overline{\text{DTACK}}$ signal, in any case no longer than 240 ns (110 ns) after the negation of its Strobe signals.
8. The MPU lifts its data off the bus by no more than 40 ns (40 ns) (t_{SHDOI} — Strobe High to Data Out Invalid) after the $\overline{\text{DS}}$ strobes negate. This is the time a memory device or port has to grab the data (forgetting about these devices' data hold requirements) after a $\_\_/\!\!\!\overline{}$ strobe edge. This already short time is reduced to 10 ns for the 20 MHz CMOS 68000 devices, and means that the design of output interface circuitry is time-critical — see page 217.

We have indicated that if the addressed device does not return its $\overline{\text{DTACK}}$ signal on time, that is just before the end of Clock State 4, the processor will idle until $\overline{\text{DTACK}}$ is eventually asserted. This situation is

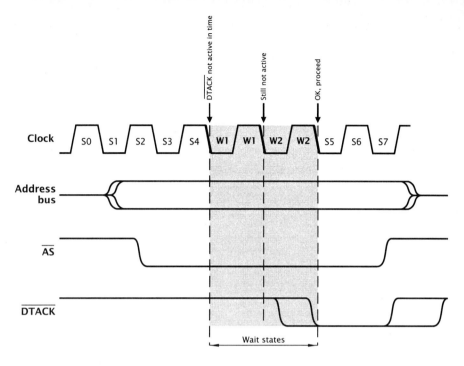

Figure 11.4 *Wait states.*

shown in more detail in Fig. 11.4, where the late arrival of $\overline{\text{DTACK}}$ causes two complete clock cycles to be inserted between State 4 and State 5. If $\overline{\text{DTACK}}$ is not active just before the ‾_ of State 4, one *complete* clock cycle, known as a **wait state**, is inserted and $\overline{\text{DTACK}}$ is again sampled on the ‾_ of this inserted clock pulse. This process continues until an active $\overline{\text{DTACK}}$ is detected.

The question to ask at this point is why use this complicated feedback mechanism at all? Older and slower MPUs, such as the Motorola 6800 or Intel 8080, use an open-loop synchronous approach, where the data is read at the end of the cycle with the assumption that it is ready — even if it isn't. The designers of the new generation of 16/32-bit MPUs at the end of the 1970s, e.g. the 68000 and Intel 8086, knew that clock speeds would be dramatically increased during the development lifetime of their products. For example, the first 68000 devices were clocked at 4 MHz[2] and the latest 68060 runs at 50 MHz. Thus many peripheral devices and memory chips would probably be unable to keep up with the required short access times. The clock speed could of course be slowed, but that would mean *all* bus cycles would be slowed (by a factor of 50% in Fig. 11.4)

---

[2]The APPLE Lisa, the predecessor of the Macintosh, in 1983 used a 5 MHz 68000 MPU.

perhaps for the sake of a single slow device. In using the **asynchronous** protocol, where $\overline{\text{DTACK}}$ is used as a kind of handshake control signal, the speed of each bus cycle can be tailored to suit the response time of the addressed device.

Before we go on to discuss the details of the interfacing circuitry in the next two chapters, we need to look at what exactly we mean by an address. Address of what? Well back in the days of eight-bit MPUs, when MPUs came of age, an address really meant the location of a byte of data, as the Data bus was eight-bits wide. Thus, from the point of view of these MPUs, the world is 'seen' in terms of an eight-bit eye, as depicted in Fig. 11.5(a). In a similar manner, we would expect the 68000 MPU to see the world with a 16-bit word-sized eye, as shown in Fig. 11.5(b). In this case the address can be thought of as a pointer-to-word.

Historically the introduction of the 16-bit Data bus 68000 MPU in 1979 was accompanied by its 68008 eight-bit Data bus little brother. The 68008[3] was entirely software compatible with its bigger brother, but sees the world through a byte-sized eye. Although this approach halves the data transfer rate (sometimes known as the bandwidth) there are many economic advantages in using this technique. First, most memory chips (and indeed peripheral interface devices) are byte-sized. Thus for small systems, such as shown in Chapter 15, this can half the memory chip count. Second, the smaller bus and package size (48- or 52-pin against 64-pin) reduces the size and complexity of the printed circuit board. It was for these reasons that the first IBM PC was powered by the eight-bit Intel 8088 (as opposed to the 16-bit equivalent 8086). The later IBM XT used the 8086 MPU. Similarly, the Intel 80386SX is a 16-bit version of the 32-bit 80386DX. Although the 68008 was withdrawn in 1995, both the 68HC001 and 68EC000 devices have an eight-bit mode, which makes these processors look rather like the, now defunct, 68008 MPU.

For these reasons, addresses in 68000 language refer to bytes, the lowest common denominator. Where the object is really a word or long-word, then its location is specified as its lowest byte address (where the most significant byte is resident). For example, the word-sized object

MSbyte $\quad$ 0E100h	LSbyte $\quad$ 0E101h

is located at 0E100h; thus move.w 0E100h,d0 copies the contents of both 0E100h and 0E101h into D0.W. Physically the 68HC001/EC000 devices express their address as the 24 address lines $a_{23} \dots a_0$. The a_0 line is inoperative (always high) when these devices are in 16-bit mode. The 68000/HC000 omit the a_0 line. This omission reflects their word-size bias (they do not have an eight-bit mode), as addresses pointing to words will go up two bytes at a time — which is

---

[3]The 68008 was used in the Clive Sinclair QL (Quantum Leap) personal computer was touted somewhat dubiously in the press as a 32-bit processor — after its register size and not its Data bus.

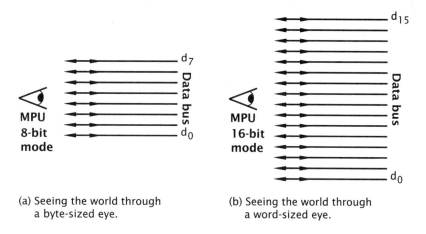

(a) Seeing the world through
a byte-sized eye.

(b) Seeing the world through
a word-sized eye.

Figure 11.5 *Looking at the outside world.*

equivalent to ignoring a_0.

Although the 68000 MPU is inherently a word-sized processor, it does have to deal with byte-sized objects, even in 16-bit mode — indeed, as we have seen, most instructions come in byte-sized (.b) versions. How is a single byte, half a word, to be read down a 16-bit Data bus; and which half of the bus will it arrive? This is especially a problem in that a_0 is missing, and so individual bytes cannot be picked out of a word directly by decoding the Address bus.

Although the least significant address bit is missing in 16-bit mode, the two Data strobes take on the role of selecting one of the two bytes which comprise a word. For example, in Fig. 11.6(a) the instruction move.b 0C000h, d0 causes the $\overline{\text{UDS}}$ alone to pulse. Although the address decoder enables *both* addresses 0C000h and 0C001h (without a_0 it cannot distinguish between them), only the upper memory chip is selected for reading by $\overline{\text{UDS}}$. In a similar manner the instruction move.b 0C001h only causes $\overline{\text{LDS}}$ to pulse, thereby only enabling the memory chip holding the odd-address bytes — as shown in Fig. 11.6(b). Thus data considered as byte-sized lumps are organized as | $\overline{\text{UDS}}$ ᴱⱽᴱᴺ | $\overline{\text{LDS}}$ ᴼᴰᴰ |. In this manner $\overline{\text{UDS}}$ is seen to be equivalent to $\overline{\text{DS}} \cdot \overline{a_0}$ (active when a_0 is low, i.e. on *even-byte* addresses) and $\overline{\text{LDS}}$ is $\overline{\text{DS}} \cdot a_0$ (active when a_0 is high, i.e. on *odd-byte* addresses). Here we use the signal $\overline{\text{DS}}$ to denote the underlying strobe whose function is to synchronize the Write bus cycle data transfer. $\overline{\text{UDS}}$ and $\overline{\text{LDS}}$ thus have the additional function of enabling a single byte to be transferred down the 16-bit Data bus from a word-organized memory space. In eight-bit mode the MPU only has a byte-sized Data bus and only the $\overline{\text{LDS}}$ is active.

A word transfer, as in Fig. 11.6(c), causes *both* $\overline{\text{UDS}}$ and $\overline{\text{LDS}}$ to be as-

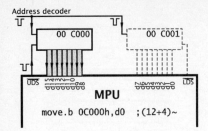

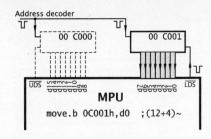

(a) Reading an even-address byte.

(b) Reading an odd-address byte.

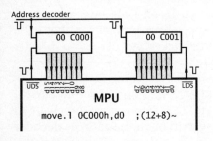

Key:
LSB   Least Significant Byte
MSB   Most Significant Byte
Execution time (fetch + execute)
~ = Clock periods
For the 68008
(a) and (b) = (24+4)~
(c)   = (24+8)~
(d)   = (24+16)~

(c) Reading a word.

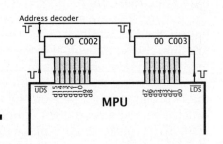

(d) Reading a long-word.

Figure 11.6 *Memory organization for the 68000/HC000 MPUs, and 68HC001/EC000 MPUs in the 16-bit mode.*

serted together, and the resulting two bytes feed the 16-bit Data bus simultaneously. Notice that the most significant byte is always located in the lower byte address (even address) of memory, in common with all Motorola MPUs. A 32-bit long-word transfer simply involves two 16-bit word transfers in sequence. As can be seen from Fig. 11.6(d), the execution time is longer by four clock periods (one bus cycle) due to the extra word transfer cycle. Byte and word execution both take a single bus cycle.

From our discussion you can see why we stipulated way back on page 66 that word or long-word instructions must only lie on *even address boundaries*. An attempt to do an odd address word access, such as:

```
move.w      0C101h,d0      ; This is erroneous
```

is an error, and the 68000 will terminate by returning to the Supervisor state (typically the operating system) via an Address Error Trap, as discussed on page 154. The 68020+ series do permit odd word addresses. These are implemented by using two bus cycles, the first bringing down the first odd byte and the second the even byte from the word across the boundary. This of course slows things down, so it is always better to organize words or long-words on even boundaries, even for these advanced processors.

In eight-bit mode the MPU only has a byte-sized Data bus and just $\overline{LDS}$ is active. There is no problem here, as address line a_0 is provided explicitly to reflect the natural byte size of the Data bus, and thus each target memory byte is individually enabled. This is exactly the same as an eight-bit MPU seeing the world through an eight-bit eye. Nevertheless, the even boundaries restriction for word and long-word memory data are retained for compatibility. Execution times for the eight-bit mode are shortest for a byte operand, word and long-word operands taking one and three extra access bus cycles respectively. Fetching the op-code also takes twice as long. At a clock frequency of 8 MHz, the 16-bit 68000 moves a word to a Data register in $2\,\mu s$, whilst an eight-bit equivalent takes $4\,\mu s$. However, moving between registers, for example:

```
move.w  d7,d0        ; A register to register move
```

takes $\frac{1}{2}\,\mu s$ in both cases. The moral being to keep as much in the Data registers as possible.

Examples

Example 11.1
The Analog Devices AD7528 dual eight-bit digital to analog converter has a worst-case access time of 230 ns to latch data successfully into its registers when powered at +5 V. How many wait states would need to be inserted into the Write cycle if a 8 MHz 68000 MPU were used? Would there be any change if a 10 MHz 68000 MPU were used?

Solution
If we assume that the converter is enabled by either $\overline{UDS}$ or $\overline{LDS}$ then from Fig. 11.3 this strobe could be as short as three clock phases less 60 ns, if t_{CLSH} was zero. At 8 MHz each clock phase is 62.5 ns, which gives an enabling duration of around 125 ns. Each wait state is 125 ns; therefore adding one wait state gives a minimum enable period of around 250 ns.

At 10 MHz each clock phase is 50 ns, giving a $\overline{DS}$ minimum width of 150 − 60 ns = 90 ns. Each wait state is 100 ns, so we would need two wait states to stretch the access past the specified 230 ns.

Powering the AD7528 with a +15 V supply reduces the access time to 80 ns in the worst case, which would allow a non-wait state operation with even a 12.5 MHz processor. Alternatively, the PM7528 (more expensive) CMOS equivalent has an access time of 100 ns at +5 V and 60 ns at 10 V.

Example 11.2

It is claimed that short-circuiting the Data bus and $\overline{DTACK}$ to logic 0 (i.e. to ground) will give a useful diagnostic function. What do you think will happen if this is done?

Solution

After reset, no matter that the processor does it will always fetch the code 0000h along its hijacked Data bus. Now the instruction so coded is ori.b #0,d0, which comprises the two words 0000 0000h, the first being the the op-code word and the latter the immediate data. Thus the processor will execute this instruction forever.

Each fetch and execute cycle will involve the Program Counter incrementing by 4 bytes. The 68000 MPU takes two bus cycles to do this (1 μs in total at 8 MHz) and twice this if in eight-bit mode. Thus the Address bus will act as a 24-bit counter. The total cycle time for the 16-bit mode is $2^{24} \times 1\,\mu s \approx 16\,s$ for a_{23}, $\approx 8\,s$ for a_{22}, $\approx 4\,s$ for a_{21}....

As the Address bus cycles through every sequence, the address decoder and various memory/port enables can be monitored. No memory, either ROM or RAM, is needed to perform this **free-run** test (see also Fig. 15.4 on page 256). As there no program memory, at what address do you think the processor will fetch its first op-code word?

Example 11.3

A student reports that his system appears to hang whenever the instruction move.w #0AAAAh,09002h is executed. It is suspected that this is due to a fault in the $\overline{DTACK}$ generator for this address. In order to prove this suspicion, the Data and Address buses are monitored when the processor hangs, together with $\overline{AS}$, $\overline{UDS}$, $\overline{LDS}$, $\overline{DTACK}$ and R/$\overline{W}$. What would you expect to see in a *16-bit mode* system if the hypothesis is correct?

Solution

If $\overline{DTACK}$ remains high during the execution of this instruction then a continual stream of wait states will extend the bus cycle indefinitely. At this point in time the Address bus will register the location 009002h with the code AAAAh on the Data bus. Both $\overline{\text{LDS}}$ and $\overline{\text{UDS}}$ will be active and R/$\overline{\text{W}}$ will be low to indicate a Write cycle. Thus in summary we have:

Address bus	0000 0000 1001 0000 0000 0010
Data bus	1010 1010 1010 1010
$\overline{\text{DTACK}}$	1
$\overline{\text{UDS}}$	0
$\overline{\text{LDS}}$	0
$\overline{\text{AS}}$	0
R/$\overline{\text{W}}$	0

Example 11.4
A diagnostic routine continually sends out the pattern 01010101b (55h) to a port located at 09000h in an *8-bit mode* system. The listing file for this program is:

```
1                             .processor m68000
2   000400   13FC0055   LOOP:   move.b     #55h,09000h
             00009000
3   000408   60F6               bra        LOOP
4                               .end
```

What sequence of states would you expect to see on the Data and Address buses as the program runs?

Solution
Table 11.1 shows the binary levels on the two buses for the 13 bus cycles comprising this two-instruction loop. Also shown are R/$\overline{\text{W}}$, $\overline{\text{DTACK}}$ and $\overline{\text{AS}}$ ($\overline{\text{LDS}}$ is similar to $\overline{\text{AS}}$).

The first instruction move.b #55h,09000h is coded as the four words 13 FC 00 55 00 00 90 00, each byte of which is seen on the 8-bit Data bus as this is fetched one byte at a time. The Address bus carries the incrementing Program Counter which points to each byte. I have used the eight-bit mode in this example, to reduce the size of the table — and omitted for the same reason the always zero $a_{23}...a_{16}$. In the case of the full 16-bit mode the fetch portion of this instruction would only take four bus cycles, with the 16-bit Data bus carrying the words 13FC 0055 0000 9000 and the Address bus going up in steps of 2 (i.e. no a_0).

Rather confusingly, the op-code word for the following instruction (60 FA) now appears on the Data bus rather than activity pertaining

Address bus	Data bus	$\overline{AS}$	$\overline{DTACK}$	R/$\overline{W}$	
Fetch move.b #55h,9000h					
0400h 0 0 0 0 0 1 0 0 0 0 0 0 0 0 0 0	0 0 0 1 0 0 1 1	⎍	⎍	1	13h
0401h 0 0 0 0 0 1 0 0 0 0 0 0 0 0 0 1	1 1 1 1 1 1 0 0	⎍	⎍	1	FCh
0402h 0 0 0 0 0 1 0 0 0 0 0 0 0 0 1 0	0 0 0 0 0 0 0 0	⎍	⎍	1	00h
0403h 0 0 0 0 0 1 0 0 0 0 0 0 0 0 1 1	0 1 0 1 0 1 0 1	⎍	⎍	1	55h
0404h 0 0 0 0 0 1 0 0 0 0 0 0 0 1 0 0	0 0 0 0 0 0 0 0	⎍	⎍	1	00h
0405h 0 0 0 0 0 1 0 0 0 0 0 0 0 1 0 1	0 0 0 0 0 0 0 0	⎍	⎍	1	00h
0406h 0 0 0 0 0 1 0 0 0 0 0 0 0 1 1 0	1 0 0 1 0 0 0 0	⎍	⎍	1	90h
0407h 0 0 0 0 0 1 0 0 0 0 0 0 0 1 1 1	0 0 0 0 0 0 0 0	⎍	⎍	1	00h
Prefetch bra LOOP					
0408h 0 0 0 0 0 1 0 0 0 0 0 0 1 0 0 0	0 1 1 0 0 0 0 0	⎍	⎍	1	60h
0409h 0 0 0 0 0 1 0 0 0 0 0 0 1 0 0 1	1 1 1 1 0 1 1 0	⎍	⎍	1	F6h
then execute move.b by sending 55h to 9000h					
9000h 1 0 0 1 0 0 0 0 0 0 0 0 0 0 0 0	0 1 0 1 0 1 0 1	⎍	⎍	0	55h
Prefetch the next word and internally execute bra					
040Ah 0 0 0 0 0 1 0 0 0 0 0 0 1 0 1 0	X X X X X X X X	⎍	⎍	1	
040Bh 0 0 0 0 0 1 0 0 0 0 0 0 1 0 1 1	X X X X X X X X	⎍	⎍	1	

Table 11.1 *Snapshot of bus activity for one pass through the loop.*

to the execution of move.b. This is because the 68000 MPU keeps two words from the instruction stream in an internal **prefetch** register buffer. As words are extracted from the queue, it is topped up at the first opportunity via bus activity. Thus now the op-code word for move.b has been extracted from the prefetch queue, it is immediately topped up by the next word — in this case the code for bra LOOP. Only then can execution proceed. This technique, sometimes referred to as **pipelining**, can enhance performance by using any idle bus cycles to keep the queue full. Thus activity on the buses is not always a straightforward progression, but may involve some out-of-sequence intermingling. This tangling is especially a problem in newer processors which use larger more intelligent prefetch buffers, known as caches. Here, when a Conditional Branch is fetched both potential destination op-code words may have been collected and lie in the cache, ready for immediate progression no matter what the outcome. The 68010 MPU, in the case of a small loop, such as above, will keep the instructions for the entire loop in its cache, and no external bus activity is seen until the loop is exited.

The execute portion of this instruction involves only one bus cycle, in which the Address bus points to the destination 09000h and the immediate byte data 55h placed on the Data bus.

With execution complete, the word following the bra LOOP in-struction is prefetched and placed in the queue. Of course this will eventually be thrown away, as the instruction bra will always cause the execution to go back to 00400h. This 'phantom' word is denoted by Xs in the table, as we have no information concerning entities at this point. If the instruction were a Conditional Branch, then this prefetched word would be the op-code for the next instruction to be executed if the condition was not met.

The execution of a Conditional Branch involves testing for the appropriate Code Condition Register flag states and then conditionally adding the offset skip to the Program Counter. This takes six clock cycles and is done internally — i.e. does not involve any external bus activity. The Unconditional Branch of this example is a special case of this, and still takes six clock cycles for internal execution.

Self-assessment questions

11.1   What state would you expect the buses to be in during the *execute* cycle of the instruction move.w d0,0E030h if D0[15:0] were FF00*h*? How many bus cycles would it take for the 16- and eight-bit modes respectively? How long would it take at a clock rate of 10 MHz?

11.2   Due to noise, which corrupts the state of the Address bus, the processor tries to fetch data from a non-existent location. What do you think would happen, and how could you use this outcome to recover from this disastrous situation?

11.3   Repeat the analysis of Example 11.4 for the program:

```
1                              .processor m68000
2 000400  33FC0055 LOOP:  move.w  #0055h,09000h
          00009000
3 000408  4E71            nop                      ; Execution time nil
4 00040A  60F4            bra     LOOP
5                         .end
```

This time assume the full 16-bit mode.

11.4   One way of debugging hardware is to single-step the processor through each bus cycle and have it freeze in the middle, where the various logic levels can be examined (not forgetting the prefetch interleave discussed in Example 11.4). The best way of doing this is to disable the $\overline{\text{DTACK}}$ feedback, which will then insert wait states and effectively freeze the state of the buses (see Example 11.3). Once this has been done, a manual debounced switch can be used to enable the $\overline{\text{DTACK}}$, which will then allow the system to proceed to the next bus cycle and repeat the process.

Design a simple circuit that will:

1. Gate through $\overline{\text{DTACK}}$ on a ⌐ from the single-step switch.
2. Inhibit $\overline{\text{DTACK}}$ on a ⌐ from $\overline{\text{AS}}$.

Typically this will involve D flip flops and an AND gate.

Why do you think it would be necessary to debounce the single-step switch?

CHAPTER 12

Address decoders

One of the first tasks of the hardware designer of an MPU-based system is to decide where everything is to reside in memory space: RAMs, ROMs, parallel ports, serial ports etc. Circuitry must then be designed to implement this topology. In essence, such decoding circuitry is akin to the exchange in a telephone system, in that this is what determines which subscriber responds to a specific number.

When you have completed this chapter, you will:

* *Understand the concept of the memory map.*
* *Appreciate the function of and need for an address decoder.*
* *Know how to split the memory space into zones.*
* *Appreciate the role of* $\overline{AS}$ *in decoding circuitry.*
* *Know how to design circuitry to divide a zone into select signals for individual devices.*
* *Understand the phenomenon and danger of multiple selection.*
* *Appreciate the concepts of image and base addresses.*
* *Comprehend how the FC2 signal can be used to switch between Supervisor and User address space.*
* *Know how to generate a* $\overline{DTACK}$ *signal for peripheral devices that require the insertion of wait states or can go ahead at full speed.*

A selection mechanism is necessary to the operation of an MPU, so that of the various things which use the common Data highway to communicate, only one will be active at any time. The topology of this arrangement was shown in Fig. 11.1 on page 177. Here the box labelled 'Decoder' picked up patterns on the Address bus and used these to enable the appropriate device which was to respond to particular patterns or **addresses**. From this description we see that an **address decoder** is simply a combinational logic circuit, configured to recognize specific code patterns, in the manner described in Chapter 2. Implementation hardware can range from SSI gates through MSI and to LSI programmable logic arrays. Here we will look at the design of some straightforward decoder circuits, together with their characteristics.

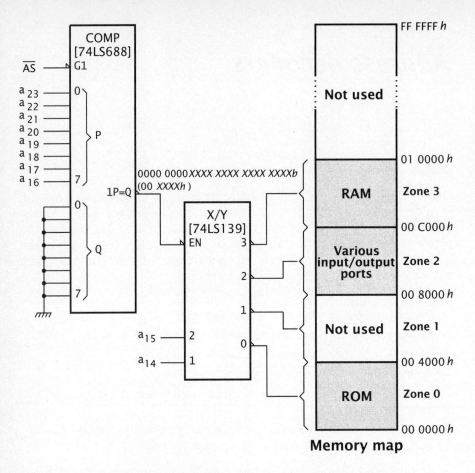

Figure 12.1 *Memory map and configurable zone decoder.*

Consider a simple system which will require ROM memory of not more than 16 Kbytes, RAM memory of a similar capacity and various input/output ports. This arrangement is shown diagrammatically as a map to the right of Fig. 12.1. This **memory map** shows the address range between 00 0000h and 00 FFFFh split into four zones, each of 16 Kbyte capacity (i.e. spanning 2^{14} byte addresses). The RAM memory has been located in the top zone, followed down by a space for up to 16,384 (16 K = 2^{14}) byte-sized input/output ports. Finally, the bottom zone is reserved for ROM, with the middle bottom space unallocated. In the same manner all memory up from 01 0000h to FF FFFFh is not used.

A $\frac{1}{2}$74LS139 2- to 4-line natural decoder (see Fig. 2.5(a) on page 19) uses address lines a_{15} and a_{14} to generate the four Zone Select lines. This device is in turn enabled by a 74LS688 eight-bit equality detector (see

Fig. 2.7 on page 21) which is active when all of the address lines $a_{23}...a_{16}$ are 0. Thus the 74LS139 is only enabled when these address lines are equal to zero, that is when an address fits the template 0000 0000 *XXXX XXXX XXXX XXXXb*.

Each output line of the 74LS139 responds to any address within this template further qualified by the address lines a_{15} and a_{14}. Thus the line enabling the ROM is active for any address fitting the template 0000 0000 **00***XX XXXX XXXX XXXXb*, i.e. 00 0000-00 3FFF*h*. Similarly, the ports will lie within the template 0000 0000 **01***XX XXXX XXXX XXXXb*, or in the range 00 8000-00 BFFF*h* and the RAM will be defined by the template 0000 0000 **11***XX XXXX XXXX XXXXb*, range 00 C000-00 FFFF*h*.

The choice of these address ranges is rather arbitrary, except — as we saw in Chapter 9 — that the ROM must lie from address 00 0000*h* upwards, as it has to hold the Reset and other exception vectors. However, the zone size is easily increased. For example, grounding the Comparator's P_7 and P_6 input pins, and using $a_{17}a_{16}$ in place of $a_{15}a_{14}$ in the 74LS139 decoder, gives four zones of 64 Kbytes each. By changing the $Q_7...Q_0$ connections, the four zones can be bodily moved to anywhere within the address space.

Irrespective of address line patterns, the decoder will not operate unless $\overline{\text{Address Strobe}}$ is active. We see from Figs. 11.2 and 11.3 on pages 183 and 185 that the address is stable when $\overline{\text{AS}}$ is low. If $\overline{\text{AS}}$ were not used as a qualifier, then the decoder may detect the various transient Address bus states at the beginning and end of a read or write cycle, resulting in glitches (spurious responses) at its output.

Within any zone (akin to a telephone area code) we will usually need to select between many individual devices. This may mean enabling an individual chip from a memory bank or one of many peripheral interface input/output ports. A memory chip of course does not appear as a single address, as it comprises many addressable cells; see Fig. 2.17 on page 31. As a consequence of this a memory chip has an on-board decoder. When enabled by the external address decoder, this internal decoder selects an individual location inside the memory chip, which is then connected to the Data bus.

To illustrate secondary decoding we will take for our example the specification that eight byte-sized peripheral interface ports are to be located anywhere in Zone 2 (i.e. 00 8000-00 BFFF*h*). We will look at three different implementations and examine their characteristics.

The first of these is shown in Fig. 12.2. **Linear decoding** uses a single gate to generate each device select signal. In this case, a single individual address line is used in conjunction with the Zone 2 template in order further to qualify each select output.

Although our circuit works, it does have one rather disconcerting "feature". There are certain addresses that will activate more than one select

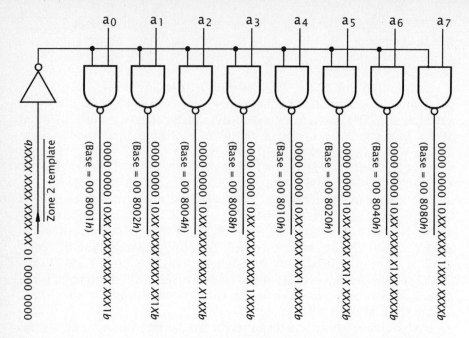

Figure 12.2 *Linear decoding.*

line at the same time. Thus the address 00 8003h will simultaneously activate the two lower (leftmost) lines, as can be seen from the binary form of the address 0000 0000 1000 0000 0000 0011b. Even worse, the address 00 80FFh will activate *all* outputs simultaneously.[1] Provided that the software is well behaved, i.e. never uses such errant addresses, there will be no problem with **multiple selection**. However, physical damage may potentially occur! Consider a washing machine controller which simultaneously turns on the spin motor and the water inlet solenoid, whilst at the same time turning off the outlet pump! Although the software may be fixed in ROM and debugged, there really is no such thing as 100% reliable software. For instance, noise could force the processor into an area of memory which accidentally sends out the address 00 8FFFh and — meltdown!

Apart from the problem of multiple selection, the linear decoder does not make very efficient use of available memory space. Using the setup shown here, a total of 14 peripherals (using $a_0...a_{13}$) could be selected from a zone which potentially could support 16,384 (2^{14}) such devices. It does however fulfil our specification. A greater address packing density can be achieved using gates with more than two inputs and a combination of address lines (see self-assessment question 12.4). However, the only advantage of this circuit, namely its simplicity and low cost, is compromised.

---

[1] Can you work out any other such addresses in Zone 2? There are lots of them!

In summary, for linear decoding we have the following advantages and disadvantages:

- Advantages:
    1. Simple.
    2. Cheap.
- Disadvantages:
    1. Inefficient use of memory space.
    2. Multiple selection.
    3. Inflexible (difficult to alter addresses).

The circuit shown in Fig. 12.3 gets round the problem of multiple selection by using a 74LS138 3- to 8-line natural decoder (see Fig. 2.5(b) on page 19) to qualify the Zone template with the eight *unique* combinations of $a_2\,a_1\,a_0$. By definition, a natural decoder cannot have more than one output active at a time.

With the connections shown, the eight select addresses are 8000–8007h. If the peripheral devices were word-sized, then $a_3\,a_2\,a_1$ could be used in place of $a_2\,a_1\,a_0$, giving eight even addresses from 8000h to

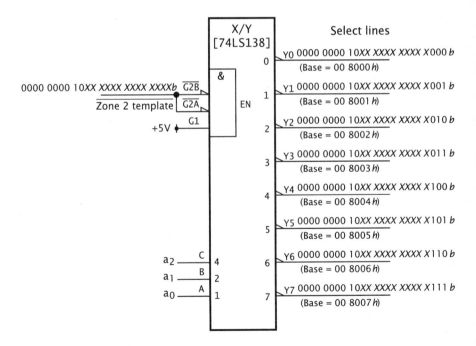

Figure 12.3 *Partial decoding.*

800Eh. This could also have been done with the linear circuit by using lines $a_1...a_8$ as qualifiers.

Like the previous circuit, not all address lines partake in the decoding equation; in this case $a_{13}...a_3$. Each one of these omitted lines is indicated by a don't care X in the diagram. The value of any X does not affect the output in any way, and thus such a signal can respond to more than one address. In this circuit there are 11 omitted variables, so that each select output will respond to $2^{11} = 2048$ different addresses; for example, Y_0 answers to 00 8000, 00 8008, 00 8010 ...00 BFF8h. Although this applies to each output; for example, Y_1 responds to 00 8001, 00 8009 ...00 BFF9h, the addresses do not overlap; that is there is no multiple selection.

The address where all Xs are 0 is known as the **base address**, and all higher combinations are **image addresses**. In general, with n omitted address lines, there are $2^n - 1$ images. Thus, in our linear select circuit there are $2^{13} - 1 = 8191$ images. Unlike multiple selection, there are no harmful effects due to images, although the more images there are the lower is the packing efficiency. Images may be reduced by using additional decoding operating on omitted address lines, but this is only economically efficient if simple circuitry cannot place the desired complement of devices in available memory space.

In summary, for partial decoding we have the following advantges and disadvantages:

- Advantages:
    1. No multiple selection.
    2. Relatively cost-effective and simple.
- Disadvantages:
    1. Inflexible (difficult to alter addresses).
    2. Still not very efficient use of address space.

None of our circuits have been very flexible if the address range needs to be changed. For example, if we wanted the eight addresses of the partial decoding circuit to move to 9000-9007h, then we could connect a_{12} to G1. This is easy enough, but each case is different, and most would need additional circuitry to implement. Where this flexibility is important, for example if the decoder were destined to be part of a plug-in card for a personal computer, then the extra complexity of the circuit shown in Fig. 12.4 is warranted.

The 74LS688 equality detector enables the front-end 74LS138 natural decoder only when the address lines $a_{13}...a_6$ equal the state of the eight switches; here shown set to 0100 0000. With these settings, the range is now 9000-9007h. Changing this range, within the chosen zone, is simply a matter of altering the switch settings. If these switches are replaced by

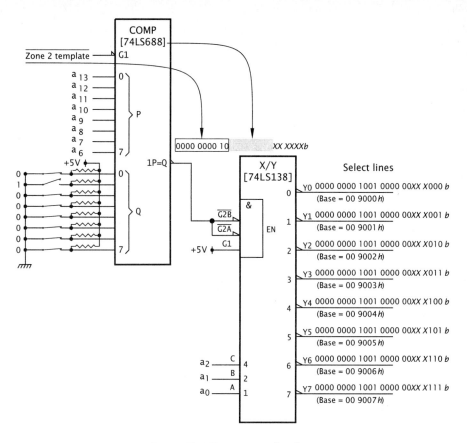

Figure 12.4 *Comparator decoding.*

latches, the MPU can change the peripheral addresses on startup to suit itself, and this is the technique used by 'plug and play' cards for IBM-type PCs. In any case, as a side effect the number of images has been reduced to seven.

In summary, for comparator decoding we have the following advantages and disadvantages:

- Advantages:

    1. Very flexible.

    2. Efficient use of address space.

- Disadvantages:

    1. Relatively expensive.

    2. More complex circuitry.

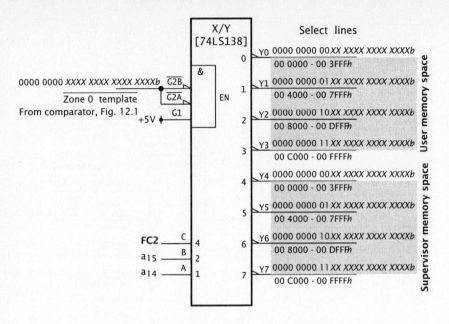

Figure 12.5 *Supervisor and User state memory.*

On page 67 we discussed the desirability of using separate memory for the Supervisor and User states. Supervisor memory should be invisible to User programs. External circuitry can tell which state the processor is operating in by monitoring the Function Code 2 (FC2) pin (see page 180), which is 1 for the Supervisor state and 0 for the User state. If this two separate memory universe strategy is to be implemented, FC2 can be used to switch in one or other address decoder, each enabling the appropriate memory bank. A simple example of this is shown in Fig. 12.5. Here the 74LS138 3- to 8-line natural decoder replaces the 74LS139 2- to 4-line equivalent in Fig. 12.1. FC2 is used to select which output is active in addition to a_{14} and a_{15}. The net effect of this is potentially to activate one of the four outputs $Y_0...Y_3$ if FC2 is low (the User state) and $Y4...Y_7$ when FC2 is high (the Supervisor state). The zone addresses are the same for corresponding pairs; for example, zone Y_0 activates ROM between 00 0000h and 00 3FFFh as does zone Y_4. However, the former ROM will be that containing user application programs, and the latter the operating system ROM.

Our final topic here considers the $\overline{\text{Data Transfer ACKnowledge}}$ control signal. You will recall from Chapter 11 that $\overline{\text{DTACK}}$ is the signal a selected device or port must *return* to the MPU when it is ready to communicate via the Data bus. If $\overline{\text{DTACK}}$ is not returned on time, the processor idles until this happens, as shown in Fig. 11.4 on page 187. These wait states

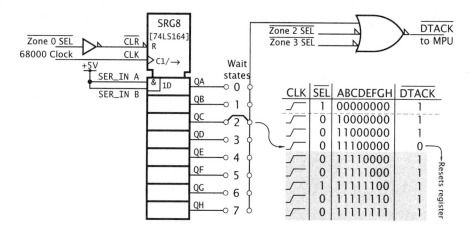

Figure 12.6 *Generating the* $\overline{\text{DTACK}}$ *signal for a slow device.*

enable the processor to adapt to peripheral devices with varying response times.

Although Motorola have a family of interface devices compatible with the 68000 family, such as the 68230 PI/T (Parallel Interface and Timer), which can generate a $\overline{\text{DTACK}}$ signal automatically, the majority of general-purpose interface ports and memory devices do not. In such cases, the hardware engineer has to provide additional circuitry to perform this task. Where these devices can respond quickly enough so that no wait states are required,[2] the various select signals from the address decoder can simply be OR-gated together and fed back to the MPU's $\overline{\text{DTACK}}$ pin. In some situations it may even be permanently conected to ground, as shown in Fig. 15.3 on page 254.

Where devices are too slow to respond, typically ROMs and liquid crystal display interfaces, then a delay circuit is needed for each such $\overline{\text{DTACK}}$ reply. This may typically be implemented as a monostable, counter or shift register. An example of the latter is given in Fig. 12.6, where we assume that Zone 0 is to a slow ROM, and Zones 2 and 3 do not require a delay. Normally when the ROM is not being accessed, the $\overline{\text{Zone 0}}$ select signal is high and all shift register outputs are reset low. When the ROM is enabled, the Zone select line goes low, thus releasing the 74LS164's $\overline{\text{CLR}}$ input. As the Serial inputs are held high, the flip flops will each in turn become high, advancing from Q_A to Q_H on the rising edge of the 68000's Clock. This gives a selectable delay of up to seven clock periods according to the position of the adjustable link. Once the high reaches the link, the OR gate brings the MPU's $\overline{\text{DTACK}}$ pin low and the processor completes its delayed cycle. The $\overline{\text{Zone 0}}$ select line then goes back high and the register resets again.

---

[2]Around 120 ns for an 8 MHz clock; 60 ns for 12.5 MHz is more than adequate.

Examples

Example 12.1

Design an address decoder that will enable up to four separate *word-sized read-only* peripheral devices at 09000–09006h and up to four separate *word-sized write-only* devices within the same address range.

Solution

As can be seen from Fig. 12.7, we use a 74LS138 enabled when in Zone 2 by the pattern $a_{13} a_{12} = 01$. The clever part is to use $R/\overline{W}$ as the upper channel select, which enables outputs $Y_0 Y_1 Y_2 Y_3$ when a write cycle is in progress (see Fig. 11.3 on page 185) — $R/\overline{W} = 0$ — and $Y_4 Y_5 Y_6 Y_7$ when a read cycle is in progress (see Fig. 11.2 on page 183) — $R/\overline{W} = 1$. The remaining channel selects are driven by a_2 and a_1, and pick one of four addresses within each band. a_0 is omitted, so addresses go up in twos, as required to enable word-sized ports (see Fig. 13.7 on page 223). Assuming that the Zone 2 decoder has no images, each output has $2^9 - 1 = 511$ image word locations.

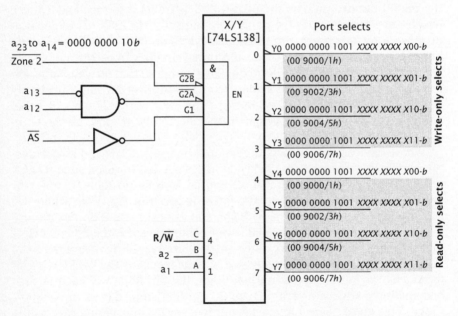

Figure 12.7 *Decoding for four read-only and write-only word-sized peripherals.*

Example 12.2

Circuitry is to be designed so that a lamp or buzzer can be turned

off by the MPU. Using a minimum of hardware in addition to *any* two
address decoder outputs, show how this could be done.

Solution

A simple solution to this problem is shown in Fig. 12.8. Here a
cross-coupled NAND latch (see Fig. 2.13 on page 27) can be set by
bringing its $\bar{S}$ input low. As shown, this could be done in software
by using the instruction move.b d0,08001h. In a similar fashion an
instruction that accesses address 08002*h* would reset the latch.[3]

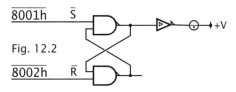

8001h $\bar{S}$

Fig. 12.2

8002h $\bar{R}$

+V

Figure 12.8 *Controlling the state of a lamp.*

Any instruction that targets the appropriate address will activate
the latch, but read–modify–write instructions (see page 91), such as
clr.b 08001h or addq.b #1,08001h, can sometimes have unex-
pected outcomes, as they access the address twice. Firstly the data in
memory is read, and then the following write back into memory; e.g.
bring in data from 08001*h* — add #1 to it — return it to 08001*h*. In
the case of a decoder like that in Fig. 12.2 this will mean that $\bar{S}$ will be
pulsed twice, which causes no problem. However, with decoders that
distinguish between read and write cycles, such as that in Fig. 12.7,
then two *different* decoder lines will pulse, possibly with mayhem
occurring!

This is a rather unorthodox way to control peripheral devices, as
the Data bus is not involved. Thus the instruction move.b d7,08001h
or move.b #26,08001h gives exactly the same interaction of software
with hardware. As we shall see in the next chapter, the Data bus is
key to the interface function. In our telephone analogy, this is rather
like using the signalling function to pass a message; for example
telling your visitor to phone when they arrive home safely and hang
up when the bell rings twice. A rather limited form of communication
— not encouraged by the telephone companies!

Example 12.3

The decoder circuit shown in Fig. 12.9 is based on an expansion
memory card for the original IBM PC which could add either one or

---

[3]The decoder shown in Fig. 12.2 has multiple selection; so what would happen if the
instruction move.b d0,08003h were executed?

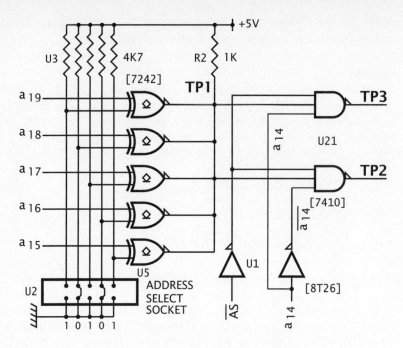

Figure 12.9 *A memory card decoder.*

two banks each of 16 Kbyte capacity. The position in the memory bank could be selected by setting up an appropriate pattern of links. Given the pattern shown, determine the address space occupied by each bank. Note that there are no images, as the PC used an Intel 8088 MPU, which only has address lines up to a_{19}, giving a total address space of $2^{20} = 1$ Mbyte.

Solution

The 7242 comprises five ENOR gates, each of which acts as a one-bit equality detector in the manner described on page 14. As these gates are open-collector, if the two input logic levels are the same, the output goes off (logic 1). If *all* gates register equality, then Test Point 1 (TP1) will be pulled up to +5 V by R2. If *any* ENOR gate is logic 0, then TP1 will be grounded. With the links as shown, TP1 will be high for addresses in the range 1011 1*XXX XXXX XXXX*b. Address line a_{14} is further used with two 7410 NAND gates to expand this to two select lines as follows:

TP2 = 1010 10*XX XXXX XXXX XXXX*b = A8000–ABFFF*h*
TP3 = 1010 11*XX XXXX XXXX XXXX*b = AC000–AFFFF*h*

Note that although AS is shown as a qualifier, this is a 68000-family control signal. The nearest equivalent in the 808X family is ALE for Address Latch Enable.

Memory expansion of this size today is derisory. How would you adapt this circuit to give two banks of 16 Mbyte capacity? Remember that MPUs like the 68020 and above, as well as the Intel 80286 and above, have address lines up to a_{31}. What capacity does 2^{32} represent?

Self-assessment questions

12.1 How would you eliminate all images in Fig. 12.3?

12.2 What would happen in Fig. 12.6 if the link fell out?

12.3 What effect would using a_3 to drive $\overline{G2B}$ and a_4 connected to G1 have in Fig. 12.3?

12.4 In Fig. 12.2, how could you use 3-I/P gates with a selection of address lines to increase the efficiency of the circuit, using only address lines $a_0...a_4$ to generate eight selections?

12.5 In Fig. 12.1 as an economy measure, configurability is not required. Suggest how the circuit could be simplified.

12.6 Design an address decoder using any technique to enable four byte devices in the range 8080–808Fh.

CHAPTER 13

Interfacing

Having made contact using the address decoder, the next problem is engineering a connection between the peripheral device and the Data bus, in the manner of Fig. 11.1 on page 177. Once this connection has been made, data can be passed to or from the MPU. Two scenarios are possible. The MPU can gate data *from* a peripheral device to the Data bus and read it into an internal register. The alternative is to write data out from a Data register via the data bus *to* a peripheral device, which must grab and hold this data. Irrespective of the direction of data flow, in or out, circuitry is necessary to interface the Data bus, which is a *common resource*, to the appropriate device. Such circuitry is called a peripheral interface **port** (so called after a way into or out of a country).

In this chapter we will look at some simple input and output ports, together with the analogous problem of interfacing to memory chips. For simplicity, initially we will assume that the MPU is operating in eight-bit mode (or is a 68008 device), and that an address decoder similar to that in Fig. 12.7 on page 206 is in situ. Later we will extend the discussion to 16-bit Data buses. After reading this chapter you will:

- *Know why input ports are implemented using three-state buffers.*
- *Realize that such ports are read-only and that instructions that attempt to write to such a port will fail.*
- *Be able to design hardware and software to interrogate any number of peripheral digital signals.*
- *Know why output ports are implemented using latch or flip flop memory elements.*
- *Understand how to deal with the critical race timing situation when writing to an output port.*
- *Realize that such ports are write-only and that instructions that attempt to read from such a port will fail.*
- *Understand the function of handshake lines and be able to distinguish between protocol and data interchange.*
- *Be able to interface memory to the MPU's buses.*
- *Appreciate the technique of serial data transmission, both sychronous and asynchronous.*

Consider that we want to interrogate the state of a single switch. For example, it could be the economy control on a dishwasher or the push switch on a pedestrian road crossing. Now, such a switch could not be directly connected to the Data bus, as this is a *shared resource*. The whole system would seize up if one of these lines were to be permanently grounded or connected to the logic circuitry's power supply!

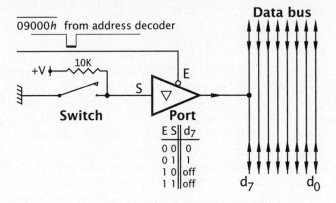

Figure 13.1 *A one-bit input port.*

With this consideration in mind, our approach is to connect the switch to a Data line only when enabled by the address decoder — at all other times it should be disconnected. Thus the properties of a suitable interface port must be:

- When enabled, input signals must pass through to the Data bus line.
- When disabled, the path between switch and bus must be disconnected.

The **three-state buffer** of Fig. 2.4 on page 18 can be used for this purpose. Thus in Fig. 13.1 we interpose a three-state buffer between the switch and one of the Data lines. This serves as the input port for the switch. In the normal state of events, when the address decoder output (arbitrarily shown in the diagram as 09000h) is inactive, i.e. high, the three-state buffer is disabled and its output is high-impedance (practically off). The Data line (again, arbitrarily shown as d_7) is then free to be used for other purposes. However, when address 09000h activates the decoder, for example during the execute cycle of the instruction move.b 09000h,d4, the three-state buffer will be enabled and the state of the switch connected to line 7 of the Data bus, whence it can be read by the MPU at the end of the read cycle (see Fig. 13.2(b)).

To check the state of this switch, a software construction such as:

```
LOOP:   btst #7,09000h  ; Check only bit 7 of the input port
        bne  LOOP       ; IF =1 (switch open) THEN try again
        .... .....      ; ELSE continue as switch is closed (=0)
```

will repetitively interrogate the state of d_7 at address $09000h$. If the switch is open, then the voltage at node S will be $+V$ (logic 1).[1] This will be gated through to d_7 when the address $09000h$ is output by the execution of the btst (Bit TeST) instruction.[2] As this reads a 1 at bit 7, the following bne will take the execution back to LOOP and the switch will be interrogated again. As soon as the switch is closed, node S will go low, and this will be reflected on d_7 whenever btst #7,09000h is next executed. This will cause the **Z** flag to set (as bit 7 is zero) and the following Branch will fail. The program now exits the loop and proceeds to the next segment.

Up to eight switches can be accessed in one byte-sized read cycle by simply using the appropriate number of three-state buffers. The input port shown in Fig. 13.2(a) uses the 74LS244 as a single-chip implementation of an eight-bit input port operating in exactly the same manner as the single-bit port. The 74LS244 is especially useful, as its output can drive a larger current than normal, which serves to charge/discharge the capacitance of long bus lines more quickly.[3]

The waveform diagram of Fig. 13.2(b) shows the decoder's output dropping low whenever the address $09000h$ is on the Address bus and when Address Strobe ($\overline{\text{AS}}$) is active — after a short propagation delay. Typically this would be the situation during the execution cycle of btst #n,09000h or move.b 09000h,dm. The state of the eight switches then appears on the Data bus, again after the 74LS244's short propagation delay. The MPU then reads in this data, in the usual way (see Fig. 11.2 on page 183) at the end of clock phase S6, assuming that DaTa Transfer ACKnowledge ($\overline{\text{DTACK}}$) has been asserted.

As in our previous program fragment, we can examine any single switch, for example btst #3,09000h for switch 3. For more sophisticated processing, we can copy the switch state to a Data register. As an example of this, consider a subroutine that will sample the current state of the switches and only return whenever 1000 successive reads show no change.

Program 13.1 commences by copying the state of the switches to D7.B and clearing the count which is held in D0.W. The inner loop simply compares this original reading with the current reading (line 10), and if they are not the same returns execution to G_START, which resets the count and begins the process all over again. Otherwise the count is incremented and

---

[1] As dictated by the 10 kΩ pull-up resistor. The resistance should be neither too low, as it will conduct a high current to ground when the switch is closed, nor too high, as it will not dampen down induced noise.

[2] Remember from Table 6.5 on page 100 that btst is byte-sized for memory accesses and long-word-sized for data registers. Thus word or long-word ports will need to be read into a Data register before this instruction is used.

[3] Or match the transmission line characteristic impedance more closely, depending on your point of view.

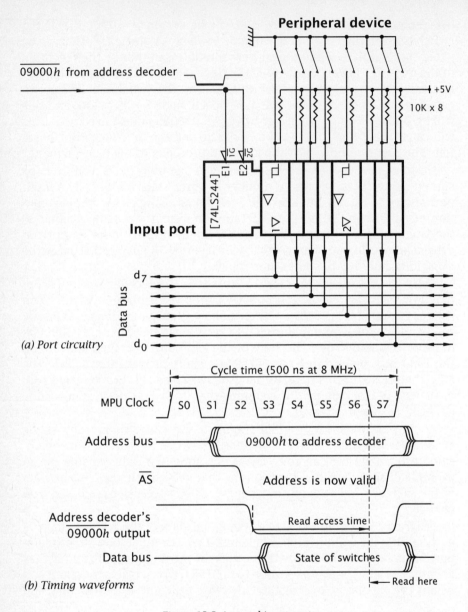

Figure 13.2 *An octal input port.*

another comparison is made. If this latter process is repeated successfully 1000 times, then the switches are assumed to be in a stable state and the subroutine exits with the original reading still in D7.B. The subroutine is transparent, as the counter register D0.W is restored on exit.

Program 13.1 *Sampling the switches for stability.*

```
; **************************************************************
; * FUNCTION: Returns a stable switch state              *
; * ENTRY   : None                                       *
; * EXIT    : Switch state in D7.B                        *
; **************************************************************
            .define  SWITCHES = 09000h
GET_IT:     movem.l  d0,-(sp)       ; Save register
G_START:    move.b   SWITCHES,d7    ; Get original settings
            clr.w    d0             ; Use D0 as counter
G_LOOP:     cmp.b    d7,SWITCHES    ; Compare original with current values
            bne      G_START        ; IF not same, restart all over again
            addq.w   #1,d0          ; ELSE chalk up one more success
            cmp.b    #1000,d0       ; Reached 1,000 yet?
            bne      G_LOOP         ; IF not THEN go again
            movem.l  (sp)+,d0       ; ELSE restore the value of D0
            rts                     ; and exit with switch state in D7.B
```

This subroutine is of practical importance, as mechanical switches do not make clean contact and bounce (literally) for several milliseconds before settling down. During this period, any readings will be unreliable. Some form of debouncing, as a form of signal conditioning, is therefore frequently required. We have already seen in Fig. 2.13 on page 27 that this can be done in hardware, but provided that the MPU has enough processing time in reserve, this software solution is more economical.

One point to be careful of is that although our switch port can be read as if it were a normal memory location, it most decidedly does not behave in the same manner. Data at this address is *read-only* and *cannot be changed by software* — only by the tame human outside. Unlike an analogous ROM location, the contents of which must also be treated as read-only, the contents of an input port can change, but it appears to the MPU to alter spontaneously. In the **C** language such a variable is called **volatile**. On this basis the following program will fail

```
; This program is supposed to do something n times,
; where n is the switch setting
LOOP:    subq.b   #1,09000h      ; For as long as n>0
         jsr      DO_SOMETHING   ; go and do something
         tst.b    09000h         ; Is count down to zero yet?
         bne      LOOP           ; IF not THEN go again
```

as it tries to alter the contents of $09000h$. Of course subq.b #1,09000h is an example of a read-modify-write instruction. It does its work by bringing in the contents of $09000h$ into a temporary MPU register, decrements it (both of these are OK) and back — which fails. *You cannot write a value into an array of switches!*

What if you have to read more than eight digital lines? Take as an example 32 infra-red sensors, which are part of an industrial building intruder alarm. Simply use as many eight-bit input ports as is necessary, each located at a unique address, as shown in Fig. 13.3. Each port can then be interrogated as and when this is necessary. Actually, the complete array shown in Fig. 13.3 can be loaded into a Data register in a single instruction, e.g. move.l 09000h,d0. In reality when the processor is in eight-bit mode there will be four sequential read cycles at $09000h$, $09001h$, $09002h$ and $09003h$. The whole will be companded in the destination Data register

24	16	8	0
Port3	Port2	Port1	Port0

D0 in that order and can be examined using the btst or any other relevant instruction.

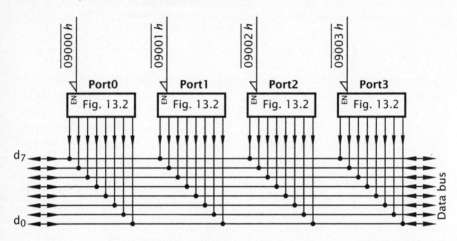

Figure 13.3 *Reading 32 switches.*

Suppose the MPU wants to send out data, perhaps to light a lamp or close a relay. Output peripherals cannot be hung directly on to the Data bus, as this is a *common resource* and will accordingly change during each bus cycle. Something must be interposed between such a peripheral and the bus; this something is an **output port**.

The functions of an output port are:

- To sample data on the bus when such data is valid during the relevant write cycle.
- To hold such data until the next update, irrespective of what is happening on the Data bus.

These properties can be implemented using either flip flops or latches as a digital sample and hold.

In Fig. 13.4(a) a D latch is fed from (arbitrary) d_0, and is enabled when the (arbitrary) $\overline{09001h}$ decoder output is low. The state of d_0 passes

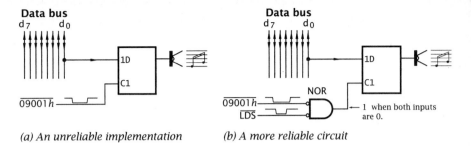

(a) An unreliable implementation (b) A more reliable circuit

Figure 13.4 *A one-bit output port.*

through the transparent latch as long as the address decoder output is active, and the value at the time the decoder goes back up high is that which is held. If we assume that the buzzer is activated on a high voltage, then the routine

```
BUZZ: move.b  #1,09001h   ; Send 00000001b to the port
      jsr     DELAY_1_SEC ; Hang around for 1 second
      move.b  #0,09001h   ; Turn buzzer off (or use clr.b)
```

will sound the buzzer for one second.

Although the circuit of Fig. 13.4(a) will function 90% of the time, there is an inherent weakness in the design. The problem is that the data on the bus disappears in a few tens of nanoseconds after Address Strobe ($\overline{AS}$) deactivates, near the end of the write cycle (t_{SHDOI} in Fig. 11.3 on page 185). Thus, by the time _／ from the address decoder freezes the D latch the data may have gone! Even though the address decoder is usually qualified by $\overline{AS}$, its propagation time plus any setup time demanded by the latch may well exceed this window of opportunity, as is depicted in Fig. 13.5(b). Thus we have a **critical race** between the decoder relaxing and the data collapsing. To ensure that the port wins the race, in Fig. 13.4(b) the decoder output is qualified with the Lower Data Strobe. This by-passes any decoder delay by directly clocking the flip flop (colloquially, kicking the flip flop up the backside).[4] When the MPU is in eight-bit mode the $\overline{LDS}$ goes low whenever data is stable.[5] When the MPU is in 16-bit mode then either $\overline{LDS}$ or Upper Data Strobe ($\overline{UDS}$) may be used, as shown in Fig. 13.7.

Up to eight output lines may be simultaneously controlled at a single byte address by enabling eight D flip flops or latches in parallel. Figure 13.5(a) shows eight light-emitting diodes (LEDs) as the output peripheral, optionally as segments of a seven-segment display (plus decimal point). An LED is a semiconductor diode where some[6] of the energy lost

---

[4]Actually the NOR gate will have some propagation delay; but not too much.
[5]In the eight-bit 68008 MPU, this is labelled $\overline{DS}$.
[6]Typically only a few per cent.

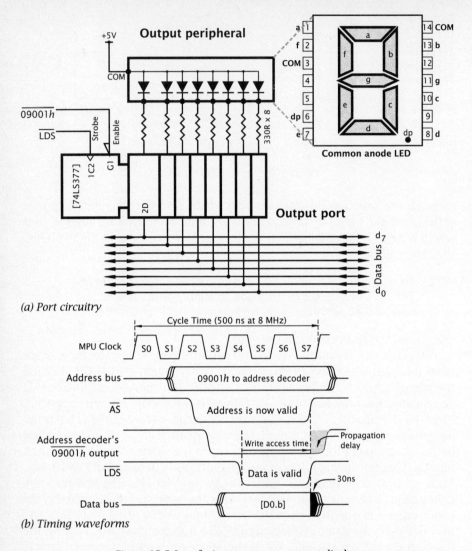

(a) Port circuitry

(b) Timing waveforms

Figure 13.5 *Interfacing to a seven-segment display.*

by charge carriers crossing the junction is emitted as light. It has a nominal 2 V junction drop, unlike the 0.7 V silicon equivalent, and the series resistors shown limit the current to around 10 mA for a 5 V supply.

The 74LS377 octal D flip flop, first introduced in Fig. 2.15, is used as the port's sample and hold. This device is convenient as it effectively integrates the NOR gate of Fig. 13.4(b). When enabled by the decoder's $09001h$, a _/‾ on $\overline{LDS}$ clocks the data into the flip flop array. Of course, kicking the port at this instant ensures that the critical race is won. I

Program 13.2 *Seven segment count down to zero.*

```
;  ****************************************************************
;  * FUNCTION: Counts down 7-segment display 0-9 at 1 s intervals*
;  * ENTRY    : None                                             *
;  * EXIT     : No change                                        *
;  * SUPPORT  : SVN_SEG natural BCD to 7-seg; DELAY_1_S           *
;  ****************************************************************
              .define  DISPLAY = 09001h
ANNUNCIATE:   movem.l  d0/d7,-(sp)    ; Save used registers
              moveq    #9,d0          ; Initialize counter to 9
ANN_LOOP:     jsr      SVN_SEG        ; Convert count to 7-seg code
              move.b   d7,DISPLAY     ; Returned in D7.B; display it
              jsr      DELAY_1_S      ; Hang around for 1 second
              subq.b   #1,d0          ; Decrement count
              bcc      ANN_LOOP       ; until drops below zero
              movem.l  (sp)+,d0/d7    ; Returned used registers
              rts                     ; and exit
```

have depicted the address decoder's propagation delay (shown shaded) in Fig. 13.5(b), as being longer than the persistence of data on the bus, shown blackened. If we used $\overline{09001h}$ alone as the trigger in this situation, the incorrect data would be grabbed from the bus. In contrast with the previous situation, we have used D flip flops rather than latches, but either will do the job.

As an example of the hardware–software interface, consider a subroutine that uses the seven-segment display as an annunciator to count down from 0 to 9 at a one-second rate. The count is kept in D0.B and converted to seven-segment code using the SVN_SEG subroutine from Program 8.6 on page 139. The one-second timing is courtesy of the DELAY_1_S subroutine of Program 8.1 on page 131. From our point of view here, the key line is 11, where the data (the active-low seven-segment code representation of the count in D7.B) is copied out to the port.

It must be understood that memory location $09001h$ is not like an ordinary RAM location, in that it is **write-only**. That means that instructions such as subq.b #1,09001h will not succeed, as the current state of this address must be *read* first — clearly impossible — before being processed and sent back out again.[7]

More than eight outputs can be controlled in the same manner as that shown in Fig. 13.3. Specifically, in the case of LEDs, it is possible to multiplex the displays. By this means, two eight-bit ports can control up to 8 eight-bit displays separately. This is done by enabling each display in

---

[7]It would of course be possible, but not particularly useful, to build a combination input and output port responding to the same address in which this could be done. How would you go about doing this?

turn and latching the appropriate data. If this performed rapidly enough, and higher currents used, the eye is fooled into thinking that the displays are individually controlled. Of course, this saving of hardware is at the expense of computing power, the processor spending a great deal of time performing the endless scan. Thus it is probably more cost-effective to offload this task on to hardware and let the MPU get on with its other tasks.

Reading switches and controlling lights are fairly undemanding tasks, as these various peripherals are fairly dumb. Thus switches can be read at any time, as and when the processor desires. However, many situations demand more of their interfaces than just plain three-state buffers or latches. Consider as an example, designing the intelligence into a printer. Data is transmitted, fairly rapidly and at an unknown speed from, say, a personal computer. How is the printer's MPU to know when new data has arrived? It may be several identical characters, such as a space sequence; how is the MPU to distinguish between them? Perhaps the printer's buffer is full or it is out of paper. How is the PC to know, and thus take the appropriate action?

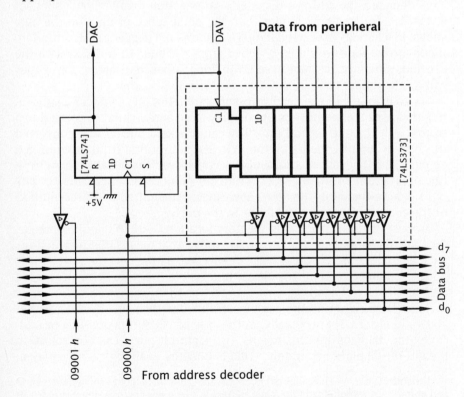

Figure 13.6 *A latched input port with handshake.*

One possible solution is shown in Fig. 13.6. Here the standard three-state buffer input port is augmented by a 74LS373 octal latch on the peripheral side. This allows the peripheral to latch its data and then move on to other things. To do this the peripheral (the PC printer port in our example) must be able to send a "Hello, here it is" signal to the port, designated as Data Valid ($\overline{DAV}$) in the diagram. If $\overline{DAV}$ is also used to set a flip flop, then this can be read at any time by the MPU via a one-bit input port — in our case as bit 7 of address $09001h$. Thus the MPU can check for the arrival of new data. This flip flop is also used to generate the status signal labelled Data ACcepted ($\overline{DAC}$). When the processor eventually reads the data, the Flag flip flop is automatically clocked back to zero. Thus the PC can tell that its last data byte has been read and it is clear to send the next character. Indeed, sometimes this line is labelled $\overline{CTS}$.

Both signal lines $\overline{DAV}$ and $\overline{DAC}$ are not data in themselves, but are involved in the protocol of interchanging the data. This protocol is of the form:

- The Peripheral
    - Hello, how are you? Are you ready for new data?
    - Here it is.
    - *Data is sent.*
- The MPU
    - Is there new data for me?
    - Thank you, see you again.
    - *Data is read.*

Such control and status lines are collectively known as **handshake** signals, which signifies their greeting (or protocol) role.

The complete sequence of operations is then:

1. PC checks the state of $\overline{DAC}$ to confirm that the printer's MPU is ready to accept the next character byte.
2. If clear to send then data is output and $\overline{DAV}$ pulses ($\neg\_\diagup\neg$) to latch it into the port's receive latch.
3. Simultaneously the Flag flip flop is set to 1.
4. Subsequently the MPU can read the state of this flag to check if new data is available.
5. If there is, then it is read in the normal way and the Flag flip flop is cleared. This signals the PC that the data has been read.

A simple subroutine that returns the value of any new data, and times out if nothing appears after 65,536 tries, is shown in Program 13.3(b). The byte-sized data is extended by padding out with 0s to word-size before

Program 13.3 *Handling the handshake port.*

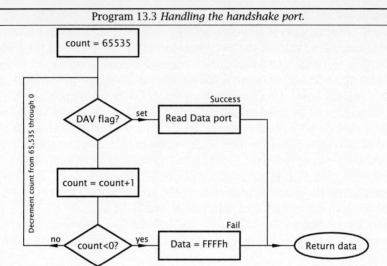

(a) Flowchart

```
;  ***********************************************************
;  * FUNCTION: Acquires new data from PC printer port        *
;  * ENTRY    : None                                         *
;  * EXIT     : Data in D7.W or else -1 if fail              *
;  ***********************************************************
             .define DATA = 09000h, FLAG = 09001h
GET_CHAR:    move.w  #0FFFFh,d0   ; D0 is the tries counter
GET_LOOP:    btst    #7,FLAG      ; Check the DAV Flag flip flop
             bne     GET_SUCCESS  ; IF =1 THEN success!
             subq.w  #1,d0        ; ELSE record failure and try
             bcc     GET_LOOP     ; again, unless underflowed
             move.w  #0FFFFh,d7   ; ELSE flag error by
             bra     GET_EXIT     ; exiting with -1 in D7

GET_SUCCESS:clr.w    d7           ; Get byte data into D7.W
             move.b  DATA,d7      ; with upper byte zero
GET_EXIT:    rts
```

(b) Coding

return. If the attempt fails, −1 (FFFF*h*) is returned as an error marker. This pattern can never be legitimate data, as the upper byte is normally all zeros. Of course the act of reading the port clears the handshake flag.

This is only a simple example; there are many other configurations possible. For example, the $\overline{\text{DAC}}$ handshake may pulse for a fixed time whenever the processor reads the data. A more reliable technique would be to reset or pulse $\overline{\text{DAC}}$ whenever the MPU reads the Flag flip flop *followed* by reading the data, rather than simply reading the data alone.

Of course output ports may also have handshaking to tell the peripheral that there is new data for it. When the peripheral gets around to reading the data, it then sets a flag which can be read by the MPU. In this way a properly synchronized flow of data between MPU and peripheral is established.

Up to this point all our examples have related to interfacing to an eight-bit Data bus, i.e. when the processor is in eight-bit mode, or to the 68008 MPU. The principles are exactly the same when the 16-bit mode is used or the original 68000 MPU is used, but this time we need 16 latches, flip flops or three-state buffers.

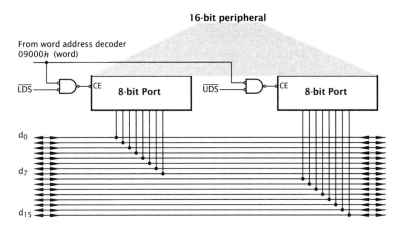

Figure 13.7 *A 16-bit port.*

The circuit shown in Fig. 13.7 is really only a more detailed exposition of the situation depicted in Fig. 11.6(c) on page 190. Here we effectively use two eight-bit ports, the one connected to the lower eight Data lines being qualified by the $\overline{\text{LDS}}$ and the one connected to the upper eight Data lines being qualified by the $\overline{\text{UDS}}$. Both ports are simultaneously enabled by the address decoder output. Like the address decoder of Fig. 12.7 on page 206, a decoder used for such ports must omit a_0[8] so that it goes up in steps of 2 (two bytes to a word). As an example, assuming an input port, to access all 16 lines of the peripheral we would have:

```
move.w  09000h,d0  ; Reads 16-bit peripheral into D0.W
```

What if you have an eight-bit peripheral device and a 16-bit bus? Well, either the left or right port circuitry would suffice, as shown in Fig. 11.6(a) or Fig. 11.6(b) on page 190. Thus to read the upper port we have:

```
move.b  09000h,d0  ; Reads rightmost 8-bit peripheral into D0.B
```

---

[8]Remember anyway that Address line 0 is not valid in 16-bit mode and not available on the original 68000 or the 68HC000 MPUs. The two signals $\overline{\text{LDS}}$ and $\overline{\text{UDS}}$ take its place as described on page 190.

and in a similar manner the lower port is read as:

```
move.b   09001h,d0   ; Reads leftmost 8-bit peripheral into D0.B
```

Of course it is not just ports that need to be interfaced to the Data bus, but also ROM and RAM memory. Fortunately the vast majority of such devices are designed to be compatible with the common bus topology and can be hung directly on to the Data bus. Thus both ROM and RAM chips have integral three-state buffers for reading from (enabled in both cases from the Output Enable ($\overline{\text{OE}}$) pin).

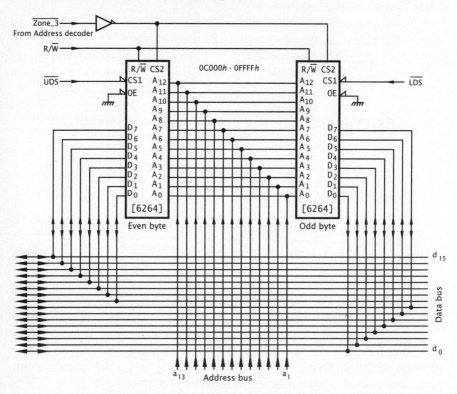

Figure 13.8 *Interfacing 6264 RAM ICs to the 68000 MPU's 16-bit Data bus.*

Our example, shown in Fig. 13.8, uses two 6264 8 K × 8 RAM chips (see also Fig. 2.17 on page 31) feeding the 16-bit Data bus. The zone address decoder enables both devices in parallel, with each half of the pair being enabled by the appropriate Data Strobe, in the manner of Fig. 13.7. To the MPU, each RAM pair appears as 8192 (8 K) *words* located in the address space 0C000-0FFFFh. The actual cell pair activated is a function of the Address lines $a_{13}...a_1$, which drive the 6264 internal decoders. Thus the instruction move.w 0C102h connects the two byte cells 81h (102$h \div 2$) to the Data bus, and with R/$\overline{\text{W}}$ high the 16 bits of data will be read into the D0.W Data register.

Single cells can still be accessed by using byte-sized instructions, with even addresses for the left RAM (e.g. `move.b d0,0C102h`) and odd addresses for the right 6264 RAM (e.g. `move.b d0,0C103h`). In the former case, only $\overline{\text{UDS}}$ will pulse $\overline{}\underline{}\diagup$, in the latter case $\overline{\text{LDS}}$ will $\overline{}\underline{}\diagup$. Word-sized accesses pulse both. Notice that a_0 is not used in this circuit, as the configuration is word-oriented.

One final question remains. Most memory chips come in a variety of access speed selections, typically from 250 ns down to 60 ns and faster. Also the shorter the access time the more expensive is the device.

Given the configuration of Fig. 13.8, what is the longest access time we can get away with? Essentially the RAM is enabled by one of the Data Strobes. During the read cycle, this is coincident with $\overline{\text{AS}}$ (see Fig. 11.2 on page 183) but during the write cycle this is somewhat shorter, so we will concentrate on a write action. From Fig. 11.3 on page 185 and also Fig. 13.5(b), we see that the $\overline{\text{UDS}}/\overline{\text{LDS}}$ width is three clock phases plus t_{CLSH} less t_{CHLS}. As an extreme worst case we can ignore the first propagation delay and take the latter as being one clock phase. This gives a figure of two clock phases. Thus at a clocking rate of 8 MHz a 120 ns speed selection would be more than adequate, reducing linearly to a 60 ns for a 16 MHz rate.

Although we have used RAMs as our example, ROM chips interface in the same way. However, ROMs usually have a longer access time, so for clock rates above 8 MHz they are often selected by using $\overline{\text{UDS}}/\overline{\text{LDS}}$ to drive $\overline{\text{OE}}$ to enable the integral three-state buffers, and the longer address decoder pulse to drive the two memory chips' slower $\overline{\text{CE}}$ input (sometimes ANDed with R/$\overline{\text{W}}$ to prevent accidental writes to ROM). The access time from a ROM's $\overline{\text{OE}}$ is normally much shorter than from its $\overline{\text{CE}}$. Even so, it may be necessary to insert wait states when accessing a ROM.[9]

Examples

Example 13.1
The GEC Plessey ZN508 is described in its data sheet as a "Dual eight-bit Microprocessor Compatible D-A Converter". The ZN508 has two built-in octal D latch registers, each of which drives a resistor network giving in turn an analog equivalent voltage at $V_A$out and $V_B$out respectively in Fig. 13.9. By treating the ZN508 as two normal output ports, selected via input $\overline{\text{DAC A}}$/DAC B, either DAC A or DAC B can be targeted. Other digital inputs are Write ($\overline{\text{WR}}$) and Enable ($\overline{\text{EN}}$),

---

[9]In high-speed IBM-type PCs, the ROM-based operating system (the Basic Input/Output System or BIOS) is often loaded into higher-speed RAM during boot-up to avoid wait states.

being the registers' Clock input and the Clock Enable respectively. Show how you would interface this device to a 68000 MPU in eight-bit mode.

Solution
One strategy is shown in Fig. 13.9. Here the device is clocked as usual by $\overline{\text{LDS}}$ (see Fig. 13.4) to prevent the output critical race. The chip is enabled by the output of a word address decoder. A word-sized decode is necessary as a_0 is used to select ADC A or ADC B. This maps the former to $09000h$ and latter to $09001h$.

As an example of the software interaction with this dual output port, consider a routine continually to output a synchronized up-ramp from DAC A and down-ramp at DAC B:

```
D_A_LOOP:   move.b    d0,09000h    ; Send count to DAC A
            not.b     d0           ; Invert count
            move.b    d0,09001h    ; and send to DAC B
            not.b     d0           ; Restore count
            addq.b    #1,d0        ; Increment count (ramp)
            bra       D_A_LOOP     ; and repeat forever
```

It is possible to use the ZN508 on a 16-bit mode processor. Here a_0 does not exist, so a_1 is used instead. This maps DAC A to $09000h$ and DAC B to $09002h$.

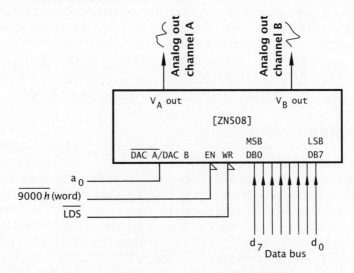

Figure 13.9 *Interfacing the ZN508 dual D/A.*

Example 13.2

The Maxim MAX191 12-bit analog to digital (A/D) converter has four control lines as follows:

- The $\overline{CS}$ must be low (minimum pulse width 150 ns) for the A/D converter to recognize ReaD ($\overline{RD}$) and High-Byte ENable (HBEN).

- The $\overline{RD}$ input must be low to enable the integral three-state buffers (access time 160 ns maximum). If both $\overline{CS}$ and HBEN are low, then bringing $\overline{RD}$ low starts the A/D converter's conversion cycle.

- The $\overline{BUSY}$ output is low whenever the MAX191 is busy doing a conversion from analog to digital. With the clock capacitor shown, conversion time varies from 6 to 18 μs.

- When HBEN is high, 0000D11D10D9D8 is output, that is the upper nybble of the 12-bit word padded with zeros. When HBEN is low, the eight lower bits D7D6D5D4D3D2D1D0 are output. Reading the MAX191 when $\overline{CS}$ and HBEN is low also starts a new conversion behind the scenes.

How would you go about interfacing this device to the Data bus of an eight-bit mode 68000 MPU?

Solution

One possible solution is shown in Fig. 13.10. Data in the internal registers may be read on to the bus via the internal three-state buffers at *word* address 09000h from the appropriate address decoder output. The $\overline{CS}$ input is also activated at the same time. The

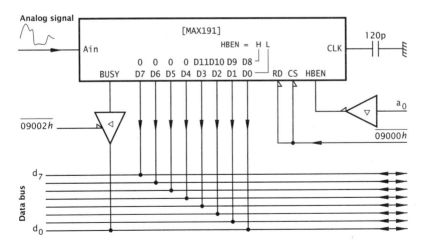

Figure 13.10 *The digital interface to the MAX191 12-bit A/D converter.*

state of HBEN determines if the higher or lower byte is read. If we want to use a word-sized Move to acquire the data in one instruction, then we need to enable the high byte first at 09000h and low byte next at 09001h. By driving HBEN from $\overline{a_0}$ an access at 09000h will force HBEN high (high byte) and at 09001h HBEN will be low (low byte). Finally, the state of the $\overline{\text{BUSY}}$ output can be assessed by examining bit 7 at address 09002h via an external three-state buffer in the manner of Fig. 13.1.

As an example of the interaction of the port with software, consider an endless loop reading the analog input (for example a sine waveform), squaring it and sending the most significant byte of the 24-bit product to a digital to analog port at 09006h (see Example 13.1).

```
SQUARE: btst   #7,09002h ; Check is A/D busy?
        beq    SQUARE    ; IF yes THEN try again
        move.w 09000h,d0 ; Read 12-bit data/start new convert
        move.w d0,d1     ; Copy data
        mulu   d0,d1     ; Square to 24 bits
        swap   d1        ; High word of which in bottom of D1
        move.b d1,09006h ; Send out byte to D/A (bits 23-16)
        bra    SQUARE    ; and repeat
```

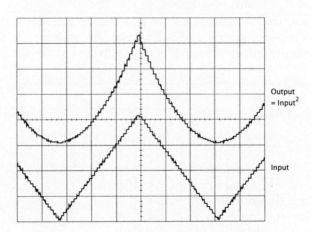

Figure 13.11 *Squaring a triangular analog input.*

The only trick here is to note that squaring a 12-bit quantity gives a 24-bit product. In a 32-bit register, swapping the upper and lower words (line 6) puts the upper byte of the 24-bit product in the lower byte of the register, whence it is sent to the output at 09006h.

Figure 13.11 shows what it looks like in an actual oscilloscope trace.[10]
Also notice that the last execute cycle of the move.w 09000h instruction enables the chip with HBEN low (i.e. 09001h). This automatically begins the next conversion. Also, if the MAX191 is going at its maximum internal clock rate and the processor is running at 8 MHz then it takes 19.5 μs to complete a loop, ignoring the Test and Branch if Busy instructions. As this is longer than the maximum conversion time, the external three-state buffer could be dispensed with as an economy measure.

Finally, if you wish to interface the MAX191 to a 16-bit bus, then connection of each Data line is duplicated for the upper Data bus, e.g. D7 to both d_7 and d_{15}; D6 to d_6 and d_{14} etc. As a_0 is not available in this mode, $\overline{\text{LSD}}$ should be directly connected to HBEN. Reading data now becomes

```
move.b   09000h,d0    ; Get upper byte from A/D, HBEN=1
lsl.w    #8,d0        ; Align it upwards
move.b   09001h,d0    ; Get lower byte (HBEN=0)
                      ; Starts next conversion
```

which ends up with the 12-bit word in D0.W.

Example 13.3
Where speed is not an issue, a considerable economy of hardware can be effected by sending or receiving data one bit at a time. As an example, the Texas Instruments TLC549 is described as an eight-bit A/D converter with serial control. From Fig. 13.12 we see that only three lines are necessary to control and access the data. The sequence of operations using these lines is:

- When $\overline{\text{Chip Select}}$ is brought low, after a short delay (for internal synchronization) of around 1 μs the most significant bit of the previous conversion result will appear at the DATA_OUT pin.
- Each I/O_Clock ⌐_ shifts out a subsequent data bit, with the least significant bit appearing after the seventh ⌐_. The maximum shifting rate is 1.11 MHz, with a minimum high or low clock duration of 400 ns.
- An eighth ⌐_ starts the next conversion, which takes around 17 μs to complete. To ensure no interruption of the analog sample and conversion sequence, $\overline{\text{CS}}$ should go back high before any _/⁻ on the I/O_Clock.

Show how the TLC549 could be interfaced and controlled from the MPU.

---

[10]The glitches in the waveform are artefacts due to the sampling action of the oscilloscope.

Solution

One possible solution, shown in Fig. 13.12, uses two lines from an output port to control $\overline{CS}$ and the I/O_Clock, with the serial bits being examined using a one-bit input port (three-state buffer). With this hardware, a viable subroutine to acquire one byte is shown in Program 13.4. Notice how in lines 11 and 12 the single data bit is shifted first into the **X** flag and then into the parallel data byte building up in **D7.B**. After eight of these load-and-shift actions, a full eight-bit byte will be assembled.

All this takes a considerable time, but only three physical lines are required. Indeed the TLC548 version of this device can support I/O_Clock rates of 2 MHz and could be clocked directly from the address decoder of a 68000-based system running at up to 10 MHz, which further reduces costs. There are versions of the TLC540 series that have up to 19 input analog channels and up to 10-bit resolution, still using the same three lines plus one extra for the channel address.

Lowering the number of data lines is especially important where the peripheral device is remote from the processor. Apart from the cost of the conductors, special techniques, such as modulation or/and opto-isolation, are needed for reliable long-distance communication, and these are expensive on a per-line basis. Here the economy of serial communications is obvious, and most manufacturers provide a family of serial peripheral interface chips for such situations.

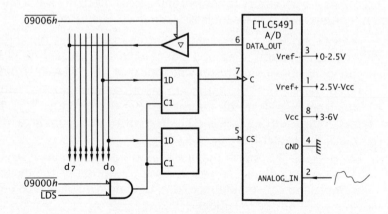

Figure 13.12 *Controlling the TLC549 serial A/D converter.*

Program 13.4 *Reading one byte from the TLC549.*

```
;   ********************************************************
;   * FUNCTION: Acquires one byte of data in serial        *
;   * ENTRY    : None                                      *
;   * EXIT     : Data in D7.B, no other alterations        *
;   ********************************************************
            .define OUT = 09000h, IN = 09006h
SER_GET:    movem.l  d0/d6,-(sp)  ; Save auxiliary registers
            moveq    #8,d6        ; D6.b is the bit counter
            move.b   #0,OUT       ; CS active, clock low

S_LOOP:     move.b   IN,d0        ; Get data in bit 7
            lsl.b    #1,d0        ; Put data in X flag
            roxl.b   #1,d7        ; and shift into D7
            move.b   #10b,OUT     ; Now pulse I/O_Clk, first high
            move.b   #00b,OUT     ; then low again
            subq.b   #1,d6        ; Decrement count
            bne      S_LOOP       ; and go again

S_EXIT:     move.b   #01b,OUT     ; CS back high on exit
            movem.l  (sp)+,d0/d6  ; Pull back saved registers
            rts
```

Example 13.4

Serial transmission such as that demonstrated in Example 13.3 is known as synchronous, as the synchronizing clock signal is transmitted along with the data. The alternative, illustrated in this example, uses an asynchronous technique where *each* data byte is preceded by a logic 0 start bit and followed by a minimum of one logic 1 stop bit, as shown in Fig. 13.13. While the line is idling, a logic 1 (break level) is transmitted.

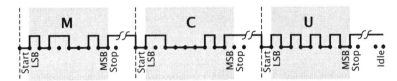

Figure 13.13 *Transmitting the message "MCU" in the asynchronous serial mode.*

This standard[11] was adopted by the computer industry in the 1940s from the existing telex communications service, which used the teletypewriter (TTY)[12] as a terminal for alphanumeric characters sent over telephone and radio links in a serial manner. Until the early 1980s, TTY computer terminals were electromechanical machines driven by a synchronous electric motor. This meant that synchronization between remote terminals could only be guaranteed for short periods. To get around this problem, each transmitted

---

[11] The good thing about computer standards is that there are so many of them!

[12] Literally a 'typewriter from afar'; Greek tele = far.

word was preceded by a start bit, as shown here. In effect each word is resynchronized afresh and hence a drift of up to around ±5% between receiver and transmitter could be tolerated. Electromagnetic terminals typically print a maximum of ten characters per second, and require a double-length stop bit. With eight-bit characters this gives a transmission rate of 110 bits per second, or 110 **baud**. Faster rates utilized in purely electronic systems require only one stop bit, and are typically doubling multiples of 300 baud. Thus the serial port on an IBM-type PC can typically support rates of up to 19,200 baud (1920 characters per second).

Given the necessity for a MPU to interface in a serial manner with such a peripheral, we have the problem of converting an outgoing byte of parallel information to a serial format and sandwiching it with start and stop bits. Similarly, incoming serial data must be captured, synchronized and parallelized. This can be done using a one-bit input and output port and utilizing software to do the data handling tasks. This approach is hardware-efficient, and has been used,[13] but ties up the processor for an inordinate amount of time. The normal approach is to use a standard LSI device designed specifically for this task. These are generically known as a **Universal Asychronous Receiver/Transmitter (UART)**, and this is the approach taken by the IBM-type PC. A discussion of UARTs is beyond our scope.

For this example, we will design a subroutine using the one-bit input port of Fig. 13.1 to check for a start bit, and if found return with the character in the lower byte of D7.W, otherwise the word FFFFh (−1) is returned as an error marker. Incoming data has a baud rate of 4800 and one stop bit. We will assume any necessary delay routines are already available in situe.

Solution

A task analysis for this problem gives a possible structure:

1. Check input for logic 0 (start bit)
2. IF not start bit THEN $data = -1$
3. ELSE
    - $count = 8$
    - $data = 0$
    - WHILE $count \neq 0$
        - Delay one bit time
        - Shift $data$ left
        - LSB $data$ = input state
        - $count = count - 1$
    - Delay one bit time
4. Return with $data$

---

[13]Notably by the Apple II PC in the late 1970s.

In essence this approach exits immediately if the input state is logic 1, which is the stop or idle condition, with −1 as the return code. Otherwise each bit is read after the appropriate delay, and the data byte built up by shifting eight times. At a baud rate of 4800 the bit duration is $1 \div 4800 \approx 208\,\mu s$.

Program 13.5 *Input one asynchronous serial character.*

```
; **********************************************************
; * FUNCTION: Reads one 4800 baud character                *
; * ENTRY    : None                                        *
; * EXIT     : Character in D7.B if successful              *
; * EXIT     : No registers altered                        *
; * SUPPORT  : 208 us delay subroutine DELAY_208           *
; **********************************************************
           .define IN = 9000h   ; The input port
INCH:      movem.l d0/d1,-(sp)   ; Save temporary registers
           move.w  #-1,d7        ; The unsuccessful marker
           move.w  #8,d0         ; count = 8
           tst.b   IN            ; Check bit 7, is it 0?
           bne     INCH_EXIT     ; IF not THEN exit with -1

; WHILE count not equal zero build up character bit by bit
           clr.w   d7            ; Zero the data register
INCH_LOOP: jsr     DELAY_208     ; Wait one bit delay time
           move.b  IN,d1         ; Get bit into position 7
           lsl.b   #1,d1         ; Shift bit into X flag
           roxr.b  #1,d7         ; and into D7
           subq.b  #1,d0         ; count = count-1
           bne     INCH_LOOP     ; Repeat 8 times
           jsr     DELAY_208     ; Omit stop bit

INCH_EXIT: movem.l (sp)+,d0/d1   ; Pull temporary registers
           rts                   ; and return char in D7.B
```

Program 13.5 follows the task list closely. It assumes the delay subroutine DELAY_208 of Program 8.5 on page 138. As in Program 13.4, the data byte is built up using eight load-and-shift operations. A bit delay completes the sequence.

Although this subroutine will perform its task, it can be unreliable if the incoming data line is not sampled often enough. Obviously sampling at less than 4800 times per second may miss a start bit. Just as bad, a sample just at the edge of a start bit may cause erroneous readings if the transmitter's baud rate is slightly inaccurate. It would be better to sample around 16 times the baud rate, i.e. around 76,800 times per second, and wait until eight samples have occurred to find the approximate midpoint. This oversampling can also be used to reduce the effect of noise by allowing a majority decision to be made on when the start bit has truly been received, and sampling to occur around the middle of a bit.

Another problem occurs when synchronism is lost and a data bit is erroneously picked as the start bit. This can eventually be rectified by checking that the supposed stop bit is indeed logic 1, but detecting such framing errors and oversampling place a very high software burden on the MPU, especially where higher baud rates and continuous data streams are used. In such cases the use of a UART is virtually essential.

Self-assessment questions

13.1   The instruction `bclr #7,09001h` (see page 103) was used in an attempt to turn on the most significant LED in Fig. 13.5. Why did it fail?

13.2   As part of a control system a delay of n ms is to be created, where n is the settings of the switch port of Fig. 13.2. One student wrote this code:

```
C_LOOP:  jsr      DELAY_1_MS   ; 1ms delay
         subq.b   #1,09000h    ; Decrement n by one
         bne      C_LOOP       ; Delay until n reaches zero
```

Instead it produced an infinite delay unless n was zero. Why?

13.3   The temperature of an environment is to be altered by continually using pulse width modulation (PWM) to control a heater. PWM involves switching the load (the heater in this case) on and off with a varying mark/space (on/off) ratio digital waveform. Show how you would use an input port to give the power parameter n, which varies between 0 to 255, and a one-bit output driving the heater buffer switch. Write software around your chosen hardware to give a total cycle time of 256 ms, and a mark/space ratio of $n : (256 - n)$. Comment on the use of PWM as a digital to analog converter.

13.4   Write a subroutine called OUTCH that will transmit a byte in D0.W in asynchronous serial format via the one-bit output port of Fig. 13.4. The baud rate is to be 300. How could you adapt the subroutine to transmit a baud rate from 300 to 9600 in six doubling steps, as set by a switch port, with a single switch for each rate?

13.5 One way of saving port lines is to use serial transmission. Assume that the remote receiver has an eight-bit shift register with parallel outputs, such as the 74LS164. Two output port lines are to be used to send data one bit at a time and toggle the shift register's Clock input, which is _/‾-edge triggered. Write a subroutine to send a byte from D0.B to this receiver. Do you envisage any problems using this technique? How would you extend the receiver to cope with a 32-bit transmission?

13.6 A certain television panel game has eight contestants who will answer questions posed by the umpire. Each contestant has a single push switch, which is logic 1 when pressed, and a light at his/her desk, activated by logic 0. There is a single communal buzzer. Design a suitable port structure and a software routine that will display the *first* contestant that responds and sound the active-low buzzer for 1 s. A relax time of 10 s is to be used to filter out multiple responses.

13.7 A certain disco display is to be controlled by an MPU. The output display is a group of four differently colored lamps and the input is a microphone feeding an eight-bit analog to digital converter. The objective of the system is to light each lamp sequentially, so that the repetitive rate is nominally proportional to the amplitude of the sound.

   Pertinent details are:

   - The microphone amplifier produces a voltage from 0 V for silent to 2.55 V for ear-splitting scream.
   - The A/D converter is MPU-compatible with $\overline{SC}$ input that must be ‾_/‾ pulsed low to start the conversion, and a $\overline{BUSY}$ line which is active until the conversion is complete. The integral octal buffer is activated when $\overline{OE}$ is brought low, giving an eight-bit conversion byte in 16 μs ranging from 00h to FFh over the input voltage range 0 V to 2.55 V.
   - A lamp is turned on by a logic 0, via a buffer switch.
   - The minimum on time is 100 ms (ear-splitting scream), with the maximum being 25.5 s (silent—very rare!).

   Design a suitable interface, and based on your hardware devise a possible software routine.

13.8 Students invariably talk too long during oral examinations. It has been proposed that an MPU-based system be designed to act as an interview monitor. Once triggered, the monitor will perform the following sequence of actions:

1. When the Go switch is closed (low) the active-low green lamp only will illuminate.

2. The active-low seven-segment display will count down from 9 to 2 at nominally one-minute increments.

3. Only the amber lamp illuminates and the buzzer sounds for nominally 200 ms.

4. The seven-segment displays 1 for nominally one minute.

5. The red lamp only illuminates and the buzzer sounds for nominally 400 ms.

6. The seven-segment displays 0 for nominally one minute.

7. The active-low buzzer then sounds continually until the Stop switch is closed.

You are asked to design the interface and software for the system which will implement this specification. Assume a 200 ms delay subroutine is already available.

13.9 A dedicated 68000-based system is to be designed as an intruder alarm to monitor continually the state of a number of movement sensors at various points in a 4-storey building. Every storey has eight distributed sensors, each of which acts as a switch giving a logic 1 when activated. The system output is to be a four-lamp array showing on which floor the intruder has been detected, and a single siren active if *any* movement sensor is active. All output devices are active on a logic 0.

You are asked to design the interface hardware and software which will:

- Read the intruder alarm sensors on a per-floor basis.
- Activate the appropriate floor lamp.
- Activate the siren for a minimum of 30 s if *any* sensor is active.

Design the address decoder to map input/output to the area 09000–9FFF*h*. Assume that the MPU is running at 8 MHz and is in eight-bit mode.

Discuss any practical problems which may arise with your chosen system.

CHAPTER 14

Interrupt handling

In Chapter 9 we discussed the nature of interrupts and the minutiae of how the 68000 MPU responded to a Level-n request for service. You should now reread that chapter to refresh your memory. In this chapter we wish to consider the hardware aspects of the process of generating an interrupt request signal from an external event.

After completing the chapter you will:

- *Understand how an external event can activate the three MPU pins* $\overline{IPL2}\,\overline{IPL1}\,\overline{IPL0}$ *to give the appropriate level of request.*

- *Appreciate the necessity to use an external interrupt flag (D flip flop) to ensure a one-shot request.*

- *Know how to force the processor to handle the request as an autovector process.*

- *Understand how several external processes can generate individual levels of interrupt request.*

- *Learn how an assortment of external processes can share the one level of request.*

- *Know how to use the Interrupt Acknowledge read bus cycle as an alternative to autovectoring, to generate an external pointer into the Exception vector table.*

Any event requiring service from the MPU must generate an appropriate signal — typically a change in logic state, such as ⌐_, or a complete pulse, such as ⌐_/⌐. For example, the depth sounder's receiver of Example 9.2 on page 157 may well go low whenever an echo has been detected.

To keep things simple we will take as our event the 1 kHz oscillator providing the time base for the interrupt service routine (ISR) of Program 9.1 on page 152. Our task is to interface the oscillator to the three MPU pins $\overline{IPL2}\,\overline{IPL1}\,\overline{IPL0}$ (see page 180) so as to request a Level-5 service.

An initial attempt might result in the configuration shown in Fig. 14.1. Here the oscillator is directly connected to the $\overline{IPL2}$ and $\overline{IPL0}$ pins, whilst $\overline{IPL1}$ is permanently pulled up to the positive supply, which is logic 1. With

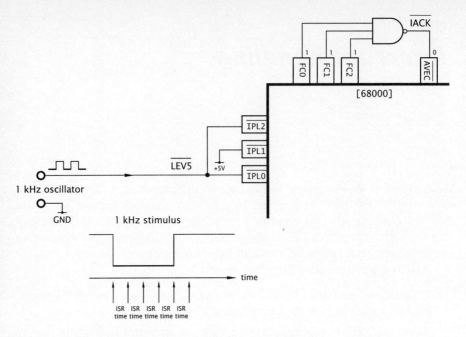

Figure 14.1 *A first try at generating a Level-5 interrupt request.*

this connection, each time the oscillator output goes low (logic 0) then the $\overline{IPL2}\,\overline{IPL1}\,\overline{IPL0}$ pins become 010 — which is active low 101 (5).

Looking back at Fig. 9.3 on page 149, we see that when the MPU responds to an interrupt request its three status lines FC2 FC1 FC0 go to logic 1 (see page 180). By NANDing these together, as in Fig. 14.1, we can generate a signal that goes low whenever an interrupt is in progress. Connecting this Interrupt ACKnowledge ($\overline{IACK}$) line to the $\overline{AVEC}$ pin forces the MPU to use the autovector process to find the interrupt service, as described in Chapter 9.

Unfortunately, if we try this together with the ISR of Program 9.1 on page 152, the outcome is a counter that runs many times faster than it ought to! Why should that be? Well, consider that the oscillator has just gone low and the processor has entered the Level-5 ISR. This proceeds to add 1 to the long-word in memory called JIFFY and then returns (rte) to the background program. However, when it gets back, the oscillator is still low, so it immediately proceeds to service the interrupt again …and again, until the oscillator goes back high. For instance taking a square waveform, the duration of the low state is $500\,\mu$s. If the ISR takes, say, $80\,\mu$s, then JIFFY increments six times per millisecond! This is illustrated in the waveform diagram in Fig. 14.1.

With this in mind we see that we have to make the event single-shot,

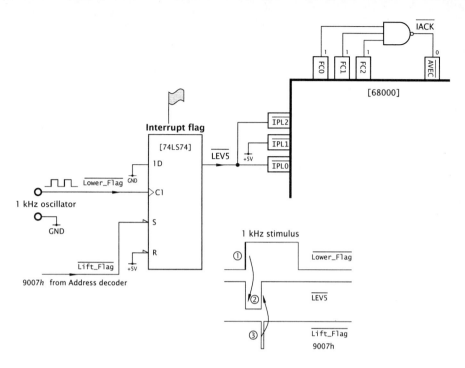

Figure 14.2 *A working Level-5 interrupt circuit.*

i.e. once only on an oscillator edge. One way of doing this would be to insert a monostable[1] or even a capacitor–resistor (CR) differentiator circuit between oscillator and MPU. In the case of our example, the period of this circuit would have to be less than 80 µs. The minimum is two clock cycles. After this point the interrupt request level is latched into the processor and becomes pending. This **latency** (the time to respond to a pending interrupt request, see page 148) can vary between 44 and 214 clock cycles in the 16-bit Data bus mode (5.5–27 µs at 8 MHz) depending on which instruction is interrupted.

Such variability, along with problems with discrete (CR) component tolerance, temperature coefficients and power supply variations, makes this technique unreliable, at least for mass-production purposes. And what if some software wizard subsequently improves the ISR and halves its execution time?

The accepted technique uses a D flip flop in a handshake role, as shown in Fig. 14.2, where it is called an **interrupt flag**. As the flip flop is edge-triggered, this fulfils the one-shot criterion, clocking through the logic 0 to "lower" the flag. By connecting the flip flop's asynchronous $\overline{\text{Set}}$ input

---

[1] Sometimes called a *one-shot*.

to a spare address decoder output, the MPU can "raise" the flag at any time to cancel the request. The process sequence is:

1. On the rising edge of the oscillator's output, the flip flop clocks the permanent logic 0 at its D input through to its output, activating ("lowering") the flag.
2. This generates a Level-5 interrupt request in the normal way by pulling $\overline{IPL2}$ & $\overline{IPL0}$ low.
3. The MPU eventually enters the Level-5 ISR. As part of the ISR, the interrupt flag is deactivated ("raised") by accessing the memory location connected to the D flip flop's $\overline{Set}$ input.

Program 14.1 *A modified interrupt-driven real-time clock ISR.*

```
; This is the foreground program
CLOCK:  clr.b   090007h     ; Lift the interrupt flag
        addq.l  #1,JIFFY    ; One more tick
        rte                 ; Return
        .end
```

A typical example of an ISR interacting with Fig. 14.2 is shown in line 2 of Program 14.1, which should be compared with Program 9.1 on page 152. Here I have used a clr instruction to reference the address 9007h. This pulses the flip flop's $\overline{Set}$ input as desired. Any byte-sized instruction that references 9007h could be used instead, such as move.b d0,9007h, but where a read-only or write-only address decoder output is used (see Fig. 12.7 on page 206) to "raise" the flag, care must be taken to use an instruction that has the appropriate address as the source or destination respectively. However, in the base 68000 family the clr instruction is read–modify–write (see page 91) and will always be caught by the address decoder at least once.[2]

The next problem to consider is how to handle interrupt requests from more than one event, perhaps even simultaneously! As our example, consider the depth sounder of Example 9.2 on page 157. Here the two events are the regular 1 kHz oscillator 'ticks' described above and the irregular return echo detector. The original example specified the former as Level 5 and the latter to request a Level-4 service.

The standard way of tackling this problem is to use a priority encoder (see Fig. 2.6 on page 20) to convert up to eight unary request lines to a three-bit binary equivalent. In turn, this binary code directly drives the three $\overline{IPL}$ MPU lines. This is illustrated for our example in Fig. 14.3, in which the request from the echo receiver is connected to the 74LS148's

---

[2]However, in 68020+ processors clr is a write-only instruction and would not be appropriate for a read-only address decoder.

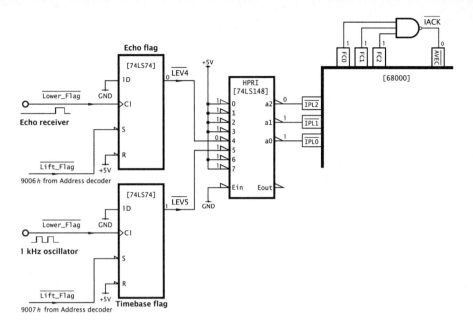

Figure 14.3 *Handling two external events wanting different levels of service.*

8- to 3-line priority encoder's $\overline{4}$ input via its interrupt flag. Similarly the 1 kHz timebase's interrupt flag drives the $\overline{5}$ input. The 74LS148 three-bit binary output $\overline{a_2}\,\overline{a_1}\,\overline{a_0}$ directly drives the $\overline{IPL2}\,\overline{IPL1}\,\overline{IPL0}$ interrupt inputs. As both the priority encoder's outputs and the MPU's interrupt inputs are active-low, a straight connection is possible.

The diagram shows the situation where the echo interrupt flag has gone low. This in turn brings the priority encoder's $\overline{4}$ input low, which gives the output 011 (active-low 100). Applied to the MPU's $\overline{IPL2}\,\overline{IPL1}\,\overline{IPL0}$ pins, this requests a Level-4 service.

If several interrupt flags are active at the same time, then the priority encoder will reflect the *highest* input at its output. Thus, the following sequence of events is legitimate:

1. The 1kHz oscillator triggers the Timebase interrupt flag.
2. The 74LS148 encodes this to 010 and the MPU enters its Level-5 ISR.
3. The Echo receiver triggers the Echo flag. The output of the priority encoder does not change.
4. The Level-5 service routine "raises" the Timebase flag.
5. The priority encoder alters its output to 011 (4). The MPU ignores this lower-level request.
6. The MPU eventually returns from its Level-5 service routine.

7. The MPU then responds to the Echo receiver's request,

8. and enters the Level-4 service routine.

9. The oscillator again triggers the Timebase flag.

10. The 74LS148 reflects this by changing its output to 010, irrespective of whether the Echo flag has been "lowered" yet.

11. The MPU moves from its Level-4 ISR to the higher-priority Level-5 ISR.

12. The Level-5 ISR "raises" the Timebase flag and eventually terminates.

13. The MPU then re-enters its Level-4 ISR, irrespective of whether the Echo flag has been "raised" yet.

14. The Level-4 ISR "raises" the Echo flag and subsequently, when completed, drops down to the background program.

As each interrupting source has its own interrupt flag, the various process requests can operate independently of each other. Each interrupt flag can be individually "raised" by connecting each D flip flop's $\overline{\text{Set}}$ input to a different address decoder output. Thus the Level-4 ISR of Program 9.3 on page 158 should be modified as shown in Program 14.2 by referencing address 09006h in line 8 — for the hardware shown in Fig. 14.3.

Program 14.2 *Evaluating the hull–river bottom distance.*

```
; ****************************************************************
; * ISR updates distance to river bottom on sounder's return    *
; * ENTRY: Global word JIFFY is time in ms since pulse is sent   *
; * ENTRY: Interrupt flag is at 09006h                           *
; * EXIT : Global byte DISTANCE in meters                        *
; ****************************************************************
DEPTH_SOUND: movem.l  d0,-(sp)      ; Save the environment
             clr.b    09006h        ; Line 8: *** Raise the flag
             move.w   JIFFY,d0      ; Read current time
             mulu     #183,d0       ; Multiply by 0.183
             divu     #1000,d0      ; To give meters
             move.b   d0,DISTANCE   ; Update the distance
             movem.l  (sp)+,d0      ; Retrieve the environment
             rte
```

Using an 8- to 3-line priority encoder, as shown here, allows up to seven completely separate events to be interrupt-serviced from Level 1 to Level 7. This should be sufficient for most applications. But what if more than this number is to be interrupt-driven?

One approach is shown in Fig. 14.4, where four peripheral devices are interfaced to the Data bus in the manner described in Fig. 13.2 on page 214. Related to each peripheral is an external event, which generates a _/‾ when it requires service. This triggers an associated interrupt

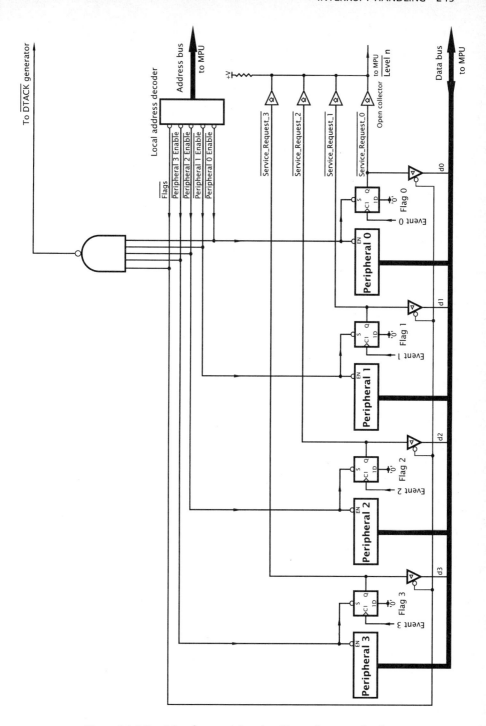

Figure 14.4 *Servicing four peripherals with one interrupt level.*

flag, the output of which drives the Level-*n* interrupt request line low via its own open-collector buffer. Wiring all four buffer outputs together to the interrupt line means that *any* flag(s) going low generate(s) an interrupt request.

The output of each flag is interfaced to the Data bus through a three-state buffer as a normal input port, which can be read by the ISR to determine which event actually occurred.

Program 14.3 *Handling multiple requests at the same level.*

```
ISR:       move.l   d0,-(sp)      ; Save environment
           move.b   FLAGS,d0      ; Read the interrupt flags
           lsr.b    #1,d0         ; Check bit 0 (Flag 0) >> into C
           bcc      ISR_0         ; IF = 0 THEN service event 0
           lsr.b    #1,d0         ; ELSE check bit 1 (Flag 1)
           bcc      ISR_1         ; IF = 0 THEN service event 1
           lsr.b    #1,d0         ; ELSE check bit 2 (Flag 2)
           bcc      ISR_2         ; IF = 0 THEN service event 2
           lsr.b    #1,d0         ; ELSE check bit 3 (Flag 3)
           bcc      ISR_3         ; IF = 0 THEN service event 3
; Common exit point
ISR_EXIT:  move.l   (sp)+,d0      ; Retrieve environment
           rte                    ; and exit
; ******************************************************************
ISR_0:     .....    .....         ; The handler for event 0
           .....    .....         ; Includes a reference to Periph 0
           bra      ISR_EXIT      ; Exit on completion

ISR_1:     .....    .....         ; The handler for event 1
           .....    .....         ; Includes a reference to Periph 1
           bra      ISR_EXIT      ; Exit on completion

ISR_2:     .....    .....         ; The handler for event 2
           .....    .....         ; Includes a reference to Periph 2
           bra      ISR_EXIT      ; Exit on completion

ISR_3:     .....    .....         ; The handler for event 3
           .....    .....         ; Includes a reference to Periph 3
           bra      ISR_EXIT      ; Exit on completion
```

Program 14.3 gives a possible structure of an ISR related to this hardware. Line 2 reads the flag port, and the succeeding code repetitively shifts the bit pattern through the **C** flag. A sequential series of Branches causes control to be transferred to one of four separate routines, each of which services one of the peripheral devices. As part of this service, the peripheral's port will be accessed. The access decoder signal automatically "lifts" the accompanying interrupt flag, thereby cancelling the request by the ISR's return. This is rather like the automatic handshake cancellation of Fig. 13.6 of page 220. Here the $\overline{\text{DAC}}$ signal can be used as a service request, and the $09000h$ port enable from the address decoder clocks the D flip flop interrupt flag to cancel the request.

Within reason, as many interrupt requests as desired may be accommodated using this configuration. For very large numbers, a priority encoder might be more efficient at converting the unary Service Request port to binary. Similarly, where large numbers of events are to be handled, the software encoding routine is likely to be more efficient if a look-up table is used to target the appropriate routine; see Example 14.2.

The ultimate hardware interrupt to an MPU is an external reset request.[3] An MPU should only be reset on power-up (cold start) or on a irrecoverable system collapse. Back in Chapter 9 we observed that on reset the processor obtains the initial value for the Supervisor Stack Pointer from the first vector table address and then the start-up address for the Program Counter in the second (see Fig. 9.1 on page 145).

The bottom line in reset hardware is that *both* the $\overline{\text{Reset}}$ and $\overline{\text{Halt}}$ pins must be driven low to initiate the reset action. In starting from cold, that is when power has just been applied, a minimum pulse of 100 ms is specified. A warm start, that is when power is continuously present, only requires activation for ten clock cycles — around $1\,\mu$s.

Unfortunately both $\overline{\text{Reset}}$ and $\overline{\text{Halt}}$ are also outputs on occasion. The privileged instruction reset will drive $\overline{\text{Reset}}$ low. If this pin is connected to external peripheral interfaces, then this will initialize such devices without affecting the processor itself. The MPU will drive $\overline{\text{Halt}}$ low on a Double-Bus fault. This occurs when the initial value of the Supervisor Stack Pointer (from the vector table) is odd or when the $\overline{\text{Bus Error}}$ pin is low during an exception. This is a catastrophic event and the MPU can only halt in such circumstances.

In order to accommodate this I/O nature, any reset circuitry should drive these pins via an open-collector (or open-drain) buffer. As discussed on page 17, such outputs are either hard low or open-circuit. In Fig. 14.5(a) a debounced switch (see Fig. 2.13 on page 27) drives $\overline{\text{Reset}}$ and $\overline{\text{Halt}}$ separately through associated open-collector buffers. When the Reset switch is up, the output of the debounce latch is high and both buffer outputs are hard low. Moving the switch down gives a low latch output and both buffers are turned off. Both $\overline{\text{Reset}}$ and $\overline{\text{Halt}}$ can now be used by the MPU as outputs.

Rather than rely on a manual-only reset mechanism, it is more satisfactory to reset automatically when power is applied, with perhaps a manual override. This problem is sufficiently well defined to warrant a class of

---

[3]In a manner of speaking, the mother of all interrupts!

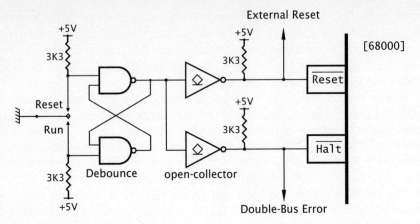

(a) A simple manual reset circuit.

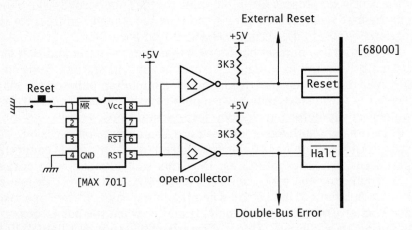

(b) A cold-start with manual override reset.

Figure 14.5 Reset circuits.

integrated circuits cataloged as MPU **supervisors**. The Maxim MAX701 shown in Fig. 14.5(b) is a simple example of this genre. When the power supply V_{cc} drops below 4.65 V, RST goes high and the MPU resets through the inverting open-collector buffers in the normal way. When the supply rises above 4.65 V, RST remains active for a least 200 ms. The manual Reset ($\overline{\text{MR}}$) input provides for a debounced override switched Reset.

More sophisticated supervisors can switch through a reserve battery on an impending power failure. This can interrupt the processor, which can then quickly store sensitive data in RAM kept alive by this backup supply. Some MPUs and MCUs have a sleep mode, in which a few microamperes of current from such a reserve will keep it "ticking over". Some supervisors can also act as a watchdog timer, resetting the processor unless it is triggered continually. This trigger is normally provided by a software routine accessing a prescribed address, which is picked up by an address decoder. If the MPU is not operating correctly, this routine is not entered and the triggering pulse is not forthcoming.

Examples

Example 14.1
When the 68000 MPU receives an interrupt request, it is latched in and becomes pending. When the current instruction is completed and provided that the request level is *above* the Interrupt mask setting, the response to the request is set in train. As part of this train of events, the MPU sets FC2 FC1 FC0 all high and executes an **Interrupt Acknowledge cycle**. During this bus cycle Address lines $a_3 a_2 a_1$ reflect the service level of the interrupt, e.g. 101 for Level-5. All other Address lines are logic 1 at this time.

Design a circuit to generate up to seven Interrupt Acknowledge signals, $\overline{IACK7}...\overline{IACK1}$, for corresponding levels of service.

Solution
Generating one of n Interrupt Acknowledge signals is simply a matter of decoding the three pertinent Address lines whenever

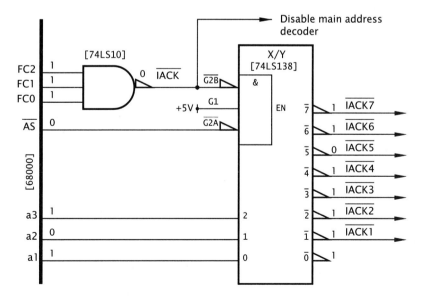

Figure 14.6 *Generating $\overline{IACKn}$ signals; showing the response to a Level-5 request.*

FC2 FC1 FC0 = 111. This is the original $\overline{\text{IACK}}$ signal shown in Fig. 14.1, and is shown in Fig. 14.6 enabling a 74LS138 3- to 8-line decoder, acting on the three select Address lines $a_3\,a_2\,a_1$. This decoder is thus only active during the Interrupt Acknowledge bus cycle, and generates seven individual Interrupt Acknowledge lines. The response to a Level-5 request ($a_3\,a_2\,a_1 = 111$) is shown in the diagram.

Strictly $\overline{\text{IACK}}$ should be used to disable the main address decoder during the Interrupt Acknowledge bus cycle. This is to prevent unintended access to devices or memory in locations FFFFF2–FFFFFFh. This bus cycle is a read cycle, and if an access to this area (or images) will cause no problems, then this qualifier may be omitted from the main address decoder circuit.

Example 14.2

The Interrupt Acknowledge bus cycle occurs whether or not the $\overline{\text{AVEC}}$ pin is activated. If $\overline{\text{AVEC}}$ is not active, then during the Interrupt Acknowledge cycle (see Example 14.1), the MPU expects to read the vector number off the Data bus, placed there by the interrupting device. Thus the peripheral device tells the MPU where in the exception table it is to get its ISR start address. Legal vector numbers are 64–255 (see Fig. 9.1 on page 145). Based on an extension to Fig. 14.6, show how this external vector number could be manually set up.

Solution

Provided that $\overline{\text{AVEC}}$ is not active, the Interrupt Acknowledge cycle is a normal read bus cycle, with the state of the Data bus $d_7...d_0$ being taken as the vector number. Internally multiplying this by 4 gives the absolute address of the vector ($64 \times 4 = 256 = 0100h$).

In consequence, Fig. 14.7 shows the Level-5 vector port to be an eight-bit three-state buffer identical to the standard eight-bit input port of Fig. 13.2 on page 214. Here the port is enabled by the $\overline{\text{IACK5}}$ output of Fig. 14.6, and consequently is only active during the Interrupt Acknowledge cycle. $\overline{\text{DTACK}}$ is generated in the normal manner. The setting of the switches, shown here as 01000000b (64), points to the appropriate vector. This is supposed to be 64–255, but there is nothing to stop it being below 64!

Peripheral interface devices specifically designed for 68000-family use, such as the 68230 PI/T (Peripheral Interface/Timer) will have integral switches/three-state buffers enabled by an $\overline{\text{IACK}}$ pin (e.g. $\overline{\text{PIACK}}$ and $\overline{\text{TIACK}}$ for the parallel port/timer parts of the 68230). On reset, the switches (actually the state of a register) will be set to 15. This points to the Uninitialized Interrupt vector. This register (called the Port Interrupt Vector and the Timer Interrupt Vector registers in the 68230) can subsequently be altered by the MPU by software in the usual manner.

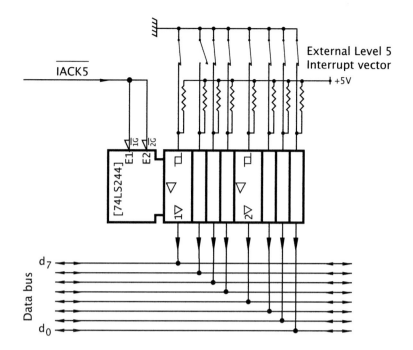

Figure 14.7 *Generating an external number at Level 5. Vector 64 shown.*

Self-assessment questions

14.1 It is proposed to use an MPU to control the signalling in a TV panel game with ten contestants. During the initial discussion a student has suggested using an interrupt scheme with ten interrupt flags in the manner of Fig. 14.4. Is this a legitimate use of interrupts?

14.2 The Shift and Branch technique to identify the source of the interrupt request used in Program 14.3 is rather inefficient. Discuss how this might be improved for larger numbers of interrupt request sources, with both hardware and software techniques being explored.

14.3 The exception vector table of Fig. 9.1 on page 145 is normally located in ROM between addresses 000000h and 0003FFh. Whilst it is necessary to locate the two Reset vectors (0 and 1) in ROM, so the MPU can always boot up from a cold start, there is actually no need for the other vectors to be held permanently in memory.

By reference to this diagram, design a hardware-related scheme to locate vectors 2–255 in RAM.

14.4 Can you think of any use for the $\overline{\text{IACKn}}$ signals generated in Fig. 14.6 besides that of enabling an external Vector port?

CHAPTER 15

A case study

Up to this point our MPU material has been presented piecemeal. To complete our study we are going to put much of what we have learnt to good use and design both the hardware and software of an actual gadget. This is not an easy task to do in a single short chapter. However, very little new material needs to be presented at this point, rather a process of coalescence.

We begin with our specification. Students invariably talk too long during their oral presentations. It is proposed that a dedicated embedded MPU-based system be designed to act as a time monitor. This monitor should default to a time-out of 10 minutes, but will have the provision to vary the allotted time from 1 to 99 minutes.

Once triggered, the monitor should perform the following sequence of operations:

1. When the GO switch is closed, a green lamp will illuminate and a dual seven-segment display will show a count-down from the time-out value to **03** at nominal one-minute intervals.
2. After a further minute, an amber lamp only will illuminate, the count of **02** will be displayed and a buzzer will sound for 250 ms.
3. After a further minute, a red lamp only will illuminate together with a display of **01**. The buzzer will sound for 500 ms.
4. Finally, after another minute the display will show **00**, the red lamp will continue to be illuminated and the buzzer will sound continuously until the STOP switch is pressed. This will reset the system to the start of the sequence. Indeed, closing the STOP switch at any time during the sequence above will cause the system to abort and return to the "touch-line" at item 1.
5. At any time the sequence can be frozen by closing the PAUSE switch. When opened, the sequence is to continue on from where it left off.
6. In order to alter the time-out from the default value of **10**, the SET switch must be closed when the system is reset. The display will then show **99** and will count down at a rate of around 2 per second. The value showing when the SET switch is released will be the new time-out and will be retained until the next manual or power-up reset.

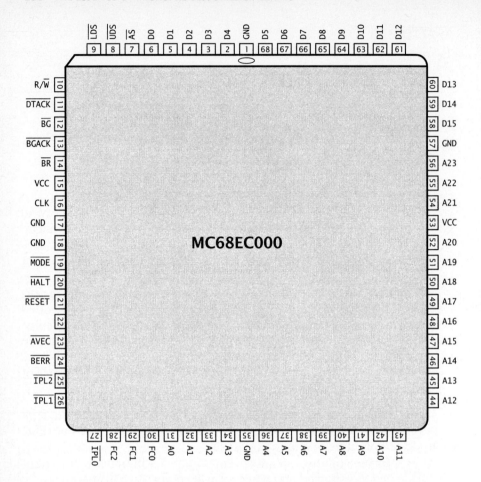

Figure 15.1 *Pinout for the 68EC000 microprocessor.*

The first decision to be made is the choice of MPU. In this case we are constrained by the need to use our book's model device, i.e. one of the 68000 series. The 68EC000 MPU,[1] whose pinout is given for reference in Fig. 15.1, has the advantage over the original 68000 MPU that it can operate in eight-bit mode (see page 179) and thus reduce the number of memory chips needed in our implementation. It also uses an order of magnitude less power than the original circuit. The 68-pin PLCC[2] 0.05″ (1.27 mm) pitch square package is more awkward to use for wire-wrapping than the 0.1″ (2.54 mm) pitch Dual-In-Line (DIL) package, but PLCC sockets to 0.1″ pitch wire-wrap adapters are available. The 48-pin DIL 68008 eight-bit 68000 MPU is an acceptable alternative, but is no longer manufactured and difficult to obtain. The 68008's VPA pin is equivalent to the 68EC000's AVEC, and IPL2 and IPL0 are internally connected to save pins. Other than this, operation is the same.

---

[1] The EC stands for Embedded Control.

[2] Plastic Leaded Chip Carrier.

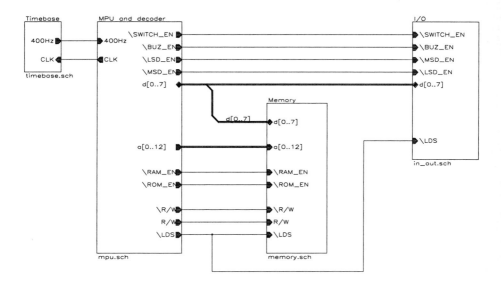

Figure 15.2 *A modular view of the hardware.*

The hardware has been structured as four modules, as shown in Fig. 15.2.

- The processor module comprises the MPU, ancillary logic and address decoder.
- A 400 Hz signal provides the timebase for general timing.
- Program, vector table, general variables and stack are stored in EPROM and RAM memory.
- The two seven-segment displays, lamps, buzzer and input switches are implemented in the input/output module.

mpu.sch

In Fig. 15.3 a 74LS138 decodes Address lines $a_{15}\,a_{14}\,a_{13}$ to provide eight fixed zones (see Chapter 12). These outputs are:

- 00000–$01FFFh$ for an 8 Kbyte EPROM chip.
- $02000h$ to enable a single output port driving the least significant (units) seven-segment display.
- $04000h$ to enable a single output port driving the most significant (tens) seven-segment display.
- $06000h$ to enable a single output port driving the lamps and buzzer.
- $08000h$ to enable a single input port for the control switches.
- $0E000$–$0FFFFh$ for an 8 Kbyte RAM chip.

Address lines $a_{23}...a_{16}$ are not used in our application.

The reset circuitry is similar to that in Fig. 14.5(b) on page 246 but with the more easily obtainable MAX702 supervisor circuit replacing the

MAX701. As the MAX702 has only an active-low output, the spare 74LS05 open-collector buffer gate U8B/R7 is used as an inverter before U8A/U8C.

The 400 Hz signal is arranged to generate a Level-7 interrupt, by connection to all three $\overline{\text{IPL2}}$ $\overline{\text{IPL1}}$ $\overline{\text{IPL0}}$ pins. A Level-7 interrupt request is special in that it cannot be locked out by the mask bits (see Fig. 4.4 on page 66) in the Status register, even if they are I2 I1 I0 = 111. Furthermore, a

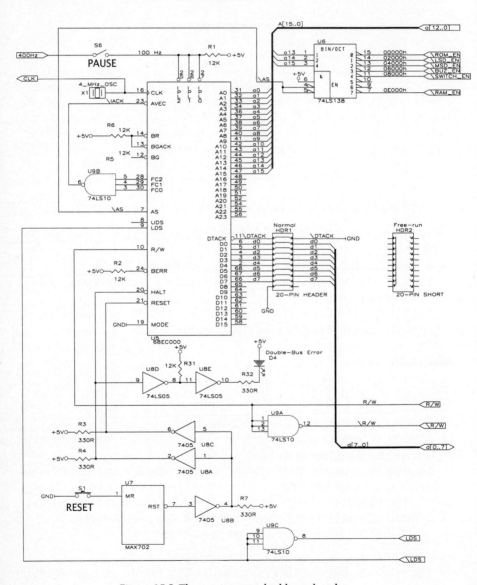

Figure 15.3 *The processor and address decoder.*

Level-7 **non-maskable** interrupt response is only initiated when the request *changes* up from a lower level, i.e. it can be considered to be edge triggered; in our case this occurs on a ⌐_ of the 400 Hz signal. Thus it can only be retriggered when the level changes down and then up again. This means that the D flip flop interrupt flag handshake mechanism of Fig. 14.2 on page 239 is not required, and the direct connection shown will suffice. Like that diagram, an Interrupt ACKnowledge signal $\overline{\text{IACK}}$ is generated by NANDing FC2 FC1 FC0. This drives $\overline{\text{AVEC}}$ low to set the processor into its autovector look-up table mode.

The PAUSE switch simply decouples the timebase output from the $\overline{\text{IPL}}$ pins. As no Jiffies are then recorded, the sequence is not advanced.

The MPU is clocked using a 4 MHz crystal oscillator module with a TTL-compatible signal output. This is also used as a convenient source for our Timebase module. If you use the more expensive 16 or 20 MHz 68EC000 versions, then you must use the minimum clock frequency of 8 MHz. The resulting 800 Hz interrupt rate can be accounted for by minor adjustments in the software, to reflect the increased number of Jiffies in a minute.

In general, hardware should be designed at the outset for testability. One simple provision here is the LED driven through two spare 74LS05 inverters from $\overline{\text{Halt}}$. During a Double-bus fault (see page 179) $\overline{\text{Halt}}$ will *output* a low level and the LED illuminate.

More significantly, a free-run facility provides for limited hardware diagnostics. By connecting both $\overline{\text{DTACK}}$ and all Data lines to ground, the processor will spend all its time executing the phantom instruction which has the op-code/operand 0000–0000h (see also page 192). This is the 4-byte ori.b #0,d0.

In Fig. 15.4 the Data bus/$\overline{\text{DTACK}}$ pair are hijacked by replacing the pass-through DIL header HDR1 by the free-run header HDR2. On reset the MPU will fetch the contents of the Reset vector, which will be 00000000h, the initial value of the Program Counter (PC). The 68000 will then begin fetching and executing ori.b #0,d0 *ad infinitum*, each fetch and execute taking four bus cycles. In doing so, the PC will increment four times on each fetch, i.e. at a rate of one increment per microsecond (at a clock rate of 4 MHz). This process will be reflected on the Address bus as the MPU fetches data down at the address held in the PC, with a_0 taking two increments to cycle (500 kHz), a_1 cycling at 250 kHz up to a_{23}, which cycles in just over 33 s! All this can be monitored through to the address decoder and to the memory circuits using a logic probe. The $\overline{\text{AS}}$ and $\overline{\text{LDS}}$ lines should be pulsing at a 1 μs rate and R/$\overline{\text{W}}$ should be permanently high. The output of the frequency divider of Fig. 15.5 should also be cycling at a 400 Hz rate. However, *the* PAUSE *switch should be open to disable interrupt requests from this source during free-run.*

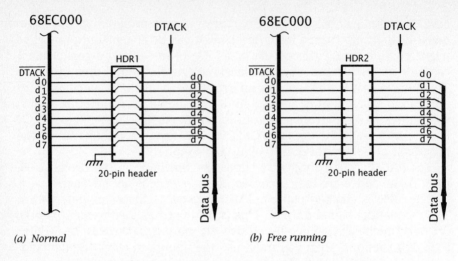

(a) Normal   (b) Free running

Figure 15.4 *Free-running an 8-bit mode 68000 microprocessor.*

Using an oscilloscope will verify these frequencies. In addition the relationship between outputs from the address decoder can be verified. Thus output $\overline{ROM\_EN}$ should cycle at a rate of approximately 131 ms, being active for one-eighth of the time, and should precede the similar $\overline{LSD\_EN}$ by one-eighth of the cycle time. As we progressively move up through the memory map, each output should appear delayed by one-eighth of the cycle.

In order to save circuitry, $\overline{DTACK}$ has been permanently grounded. This works because all memory and port interface circuitry is fast enough to respond with no wait states. Thus a smaller 18-pin header may be used for the free-run/normal headers, rather than the more general situation shown in Fig. 15.3.

timebase.sch

Given that we are going to use a regular train of interrupts to sequence our monitor's train of events, we have to generate a suitable timebase. As the timebase will be used to determine the 250 ms on-period of the buzzer, the lowest interrupt frequency is 4 Hz. Higher frequencies will be wasteful of processor resources, but in this case a modest increase in "tick" rate should not be significant.

Rather than using a stand-alone oscillator, Fig. 15.5 shows four cascaded decade counters dividing down the 4 MHz CLK signal. As each counter takes ten input clock pulses to go through its sequence of states, the output from the counter's final bit will be one-tenth the input frequency. With four counters, the final frequency ratio is 1/10,000, giving a 400 Hz output.

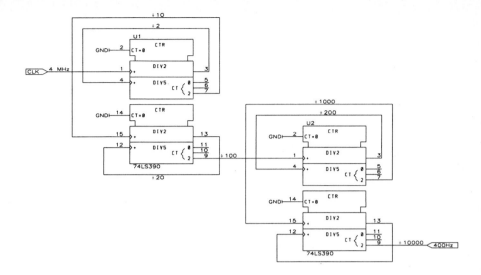

Figure 15.5 *Generating the 400 Hz timebase.*

The 74LS390 comprises two such decade counters. Each counter in turn is implemented as a divide by 2 and divide by 5 chain of flip flops. Connecting the output of the ÷2 section (e.g. pin 3) to the input of the ÷5 counter (e.g. pin 4) gives the overall ÷10 configuration.

memory.sch

Program memory is implemented in Fig. 15.6 using a 27C64 8 Kbyte EPROM. As well as being enabled by the address decoder in the range 00000–01FFFh, the device also has been enabled with R/$\overline{\text{W}}$ high, i.e. on a Read cycle. The vector table, program code and look-up data are stored in this EPROM.

Stack and general storage are located between 0E000h and 0FFFFh in a 6264 8 Kbyte RAM. The output buffers of this device are only enabled when R/$\overline{\text{W}}$ is high, i.e. on a Read cycle.

At a clock rate of 4 MHz any available access-time selection of both devices would be suitable. A 150 ns or better access-time would be needed with a 8 MHz clocking rate, and care should be taken to choose suitably rated devices, especially with the EPROM as slower versions are commonly available.

in_out.sch

The various input and output peripheral devices with their interfaces are shown in Fig. 15.7. These comprise the two seven-segment displays, the three indicator lamps, buzzer and four function switches.

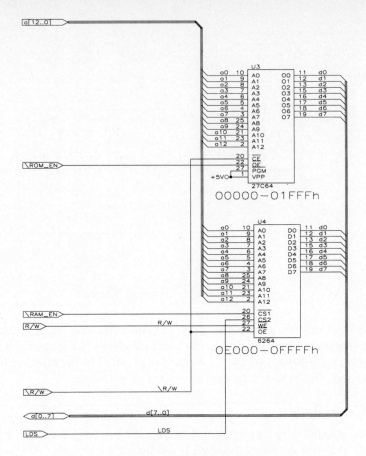

Figure 15.6 *Memory.*

The common-anode seven-segment displays shown in the diagram are packaged in a 16-pin DIL format and have both left and right decimal points (1hdp and rhdp). As these are not used here, alternatives with only one or no decimal points may be used. These typically come in 10- or 14-pin DIL formats. However, even in the 16-pin footprint, pinouts are not standardized.

Smaller-sized displays, typically below 1″/25 mm, use a single LED for each bar, with a conducting voltage drop of around 2 V.[3] Using 330 Ω series resistors limits the current to around 10 mA. The common anodes are connected directly back to the normal +5 V power supply to avoid current surges affecting the logic circuits, and should be decoupled by small tantalum capacitors. Although the displays are normally rated for

---

[3]Larger displays, e.g. 2.24″/56 mm, have typically two or four LEDs in series. In the latter case a separate 12 V supply would be needed and current buffering.

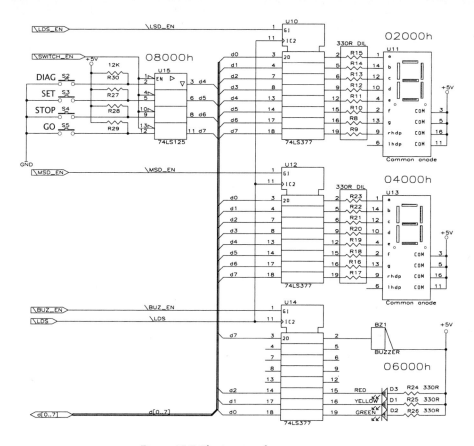

Figure 15.7 *The input and output ports.*

20 mA, restricting the current to this value gives sufficient illumination and means that the 74LS377-based output port (see Fig. 13.5 on page 218) does not need current buffering.[4]

Similar design principles apply to the 74LS377 port at 06000h. The buzzer should be a miniature solid-state device. A typical piezo-electric implementation will operate over a wide d.c. voltage range of typically 3–16 V and require little more than 1 mA at 5 V.[5]

Finally, the 74LS125-based input port allows the system to read the state of up to four single-pole push switches. If it is thought necessary, replacing the 74LS125 by a 74LS244 (see Fig. 13.2 on page 214) would expand this capability to eight switches at little additional cost.

With the hardware environment designed, we must now concentrate on the software.

---

[4]Alternatively low-current seven-segment displays are available.

[5]If you want to put paid to any possibility of the speaker continuing, a piezo-electric sound bomb producing 110 dB at 1 m distance needs a 12 V d.c. supply at 200 mA.

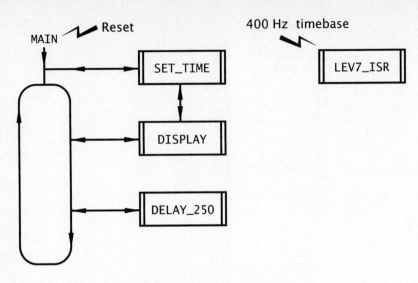

Figure 15.8 *Software modules.*

The basic modular structure for the software is shown in Fig. 15.8, where the distinctive double left/right edged box denotes a subroutine or Interrupt Service Routine (ISR). The main routine is an endless loop calling up the following subroutines:

- SET_TIME allows the user to preset the time-out period, if the 10 minutes default is not applicable.
- DISPLAY converts the current count in minutes to a binary-coded decimal (BCD) equivalent, and displays this as a two-digit seven-segment readout.
- DELAY_250 does nothing for a quater of a second (250 ms).

The order of the calling sequence in the diagram is not significant.

Separate from the MAIN routine is the ISR to which the processor is transferred on each "tick" of the oscillator. The ISR decrements the various 2.5 ms (Jiffy) counts on each transfer, and these counts may be read by the other modules.

The MAIN routine flowchart is shown in Fig. 15.9. Although this looks rather complex, it may be broken down into five phases, each of which is relatively straightforward.

1. The initial portion of the Preamble phase is *only* entered on reset. This sets the value of the countdown period to 10 minutes and then checks to see if the operator wishes to alter this default. Thus the SET switch must be held down during this time. The start of the main loop turns off all peripheral devices and waits for the GO switch to be closed.

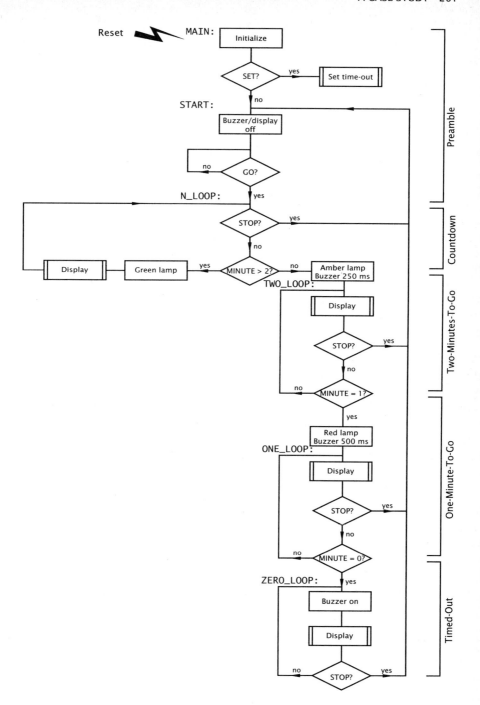

Figure 15.9 *Flowchart for the* MAIN *function.*

2. The Countdown process continuously displays the value of the MINUTE variable (updated by the ISR) and illuminates the green lamp. This inner loop continues until either the STOP switch is pressed or the MINUTE count drops below 03.

3. With Two-Minutes-To-Go, the amber lamp is illuminated and the buzzer sounded once only for 250 ms. After this an inner loop displaying 02 is exited, either back to the start if STOP is closed or on to the next phase when the MINUTE count drops to 01h.

4. With One-Minute-To-Go the red lamp is illuminated and the buzzer sounded once for 500 ms. After this the inner loop displaying 01 is exited, either back to the start if STOP is closed or on to the Timed-Out phase.

5. When the MINUTE count reaches zero, not only is 00 displayed, but also the buzzer is sounded continuously. This cacophony can only be silenced by pressing the STOP switch (or resetting).

Program 15.1 *The vector table and various declarations.*

```
            .processor  m68000

            .define  LSD      = 02000h,   ; The LSD seven-segment display
                     MSD      = 04000h,   ; The MSD seven-segment display
                     BUZ      = 06000h,   ; The buzzer/lamps port
                     SWITCHES = 08000h    ; The switch port

;   ********************************************************************

            .psect  _data     ; The data stream linked to 0E000h (RAM)

JIFFY:    .word   [1]   ; Reserve two bytes to hold the jiffy count
MINUTE:   .byte   [1]   ; Reserve one byte to hold the minute count
DELAY_n:  .byte   [1]   ; Reserve one byte for the delay parameter
TIME_OUT: .byte   [1]   ; Reserve one byte for the allowed time

;   ********************************************************************

            .psect  _text     ; The data stream linked to 00000h (ROM)

VECTOR_TABLE:
            .double 10000h    ; Stack initialized to top of RAM
            .double MAIN      ; Initial value of PC (start of program)
            .double [29]      ; Skip 29 vectors to the
            .double LEV7_ISR  ; Level-7 ISR start address
            .double [224]     ; Skip to 400h, the start of executable code
```

Before describing the coding of the MAIN routine, we need to consider the vector table and the definition of the variables used by the rest of the software. The heading of Program 15.1 equates the four constant locations of the hardware I/O ports to their name using the .define directive.

Thus for example, the instruction `btst #5,SWITCHES` in Program 15.2 is a rather more readable version of `btst #5,08000h`.

After this, space is *reserved* for the word-sized (`.word`) variable JIFFY (2.5 ms tick count) and the three byte-sized (`.byte`) variables MINUTE (the minute countdown), DELAY_n (a subsidary 2.5 ms tick count to time out 250 ms in the DELAY_250 subroutine) and TIME_OUT (the number of minutes allowed for the talk, defaulting to ten). These four variables are allocated space in the `_data` data stream using the directive `.psect`, which the linker should be configured to direct to the RAM at 0E000–0FFFFh. As well as space allocation, each variable is given the indicated name, which can be used subsequently in lieu of an address. Finally, space is reserved in the `_text` data stream, subsequently linked to the EPROM at 00000–01FFFh, for the vector table. Each address in the table is allocated a four-byte slot using the `.double` directive. The first two of these are the initial value of the System Stack Pointer (10000h is the first even address over the top of the RAM chip) and the initial value of the Program Counter (MAIN is the address of the first instruction of Program 15.2, which is 00400h).

The next 29 address slots are not used, and are skipped over. Entry 32 is the start address of the Level-7 ISR, which in Program 15.6 is labelled LEV7_ISR. Finally, skipping the next 224 address slots takes us up to the first location after the vector table, which is 00400h.

The MAIN routine in Program 15.2 is split into phases corresponding to the flow diagram of Fig. 15.9. Code from MAIN and up to BEGIN is entered and executed only on a reset. This initializes the memory location TIME_OUT to the default 10 minutes. The state of bit 5 of the Switch port is then checked and if open (high) execution moves to the start of the main endless loop. Otherwise the SET_TIME subroutine is called, which allows the operator to alter the value of TIME_OUT.

The beginning of the main loop at BEGIN intializes the MINUTE count variable to the value in TIME_OUT and also the JIFFY word to its maximum of 24,000 (60×400 Jiffies — interrupts — is a minute).[6] The two seven-segment displays and buzzer are then turned off. However, the green LED remains illuminated to reassure the user that the system is live. Finally the GO switch is continually checked and only when this is opened (high) does execution move to the start of the Countdown sequence.

The Countdown phase from N_LOOP up to TWO continually calls the DISPLAY subroutine to show the state of the MINUTE count and illuminate the green LED. Exit from this loop is back to START on a premature abort if the STOP switch is closed (bit 6 of the Switch port) or else on to the next phase if the state of the global byte MINUTE drops down to 02h.

The Two-Minutes-To-Go phase from TWO up to ONE initially turns on the buzzer, calls up the 250 ms DELAY_250 subroutine and turns it off again.

---

[6]Alter this to 48,000 if a 8 MHz clock/800 Hz interrupt rate is used.

Program 15.2 *The* MAIN *routine.*

```
; The Preamble phase *************************************************
; First initialize only on Reset
MAIN:     move.b  #10,TIME_OUT    ; 10 mins is the default time value
; Check switch settings before going on
          btst    #5,SWITCHES     ; Check the SET switch
          bne     BEGIN           ; IF not desired, check the GO switch
          jsr     SET_TIME        ; ELSE allow user to change timeout
BEGIN:    move.b  TIME_OUT,MINUTE ; Initialize the minute count
          move.w  #24000,JIFFY    ; and the Jiffy (1/400s) count
          move.b  #11111110b,BUZ  ; Turn on green LED
          move.b  #0FFh,LSD       ; Turn off displays
          move.b  #0FFh,MSD
          btst    #7,SWITCHES     ; At the touchline
          bne     BEGIN           ; Keep trying until GO switch closed
; The Countdown phase ***********************************************
; REPEAT normal loop until Minute count drops down to 2
N_LOOP:   btst    #6,SWITCHES     ; Check the state of the STOP switch
          beq     BEGIN           ; Abort if closed

          move.b  MINUTE,d0       ; ELSE get the Minute count
          jsr     DISPLAY         ; and show it
          move.b  #11111110b,BUZ  ; and turn the green lamp on

          cmp.b   #2,MINUTE       ; IF not dropped down to 2 THEN repeat
          bne     N_LOOP
; The Two-Minutes-To-Go phase ***************************************
; At a count of two sound the buzzer for 250ms & turn on the amber lamp
; Exit when minute count drops down to one
TWO:      move.b  #01111101b,BUZ  ; Turn on buzzer and amber lamp
          jsr     DELAY_250       ; For 250 ms
          move.b  #11111101b,BUZ  ; and the buzzer off

TWO_LOOP: btst    #6,SWITCHES     ; Check the STOP switch
          beq     BEGIN           ; IF closed THEN abort

          moveq   #2,d0           ; Display 02
          jsr     DISPLAY
          cmp.b   #1,MINUTE       ; REPEAT UNTIL count drops down to 1
          bne     TWO_LOOP
; The One-Minute-To-Go phase ****************************************
; At a count of one sound the buzzer for 500 ms and turn on the red lamp
; Exit when Minute count drops down to zero
ONE:      move.b  #01111011b,BUZ  ; Turn on buzzer and red lamp
          jsr     DELAY_250       ; For 250 ms
          jsr     DELAY_250       ; For another 250 ms
          move.b  #11111011b,BUZ  ; and the buzzer off

ONE_LOOP: btst    #6,SWITCHES     ; Check the STOP switch
          beq     BEGIN           ; IF closed THEN abort

          moveq   #1,d0           ; Display 01
          jsr     DISPLAY
          tst.b   MINUTE          ; REPEAT UNTIL count drops down to 0
          bne     ONE_LOOP
; The Timed-Out phase ***********************************************
; When the Minute count reaches zero, sound the buzzer continually
; until the STOP switched is closed
ZERO:     clr.b   d0              ; Display 00
          jsr     DISPLAY
          move.b  #01111011b,BUZ  ; Turn on buzzer and red lamp

ZERO_LOOP:btst    #6,SWITCHES     ; Check the STOP switch
          beq     BEGIN           ; Reset if closed
          bra     ZERO_LOOP       ; ELSE repeat
```

With the amber LED illuminated, an inner loop continually displays 0̶2̶ and again aborts if the STOP switch is closed, and forward to the next phase when the MINUTE count drops to 01*h*.

The One-Minute-To-Go phase is nearly identical but the DELAY_250 subroutine is called twice to give a total buzz on time of 500 ms. This time the red LED is lit.

Finally, the Timed-Out loop turns the buzzer on permanently and displays 0̶ 1̶. The only way out of this loop is back to the start if the STOP switch is closed.

Program 15.3 *The* DISPLAY *subroutine.*

```
; ***********************************************************************
; * FUNCTION: Converts the binary value of the Minute count into        *
; * FUNCTION: seven-segment BCD range 00 -- 99d and displays            *
; * ENTRY    : Byte (00 -- 63h) in D0.B                                 *
; * EXIT     : Value displayed at MSD:LSD                               *
; ***********************************************************************
DISPLAY:  movem.l d0/a0,-(sp)    ; Save environment
          and.l   #0FFh,d0       ; Extend byte to long-word (for div)

          divu    #10,d0         ; Dividing by 10 -> D0.L = Units:Tens
          movea.l #TABLE,a0      ; Point A0.L to seven-seg look-up table
          move.b  0(a0,d0.w),MSD ; Convert and move tens to MSD display
          swap    d0             ; Put the units digit in D0.W
          move.b  0(a0,d0.w),LSD ; Convert and move units to LSD display

          movem.l (sp)+,d0/a0    ; Retrieve environment
          rts

; ***********************************************************************
TABLE:    .byte   11000000b, 11111001b, 10100100b, 10110000b, 10011001b,
                  10010010b, 10000010b, 11111000b, 10000000b, 10010000b
          .even
; ***********************************************************************
```

The DISPLAY subroutine of Program 15.3 comprises program code and a table of the ten active-low (segment illuminated on logic 0) seven-segment codes (see Fig. 13.5 on page 218). The program itself essentially divides a copy of the MINUTE count by ten to convert the binary value into a units and tens BCD digit (quotient is tens, remainder is units); see Program 6.3 on page 107. As MINUTE is never greater than 99, the remainder from the divu instruction will be the units digit 0...9 and the quotient will be the tens digit 0...9. Remembering that divu needs a long-word dividend, D0.L is cleared and MINUTE copied in to extend the byte data to 32-bit. swap is used to place the outcome remainder in the top of D0.L into the bottom of the register. The actual conversion to seven-segment code is done by using this digit as an offset to the pointer to the start of the look-up table in A0.L, as described in Program 8.6 on page 139. This is done twice; once for the units and once for the tens display. In keeping with good practice the subroutine is transparent.

Program 15.4 *The* DELAY_250 *delay 250ms subroutine.*

```
; ********************************************************************
; * FUNCTION: Delays for 250 ms                                      *
; * ENTRY   : Assumes a 2.5 ms tick in memory @ DELAY_n updated by ISR*
; * EXIT    : No change                                              *
; ********************************************************************
DELAY_250: clr.b  DELAY_n        ; Clear the 2.5 ms tick count

D_LOOP:    cmp.b  #100,DELAY_n   ; Wait around until 100 ticks (250 ms)
           bne    D_LOOP

           rts
```

The DELAY_250 subroutine makes use of the global location DELAY_n, which byte is incremented by the ISR at the same time as the JIFFY word is decremented. By clearing this variable on entry and only exiting when it reaches 100 ($100 \times 2.5 = 250$ ms) a delay of 250 ms will be implemented.[7] This interrupt-driven delay principle is very flexible, and any delay from 2.5 ms to 0.6375 s (255×2.5) can be achieved by altering the tick constant.

Program 15.5 *The* SET_TIME *subroutine.*

```
; ********************************************************************
; * FUNCTION: Slowly counts down from 99 to 00. When the SET switch  *
; * FUNCTION: is released, the count is the new time-out setting     *
; * ENTRY   : None                                                   *
; * USAGE   : Subroutine DISPLAY entry D0.B                          *
; * USAGE   : Subroutine DELAY_250                                   *
; * EXIT    : TIME_OUT updated                                       *
; ********************************************************************
SET_TIME: move.b #99,d0          ; Start the count at 99 decimal in D0.B
T_LOOP:   jsr    DISPLAY         ; Display Set count in D0.B
          jsr    DELAY_250       ; for 500 ms (0.5 s)
          jsr    DELAY_250
          btst   #5,SWITCHES     ; Has the user released the SET switch?
          bne    T_EXIT          ; IF so THEN completed setup
          subq.b #1,d0           ; ELSE try next value down
          bne    T_LOOP          ; unless decremented to 00
          bra    SET_TIME        ; IF underflows, try again from the top

T_EXIT:   move.b d0,TIME_OUT     ; Update the new value in TIME_OUT
          rts
```

The SET_TIME subroutine is called up only on reset, and allows the operator to alter the time-out value. In Program 15.5 the contents of D0.B are

---

[7] Alter this to 200 if a 8 MHz clock/800 Hz interrupt rate is used.

decremented from an initial value of 99 at an interval rate of 500 ms (just over twice per second). The decrement rate is set by calling DELAY_250 twice in succession. This decrementation is continually displayed, and exit occurs when the SET switch is released. The release value is transferred to the TIME_OUT memory location, used by the MAIN routine at the start of the loop sequence to set the initial value of the MINUTE count. This value is maintained unless the system is reset. Should the Set count drop to zero (due to an inattentive operator) it begins again at 99.

Program 15.6 *The interrupt service routine.*

```
; ***********************************************************************

LEV7_ISR: addq.b  #1,DELAY_n      ; One more 1/400s
          subq.w  #1,JIFFY        ; One more Jiffy
          bne     ISR_EXIT        ; Exit unless reached zero

          move.w  #24000,JIFFY    ; Reset Jiffy count to 60s (1 minute)
          tst.b   MINUTE          ; Check if Minutes has reached zero
          beq     ISR_EXIT        ; IF so THEN leave alone
          subq.b  #1,MINUTE       ; ELSE decrement Minute count
ISR_EXIT: rte
; ***********************************************************************


          .end
```

The key to the operation of the software is the update of the countdown variable MINUTE and its auxiliary JIFFY count. Hardware interrupts the processor every 2.5 ms and switches processing from the background tasks already described to the foreground interrupt service routine of Program 15.6.

The core of the ISR is the decrementation of the word-sized variable JIFFY and the auxiliary byte-sized DELAY_n. This is used by the DELAY_250 subroutine to count 100 2.5 ms Jiffies. If JIFFY is not zero then the ISR exits via the ReTurn from Exception (rte) instruction. If it has reached zero then it is reset to 24,000 (400 ticks by 60 seconds is one minute) and the MINUTE variable decremented, unless it too is zero. Finally, no Data or Address registers are used, so nothing need be saved at the beginning or retrieved at the end.

The hardware and software circuits have been presented here as a simple illustrative case study to integrate many of the techniques described in the body of the text. If you decide to build your own version, construction details, parts lists, files, test waveforms, software (a diagnostic routine and a **C** coding) and ideas for experimentation are given on the associated Web site detailed in the Introduction. Good luck!

Glossary

⊐_	A negative-going edge.
_⌐	A positive-going edge.
⊐_⌐	An active-low pulse.
_⌐⊐_	An active-high pulse.
2's complement	A method of representing negative numbers. The number is changed to the opposite sign by inverting all bits and adding 1.
68020+	The 68020, 68030, 68040 and 68060 devices were introduced progressively up to 1996. They share the basic register architecture, with extras, with the 68000 MPU and are source code compatible. The 68030 and up have integral co-processors.
Address	A reference of the location of data in memory or within I/O space.
a_n	Address bus line n. The 68000 family mainly have 32 address lines and thus can access $2^{32} = 4,294,967,296$ or 4 Gbytes of memory/peripheral input/output.
An	Address register n. The 68000 family have eight Address registers in any mode, including the Stack Pointer A7. An Address register can be accessed either as a 32-bit long-word or as a 16-bit word that is, however, always sign-extended to affect all 32 bits.
A/D converter	Analog to Digital converter. Converts an analog signal, continually variable between an upper and lower level, to an n-bit digital equivalent.
Address mode	The technique an instruction uses to pin-point where in memory an operand lies.
ALU	Arithmetic Logic Unit. The digital circuitry that implements the fundamental operations, such as add, subtract, AND, OR, NOT.
ANSI	American National Standard Institute.

ASCII	American Standard Code for Information Interchange. An early and nearly universal standard equating a range of letters, numbers, punctuation and control character mapped on to a seven-bit binary code. It has been extended to various eight-bit supersets and to 16-bit Unicode as used in Microsoft's Windows 95.
$\overline{\text{AS}}$	Active-low Address Strobe signal. The 68000's way of telling the outside world that the Address bus now carries a stable address pattern.
Binary	A number system using a base of 2.
Bit	A Binary digIT. A physical variable, such as voltage or light, having two states.
BCD	Binary Coded Decimal. A hybrid decimal/binary coding technique whereby each digit of a decimal number is replaced one of ten binary patterns. Where this code is the normal 8-4-2-1 arrangement, the term natural BCD is sometimes used.
Byte	An eight-bit binary word, giving $2^8 = 256$ unique combinations.
C	Carry flag. Doubles as a borrow indicator for Subtraction and Comparison operations. Also the **C** programming language.
CCR	Code Condition Register. The lower half of the 68000's Status register, holding the flags in the order **X, N, Z, V, C**.
CMOS	Complimentary Metal-Oxide Semiconductor. A fabrication technique using both N- and P-channel field-effect transistors.
CPU	Central Processing Unit. The component of a computer that controls the interpretation and execution of instructions.
$\overline{\text{CS}}$	Active-low Chip Select signal. The standard designation on memory and peripheral devices indicating input(s) which must be active to enable that chip.
D/A converter	Digital to Analog converter. Converts an n-bit digital word to its analog equivalent.
d_n	Data bus line n. The 68000 family have variously 8, 16 and 32-bit buses. The main data flow between the MPU and the outside world is along this common Data highway.
$\overline{\text{DTACK}}$	The active-low Data ACKknowledge signal a memory or peripheral interface port must activate in order to allow the bus cycle to proceed to completion.
Dn	Data register n. One of the eight 32-bit internal registers. Each register can be used to hold and manipulate a byte, word or long-word.

ea	Effective Address. The calculated source or/and destination address according to the address mode used.
EPROM	Erasable Programmable Read-Only Memory. A PROM that can be erased under high-intensity ultra-violet light, then reprogrammed. One-time programmable (OTP) versions without the quartz window are available.
Exception	Either an external interrupt signal or an internal software exceptional event, such as an attempt to divide by zero, that causes the MPU to transfer program control to a handler routine.
FC	Three-bit Function Code status signal showing if in the Supervisor or User mode, whether fetching program or data code or if responding to a hardware interrupt request.
G	Giga, a prefix indicating a billion. Specifically in binary systems $2^{30} = 1,073,741,824$.
Handshake	The protocol used to set up, sequence and terminate a flow of data between two or more peripheral devices and a controller.
Hexadecimal	A number system with a base of 16. Usually used as a shorthand representation for binary numbers grouped in four digits.
IC	Integrated Circuit. An electronic circuit fabricated on a semiconductor material, typically silicon.
IEC	International Electrotechnical Commission.
Interrupt	A signal (see IPL) that when activated causes the MPU to transfer program control to a particular software module called an ISR.
I/O port	Input or/and Output connection providing for data communication between MPU and a peripheral device.
IPL	Interrupt Priority Level. A three-bit input signal from an interrupting peripheral indicating the level of response requested.
ISR	Interrupt Service Routine. The subroutine entered via an interrupt request or other exception. It must be terminated with an `rte` instruction rather than an `rts`.
K	Kilo, a prefix indicating a thousand. Specifically in binary systems $2^{10} = 1024$.
$\overline{\text{LDS}}$	Active-low Lower Data Strobe status signal. Indicates whenever the data on the lower byte of the Data bus is valid (see also $\overline{\text{UDS}}$).
LED	Light-Emitting Diode.
LSB	Least Significant (rightmost) Bit or Byte.

LSI	Large-Scale Integration. Describing an IC with between 100 and 1000 gate complexity (see also SSI, MSI and VLSI).
LSD	Least Significant Digit (typically of a decimal or BCD number).
M	Mega, a prefix indicating a million. Specifically in binary systems $2^{20} = 1,048,576$.
MCU	MicroController Unit. A microprocessor integrated on the same chip as support circuitry such as memory, I/O ports and timers.
MPU	MicroProcessor Unit. The ALU and control elements of a computer-like processor integrated on the one IC.
ms	Millisecond (10^{-3} s).
MSB	Most Significant (leftmost) Bit or Byte.
MSD	Most Significant Digit (typically of a decimal or BCD number).
MSI	Medium-Scale Integration. Describing an IC with between 12 and 100 gate complexity, e.g. a decoder (see also SSI, LSI and VLSI).
N	Negative flag. Reflects the state of the most significant bit after an instruction (see also Sign bit).
ns	Nanosecond (10^{-9} s).
Nybble	A four-bit binary word, giving $2^4 = 16$ unique combinations.
$\overline{OE}$	Active-low Output Enable signal, usually pertaining to the three-state output buffers in a memory or other peripheral input port.
OS	Operating System. Software that controls the execution of a computer system that links the hardware environment to the user program and may provide facilities such as debugging and multitasking.
PC	Program Counter. Instruction pointer to the instruction being fetched from memory.
PC	Personal Computer.
PROM	Programmable Read-Only Memory. Generic term for a memory chip that can be programmed once or relatively few times, usually before insertion into the circuit. typically holds program and fixed data in embedded microprocessor systems (see also EPROM).
RAM	Random Access Memory. Memory that is written into and read from in circuit, in which any location may be accessed with the same time delay. Typically holds temporary data and the stack.

Register	An array of flip flops or latches normally holding a single word in the CPU.
RTL	Register Transfer Language. A notation describing the operation of an instruction viewed from the perspective of moving data between registers and/or memory.
R/$\overline{\text{W}}$	Read/Write status signal from the microprocessor to memory and other circuitry, giving the direction of transfer of data along the Data bus.
Sign bit	The MSB of a signed word, usually 1 for negative.
Stack	A last-in first-out data structure in memory used in conjunction with the Stack Pointer to hold the return address for subroutines and exceptions and to hold register data temporarily using the *movem* instruction to push and pull data into and out of the structure.
SP	Stack Pointer. The A7 Address register automatically used to point to the current long-word in the stack.
Status register	A 16-bit register holding the System bit, Trace bit, three Interrupt mask priority bits and the CCR.
SSI	Small-Scale Integration. Describing a simple IC with typically a few gates' complexity (see also MSI, LSI and VLSI).
SSP	System Stack Pointer. The A7 Address register used when the processor is in the System mode (**S** bit in the Status register is 1).
TTL	Transistor Transistor Logic family. A common bi-polar circuit implementation largely coonfined to SSI and MSI logic circuits. The voltage and current levels are a *de facto* standard in logic circuits of any implementation type.
$\overline{\text{UDS}}$	Active-low Upper Data Strobe status signal. Indicates whenever the data on the upper byte of the Data bus is valid (see also $\overline{\text{LDS}}$).
USP	User Stack Pointer. The A7 Address register used when the processor is in the User mode (**S** bit in the Status register is 0).
VLSI	Very Large-Scale Integration. Describing an IC with a complexity of over 1000 gates, such as a memory (see also SSI, MSI and LSI).
X	The eXtended carry flag.
Z	The Zero flag. Set when the oucome of an instruction execution is zero.
μs	Microsecond (10^{-6} s).

Shortform 68000 instruction set

Instruction	Size	#	dn	an	(an)	(an)+	-(an)	$\pm K_{16}$ (an)	$\pm K_8$ (an,Ri)	Abs	X	N	Z	V	C
add [ea],dx	BWL	*	*	*	*	*	*	*	*	*	√	√	√	√	√
add dx,[ea]	BWL				*	*	*	*	*	*	√	√	√	√	√
adda [ea],ax	WL	*	*	*	*	*	*	*	*	*	•	•	•	•	•
addi #K,[ea]	BWL		*		*	*	*	*	*	*	√	√	√	√	√
addq #K_3,[ea]	BWL		*	*	*	*	*	*	*		√	√	√	√	√
and [ea],dx	BWL	*	*		*	*	*	*	*	*	•	√	√	0	0
and dx,[ea]	BWL				*	*	*	*	*	*	•	√	√	0	0
andi #K,[ea]	BWL		*		*	*	*	*	*	*	•	√	√	0	0
asl/r dx,dy	BWL										√	√	√	√	√
asl/r K_3,dx	BWL										√	√	√	√	√
asl/r [ea]	W				*	*	*	*	*	*	√	√	√	√	√
bccf [label]	BW				See table on following page						•	•	•	•	•
bra [label]	BW										•	•	•	•	•
bsr [label]	BW										•	•	•	•	•
btst #K,dx	L										•	•	√	•	•
btst #K,[ea]	B				*	*	*	*	*	*	•	•	√	•	•
clr [ea]	BWL		*		*	*	*	*	*	*	•	0	1	0	0
cmp [ea],dx	BWL	*	*	*	*	*	*	*	*	*	•	√	√	√	√
cmpa [ea],ax	WL	*	*	*	*	*	*	*	*	*	•	√	√	√	√
cmpi #K,[ea]	BWL		*		*	*	*	*	*	*	•	√	√	√	√
divs [ea],dx	W	*	*		*	*	*	*	*	*	•	√	√	√	0
divu [ea],dx	W	*	*		*	*	*	*	*	*	•	√	√	√	0
eor dx,[ea]	BWL		*		*	*	*	*	*	*	•	√	√	0	0
eori #K,[ea]	BWL		*		*	*	*	*	*	*	•	√	√	0	0
exg Rx,Ry	L										•	•	•	•	•
ext dx	WL										•	√	√	0	0
jmp [ea]					*			*	*	*	•	•	•	•	•
jsr [ea]					*			*	*	*	•	•	•	•	•
lsl/r dx,dy	BWL										√	√	√	0	√
lsl/r K_3,dx	BWL										√	√	√	0	√
lsl/r [ea]	W				*	*	*	*	*	*	√	√	√	0	√
move [ea],[ea]	BWL	*[S]	*	*[S]	*	*	*	*	*	*	•	√	√	0	0
move [ea],ccr	W	*	*		*	*	*	*	*	*	√	√	√	√	√
move [ea],sr[P]	W		*		*	*	*	*	*	*	√	√	√	√	√
movea [ea],ax	WL	*	*	*	*	*	*	*	*	*	•	•	•	•	•
movem [ΣR_m],[ea]	WL				*		*	*	*	*	•	•	•	•	•
movem [ea],[ΣR_m]	WL				*	*		*	*	*	•	•	•	•	•
moveq #±K_8,dx	L										•	√	√	0	0
mulu [ea],dx	W	*	*		*	*	*	*	*	*	•	√	√	0	0

Instruction	Size	#	dn	an	(an)	(an)+	-(an)	$\pm K_{16}$ (an)	$\pm K_8$ (an,Ri)	Abs	X	N	Z	V	C
neg [ea]	BWL		*		*	*	*	*	*	*	√	√	√	√	√
nop											•	•	•	•	•
not [ea]	BWL		*		*	*	*	*	*	*	•	√	√	0	0
or [ea],dx	BWL	*	*		*	*	*	*	*	*	•	√	√	0	0
or dx,[ea]	BWL				*	*	*	*	*	*	•	*	√	0	0
ori #K,[ea]	BWL		*		*	*	*	*	*	*	•	*	√	0	0
ori #K,sr^P	W										√	√	√	√	√
rol/r dx,dy	BWL										•	√	√	0	√
rol/r K$_3$,dx	BWL										•	√	√	0	√
rol/r [ea]	W				*	*	*	*	*	*	•	√	√	0	√
roxl/r dx,dy	BWL										√	√	√	0	√
roxl/r K$_3$,dx	BWL										√	√	√	0	√
roxl/r [ea]	W				*	*	*	*	*	*	√	√	√	0	√
rte^P											√	√	√	√	√
rts											•	•	•	•	•
sub [ea],dx	BWL	*	*	*	*	*	*	*	*	*	√	√	√	√	√
sub dx,[ea]	BWL				*	*	*	*	*	*	√	√	√	√	√
suba [ea],ax	WL	*	*	*	*	*	*	*	*	*	•	•	•	•	•
subi #K,[ea]	BWL		*		*	*	*	*	*	*	√	√	√	√	√
subq K$_3$,[ea]	BWL		*	*	*	*	*	*	*	*	√	√	√	√	√
swap dx	W										•	√	√	0	0
trap #K$_4$											•	•	•	•	•
tst [ea]	BWL		*		*	*	*	*	*	*	•	√	√	0	0

√ : Flag operates in the normal way.   • : Not affected. P : Privileged.
a$_n$: Address register n. S : Source only.   * : Available.
d$_n$: Data register n.   K$_m$: m-bit constant.   ± : Signed.
R$_n$: Data or Address register n.   ccf : Code Condition Flags.   ccr : Code Condition Reg.
sr : Status register. ΣR_m : Any collection of Data/Address registers.
B : Byte size.   W : Word size.   L : Long-word size.

Conditional Branches, Bccf					
beq	EQual	Z=1	bvc	oVerflow Clear	V=0
bne	Not Equal	Z=0	bvs	oVerflow Set	V=1
bcc	Carry Clear	C=0	bpl	PLus	N=0
bcs	Carry Set	C=1	bmi	MInus	N=1
bhs	Higher or Same	C=0	bge	Greater or Equal	N⊕V=0
bhi	HIgher than	C+Z=0	blt	Less Than	N⊕V=1
bls	Lower or Same	C+Z=1	bgt	Greater Than	$\overline{N \oplus V} \cdot \overline{Z}=1$
bcs	LOwer than	C=1	ble	Less or Equal	$\overline{N \oplus V} \cdot \overline{Z}=0$

Appendix C

Further reading

There are many texts on microprocessors and concentrating on the 68000 family. Most of these are confined to software aspects but the following also cover hardware and interfacing topics.

- Cahill, S.J.; *C for the Microprocessor Engineer*, Prentice Hall, 1994.
  My previous book to this. Covers the use of the **C** language for embedded code generation. Uses both the 6809 and 68000 processors as the engine, together with hardware and software information and a case study.
- Cahill, S.J.; *Digital and Microprocessor Engineering*, Prentice Hall/Ellis Horwood, 2nd edn. 1993.
  Good for the digital design reviewed in Chapters 1 and 2, serial data transmission etc. but its microprocessor is mainly the 6809 eight-bit device.
- Clemants, A.; *Microprocessor System Design*, PWS-Kent/Chapman & Hall, 2nd edn. 1992.
  One of the definitive texts in this area. Covers software and hardware aspects of both the 68000 and the 68020+ devices in great depth.
- Harman, T.L. and Hein, D.T.; *The Motorola MC68000 Microprocessor Family*, Prentice Hall, 2nd edn. 1996.
  Mainly software, but with consideration of serial and parallel interfacing.
- Miller, M.A.; *The 68000 Microprocessor*, Merrill, 1988.
  A mixture of hardware and software with serial and parallel interfacing and two chapters on the 68020 MPU and 68881 co-processor.
- Veronis, A.M.; *The 68000 Microprocessor*, Van Nostrand, 1988.
  A good mixture of hardware and software including the design of a microprocessor training system.
- Wilcox, A.D.; *The 68000 Microprocessor System*, Prentice Hall, 1987.
  An extremely good practical systems design text as well as designing, commissioning and testing a real 68000-based system.
- Wakerly, J.F.; *Microcomputer Architecture and Programming*, Wiley, 1989.
  Although the coverage is very much software-oriented, this is one of the best of its kind. Also covers the 68020/30 and the 68851/81 co-processors.

Index

Ollscoil na hÉireann, Gaillimh

3 1111 40037 8202